CRAIG MCLACHLAN, RAY BARTLETT & REBECCA MILNER

Contents

PLAN YOUR TRIP
- Welcome to Japan ... 4
- Our Picks ... 6
- When to Go ... 14
- Get Prepared for Japan ... 16

EXPLORE ... 18

TOKYO, MT FUJI & AROUND ... 20
- Takao-san ... 24
- Ōtake-san ... 26
- Mt Fuji Yoshida Trail ... 28
- Mitsu-tōge-yama ... 32
- Panorama-dai ... 34
- Oku-Nikkō Marsh ... 36
- Oze National Park ... 38
- Old Hakone Hwy ... 42
- Also Try ... 44

JAPAN ALPS & CENTRAL HONSHŪ ... 46
- Tateyama ... 50
- Hakuba Happō-ike ... 52
- Kamikōchi ... 54
- Nishiho-Doppyō ... 58
- Norikura-dake ... 60
- Ontake-san ... 62
- Kiso-koma-ga-take ... 64
- Nakasendō ... 66
- Senjō-ga-take ... 68
- Hakusan ... 70
- Also Try ... 72

KANSAI ... 74
- Fushimi Inari ... 78
- Daimonji-yama ... 80
- Kurama to Kibune ... 82
- Rokku Gaaden ... 84
- Kasuga-yama ... 86
- Yama-no-be-no-michi ... 88
- Kōya-san ... 90
- Kumano Kodō ... 92
- Also Try ... 96

HIROSHIMA & WESTERN HONSHŪ ... 98
- Daisen ... 102
- Sandan-kyō ... 106
- Miyajima ... 108
- Sanbe-san ... 110
- Akiyoshidō ... 112
- Also Try ... 114

TŌHOKU ... 116
- Zaō-san ... 120
- Dewa Sanzan ... 122
- Akita Koma-ga-take ... 126
- Hakkōda-san ... 128
- Tsuta-numa ... 130
- Oirase Keiryū ... 132
- Tanesashi Kaigan ... 134
- Tōno ... 136
- Also Try ... 138

HOKKAIDŌ ... 140
- Shin Sen Numa & Chisenupuri ... 144
- Asahi-dake ... 148
- Kuro-dake ... 152
- Tokachi-dake ... 154
- Meakan-dake ... 156
- Mashū-dake ... 158
- Rausu-dake ... 160
- Rishiri-zan ... 162
- Momoiwa Observatory Course ... 164
- Also Try ... 166

SHIKOKU ... 168
- 88 Sacred Temples Pilgrimage ... 172
- Ishizuchi-san ... 176
- Iino-yama ... 178
- Tsurugi-san ... 180
- Kanka-kei ... 182
- Also Try ... 184

KYŪSHŪ ... 186
- Hiko-san ... 190
- Yufu-dake ... 192
- Kujū-san ... 194
- Aso-san ... 196
- Karakuni-dake ... 198
- Kaimon-dake ... 200
- Miyanoura-dake ... 202
- Also Try ... 206

TOOLKIT ... 208
- Arriving ... 210
- Getting Around ... 211
- Accommodation ... 212
- Hiking ... 213
- Health & Safe Travel ... 214
- Responsible Travel ... 215
- Nuts & Bolts ... 216

BY DIFFICULTY ... 217
INDEX ... 218
OUR WRITERS ... 224

Welcome to Japan

Everyone has seen the images: packed trains, cramped housing and seemingly endless concrete and neon lights. Most international visitors turn up to check out Japan's unique cultural heritage – its fascinating history, temples, shrines, fine cuisine and traditional arts – and few venture far off the well-trodden path.

But what of the other Japan? This is a country blessed with two-thirds mountainous terrain, with high peaks, twisting rivers and rugged coastlines, plus the most diverse climate in all of Asia. One of the best ways to get behind that *tatemae* (public face) that Japan shows to the outsider is to hit a hiking trail. If you really want to glimpse that *honne* (private face) that few foreigners are privileged to see, walk a rocky trail, share a beer, or soak in a remote onsen after the hike with walkers you met on the track.

Unzen (p207)
KAN_KHAMPANYA/SHUTTERSTOCK ©

Our Picks

BEST FOR CITY BREAKS

Spend some time in Japan's metropolises – the greater Tokyo area known as Kantō (population 40 million) and the greater Osaka-Kyoto-Kōbe area known as Kansai (population 25 million), plus in other big cities such as Hiroshima, Fukuoka and Sapporo – and chances are you'll be craving some green. The good news is that nature is relatively close by, often only a short train or bus ride from the concrete jungle.

TOP TIP

Weekdays are good. Don't expect to be alone on the trail if you go over the weekend.

Takao-san

Friendly trails make for a fun break from Tokyo only an hour west of Shinjuku.

P24

Rokku Gaaden

Quick escape offering spectacular views of the Kansai metropolis and rock scrambling.

P84

Kurama to Kibune

Two tiny villages that have long served as rural retreats from the congestion of Kyoto.

P82

Sandan-kyō

Relax in the healing peacefulness of pristine forest north of Hiroshima.

P106

Ōtake-san

Close enough for a day trip from Tokyo, but far enough to feel like a mountain getaway.

P26

Takao-san (p24)

TOP TIP

Get an early start during the summer months; heat can be stifling in mid-afternoons. Many of the hikes close to the big cities are low altitude and walkable pretty much year-round.

Sandan-kyō (p106)

TOP TIP

Prepare well: take plenty of food and liquids as there aren't many convenience stores out there!

Our Picks

BEST OFF-THE-BEATEN-PATH WALKS

Didn't know you could get off the beaten path in Japan? This is a mountainous country that is 70% covered in forest, with 34 national parks. It's relatively easy to get off the standard visitor trail and find places where foreigners seldom go, though you'll have to be motivated and make the effort. The rewards, however, are high and these walks may well be the highlight of your visit to Japan.

TOP TIP

Do some homework on your transport options as some of these hikes aren't easy to get to.

Kaimon-dake

This Fuji lookalike at the southern tip of Kyūshū makes a great day walk with lovely views.

P200

Mashū-dake

The peak beside Hokkaidō's Mashū-ko, the lake rumoured to have the world's clearest water.

P158

Mashū-ko (p158)

Tsurugi-san

At the head of Shikoku's remote Iya Valley, Tsurugi-san is easily climbed with the help of a chairlift.

P180

Dewa Sanzan

Tōhoku's famous pilgrim trail is deep in the sacred mountains of Yamagata Prefecture.

P122

Hakusan

Rugged and remote Hakusan, in Central Honshū, is one of Japan's three holy mountains.

P70

Haguro-san (p122)

Our Picks

BEST FOR MOUNTAIN VIEWS

Japan is a mountainous land with massive views, from both higher and lower peaks. The *Hyakumeizan*, Japan's 100 Famous Mountains, are on every Japanese hiker's bucket list and 21 peaks top 3000m. Want that classic view of Mt Fuji? You're not going to get it while climbing Japan's highest mountain itself, but those iconic images can be seen from hiking trails all around Fuji-san on a clear-weather day.

TOP TIP

Check extended weather forecasts before you go as mountain weather can be extremely changeable.

Daimonji-yama

Gorgeous views out over Kyoto and its surrounding hills from this mountain behind the temple Ginkaku-ji.

P80

Mitsu-tōge-yama

Spotting Mt Fuji's perfectly symmetrical cone from the summit is nothing short of awesome.

P32

Norikura-dake

Panoramic views of the Japan Alps from atop Japan's third-highest volcano; relatively easy to summit.

P60

Karakuni-dake

Cliffs that stare into craters and vistas stretching to the sea in southern Kyūshū.

P198

Akita Koma-ga-take

Popular mountain in the middle of Tōhoku, with views over the whole region.

P126

Kirishima mountains (p198)

TOP TIP

Join local hikers by getting an early start and climbing peaks in time to watch the sun rise.

Norikura-dake (p60)

Our Picks

BEST FOR ONSEN SOAKING

Soaking in hot springs after a hike is a Japanese tradition. You'll find onsen all across the country, from relatively untouched pools of hot water in the mountains or forest (think no facilities and mixed gender) to small, developed gender-segregated places, to rollicking onsen resort towns with huge bath complexes. Wherever you go, you'll need to get naked, but don't worry – everybody else will be too.

TOP TIP

Study up on onsen etiquette before going to Japan; if in doubt, do what everyone else does.

Kumano Kodō

Excellent options once you get to Kumano Hongū Taisha, such as at Kawa-yu Onsen.

P92

Rausu-dake

Hop into the free *rotemburo* (outdoor bath) in the forest at Iwaobetsu Onsen in Hokkaidō.

P160

Nishiho-Doppyō

Down in the valley, choose from various riverside onsen options at Shin-Hotaka Onsen.

P58

Hakkōda-san

This hike starts and finishes at one of Tōhoku's most famous hot springs, Sukayu Onsen.

P128

Old Hakone Hwy

Soak in one of Hakone's day spas after a walk down this historic, cobblestone post road.

P42

Iwaobetsu Onsen (p160)

Our Picks

BEST ISLAND ESCAPES

Japan is an island country of more than 14,000 islands, 430 of which are inhabited. Ferries play a big part in the transport network, and if the idea of escaping big cities on the mainland and heading out to see a different side of Japanese life appeals, you're definitely not short of options, from the northern tip of Hokkaidō to westernmost parts of Okinawa.

TOP TIP

Carefully check ferry schedules before you go; bookings may be necessary. Ferries can be disrupted by typhoons and strong winds.

Miyanoura-dake

Magnificent walking on World Heritage–listed Yakushima, 60km south of Kyūshū.

P202

Miyajima

Cultural walking with curious deer, temples and shrines, not far from Hiroshima City.

P108

Itsukushima-jinja (p108)

Rishiri-zan

This picture-perfect volcanic cone sits 40km west off northern Hokkaidō.

P162

Kanka-kei

Superb views and gorge hiking on Shōdo-shima in the Inland Sea.

P182

Momoiwa Observatory Course

Lovely Rebun-tō, off northern Hokkaidō, erupts in wildflowers in spring and summer.

P164

When to Go

Japan's huge variety of terrain and climate means that hikers need to do some planning.

The combination of Japan's mountainous landscape and the length of the archipelago means there are significant climatic differences between Hokkaidō in the north – with short summers, lengthy winters and deep snow – and the southern islands such as Okinawa, which enjoys a year-round subtropical climate. More snow falls on the Sea of Japan side of the central mountains than on the Pacific Ocean–facing side, and more falls the further north you go. Mt Fuji has an official climbing season of 1 July to 10 September, while the peaks of the Japan Alps and those in Hokkaidō have a July to October season. Lower-altitude, lower-latitude hikes can be done year-round. Typhoons can turn up at any time between June and October to foil the best-made plans.

Accommodation

Japan has three major holiday periods when transport and accommodation can be booked solid: New Year (Shōgatsu), Golden Week (late April to early May, with four national holidays within seven days) and Obon in mid-August.

CHERRY-BLOSSOM SEASON

Spring brings Japan's legendary cherry blossoms. The season starts in Kyūshū in mid- to late March and sweeps up through the country, hitting Hokkaidō in late April. Crowds gather for blossom-viewing parties called *hanami* – a great time to hit the outdoors for short walks.

BEST WEATHER AT THE PEAKS

Shannon Walker is the Chief Experience Officer at Kodo Travel. @kodotravel

'Japanese hikers have long believed the best time to go climbing and hiking among Japan's high peaks is at *tsuyu-ake-tōka* (the first 10 days after the rainy season). While it's difficult to be exact, this is thought of as the last 10 days of July. If you plan to climb Mt Fuji or in the Japanese Alps over this period, expect clear, cool weather, plus excellent visibility. Mountain huts are likely to be packed and most climbers will be trying to be atop the nearest high peak for sunrise.'

Weather Watch (Tokyo)

JANUARY	FEBRUARY	MARCH	APRIL	MAY	JUNE
Average daytime max: **10°C**	Average daytime max: **10°C**	Average daytime max: **14°C**	Average daytime max: **19°C**	Average daytime max: **23°C**	Average daytime max: **26°C**
Days of rainfall: **3**	Days of rainfall: **5**	Days of rainfall: **8**	Days of rainfall: **9**	Days of rainfall: **8**	Days of rainfall: **11**

Tenjin Matsuri

RAINY SEASON

An extra season that slides in between spring and summer is *tsuyu* (the rainy season), characterised by high humidity, temperatures and rainfall in June and early July.

BIG EVENTS

On 25 July, **Tenjin Matsuri** sees a procession through the streets of Osaka, a parade of boats on the Okawa River, plus evening fireworks and endless food stalls selling local delicacies. **July**

A popular Tokyo festival held over three days, **Sanja Matsuri** brings the Asakusa district alive with music, food stalls and festival games; 100 *mikoshi* (portable shrines) are paraded through the streets. **May**

The 15-day **Sumo Tournaments** are held six times per year: January, May and September in Tokyo, March in Osaka, July in Nagoya and December in Fukuoka. Details on the Japan Sumō Association website.

Japan's best-known snow festival, held in in Hokkaidō's capital, **Sapporo Yuki Matsuri** attracts more than two million visitors each year. It runs over a week, with spectacular snow and ice sculptures. **February**

AUTUMN COLOURS

Leaves start to change as early as late September in Hokkaidō and many mountain areas (depending on elevation), and through November in lower latitudes. The scenery is spectacular – especially the fiery red maples – but expect to see crowds, except on more remote mountain trails.

I LIVE HERE

AUTUMN IN THE NORTH ALPS

Ken Serizawa is the General Manager of Alpine Tour Japan. @alpinetourjapan

'Hiking and climbing in the North Alps in autumn is amazing due to the magnificent colours below the treeline. The reds, oranges and yellows of the leaves mean it's hard to stop taking photographs. Then, if you climb above the treeline to some of the high peaks, it's incredible looking down on the colours in the valleys. Kamikōchi is a great place to base yourself and the best month for autumn colours is October. The Tateyama–Kurobe Alpine Route in the north of the North Alps is also superb.'

JULY	AUGUST	SEPTEMBER	OCTOBER	NOVEMBER	DECEMBER
Average daytime max: **30°C**	Average daytime max: **31°C**	Average daytime max: **27°C**	Average daytime max: **22°C**	Average daytime max: **17°C**	Average daytime max: **12°C**
Days of rainfall: **10**	Days of rainfall: **8**	Days of rainfall: **12**	Days of rainfall: **8**	Days of rainfall: **6**	Days of rainfall: **3**

Get Prepared for Japan

Useful things to load in your bag, your ears and your brain.

WATCH

Midnight Diner: Tokyo Stories (Netflix; 2016–19) Subtitled version of the Japanese classic TV series *Shinya Shokudō*.

Seven Samurai (Akira Kurosawa; 1954) Acknowledged as iconic director Kurosawa's greatest movie.

Tampopo (Itami Jūzō; 1985) Internationally acclaimed comedy based in a ramen-noodle shop.

Shoplifters (Koreeda Hirokazu; 2018) Story of a poor family trying to make ends meet.

Woman in the Dunes (Hiroshi Teshigahara; 1964) Film adaptation of the award-winning novel by Kōbō Abe.

Don't Forget

Japanese are incredibly well prepared when they head out hiking, with everything they could possibly need. Here are a few things to think about:

Sunhat, sunglasses, sunscreen The basics when heading out into the outdoors.

Comfortable backpack Bring one with you or pick one up.

Sensible clothing Have several layers suitable for the season, the hike and weather conditions.

Suitable shoes Something sturdy if you're climbing rocky trails up to mountain peaks.

Rainwear Be prepared even if the forecast is for good weather. Japanese often take an umbrella on the hike.

Walking poles Good on longer hikes and for those with bad knees.

Gloves Often useful on hikes.

Insect repellent Every hiker carries some form of mushi-yoke.

Small headlight Useful on a multiday hike or if staying in a mountain hut.

Refreshments Bring food, snacks and plenty of liquids; plan ahead.

Do your homework Research the hike to ensure you have sufficient fitness and experience.

Navigational aids Be prepared with a good map or app.

Check the weather forecast Don't head out there if a typhoon is coming!

Shrine, Matsuyama (p170)

Words

On the Trail

Good luck! Gambatte!
Mountain track Yama-michi
Mountain hut Yamagoya
Campsite Kyampu-jō
Summit Sanchō
Where is…? …wa doko desu ka?
Does this trail go to…? Kono michi wa … e ikimasu ka?
How many minutes to…? …made nanpun desu ka?
What's this place called? Koko wa nan to iu tokoro desu ka?
We're walking from…to… …kara…made aruite imasu.
How much is it per night? Ippaku oikura desu ka?
I'd like to make a booking. Yōyaku o onegai shimasu.

Directions & Transport

Right Migi
Left Hidari
Straight ahead Massugu
Parking area Chūsha-jō
What time does it leave? Nan-ji ni demasu ka?
Where does it leave from? Doko kara demasu ka
Does it stop at…? …ni tomarimasu ka?

Weather

How's the weather today? Kyō no tenki wa ikaga desu ka?
Clear weather Hare
Rain Ame
Thunder and lightning Kaminari

LISTEN

First Love
(Hikaru Utada; 1999) Released when the artist was only 16, it became Japan's best-selling album of all time.

Umi No Yeah!!
(Southern All Stars; 1998) Greatest-hits double album by Keisuke Kuwata's legendary rock band.

Momentary Sixth Sense
(Aimyon; 2019) Second release by the popular singer and songwriter.

Abroad in Japan
(abroadinjapan.com) Podcast discussing culture, current events and all things weird and wacky in Japan.

READ

The Roads to Sata
(Alan Booth; 1985) Tales from a 3200km walk across the length of Japan.

Bashō: The Complete Haiku of Matsuo Bashō
(Andrew Fitzsimons; 2022) Japan's best-known travelling poet.

Japanese Pilgrimage
(Oliver Statler; 1983) A walk around the 88 Sacred Temples of Shikoku.

100 Mountains of Japan
(Kyūya Fukada; 1964) Inspiration for Japan hikers.

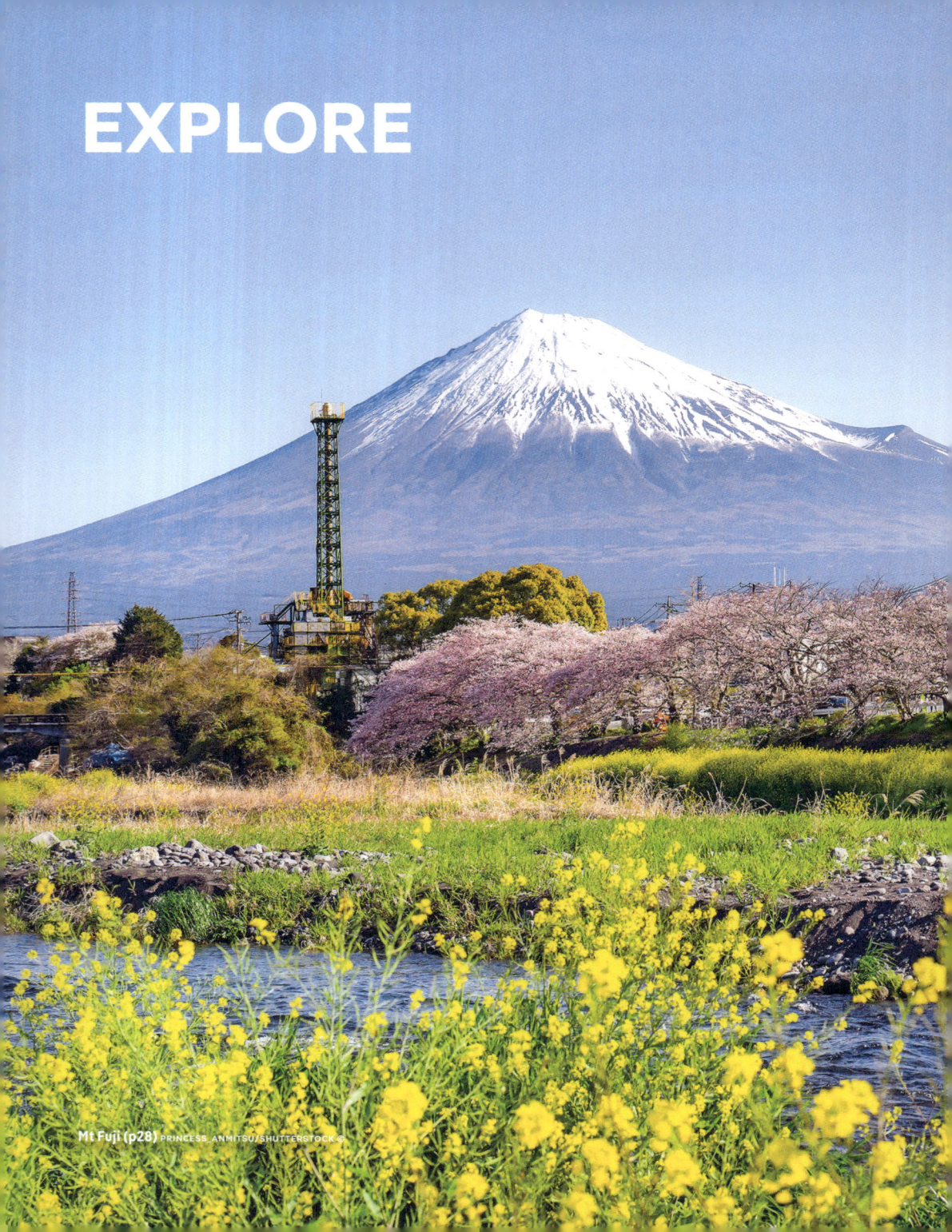
EXPLORE

Mt Fuji (p28) PRINCESS_ANMITSU/SHUTTERSTOCK ©

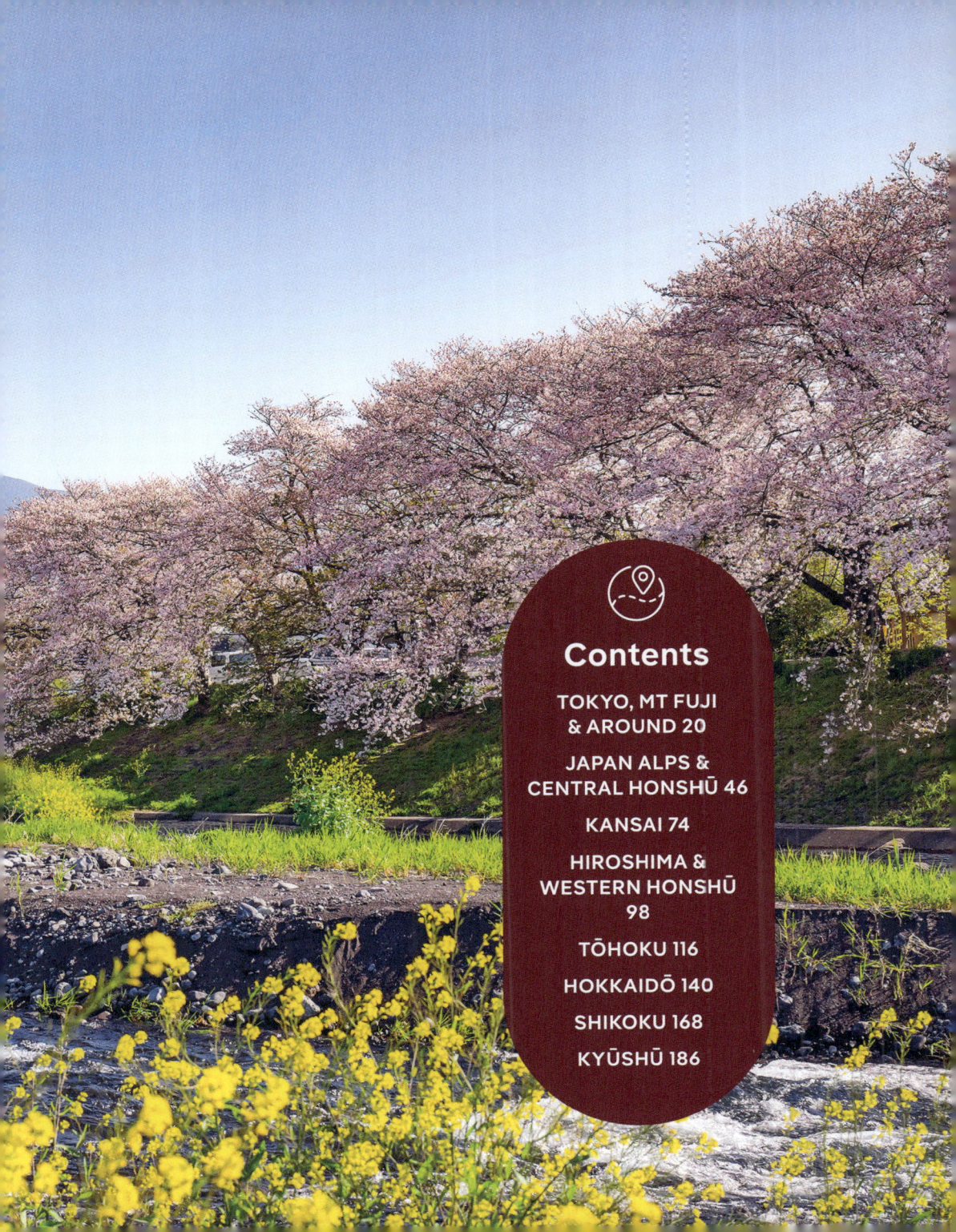

Contents

TOKYO, MT FUJI & AROUND 20

JAPAN ALPS & CENTRAL HONSHŪ 46

KANSAI 74

HIROSHIMA & WESTERN HONSHŪ 98

TŌHOKU 116

HOKKAIDŌ 140

SHIKOKU 168

KYŪSHŪ 186

Oze National Park (p38)

Tokyo, Mt Fuji & Around

01 Takao-san
Tokyo's very own mountain, just an hour from the centre of the city. **p24**

02 Ōtake-san
Ōtake-san Cedar forests and an ancient shrine in far-west Tokyo. **p26**

03 Mt Fuji Yoshida Trail
Mt Fuji Yoshida Trail The classic route up Japan's tallest mountain is a summer rite of passage. **p28**

04 Mitsu-tōge-yama
Walk through broadleaf woods to see Mt Fuji in a different light, rising above Fuji Five Lakes. **p32**

05 Panorama-dai
A short, year-round climb from the caldera lake, Shōji-ko, with a Fuji view. **p34**

06 Oku-Nikkō Marsh
Oku-Nikkō Marsh Wetlands, waterfalls and hot springs in Nikkō National Park. **p36**

07 Oze National Park
Long walks over Japan's largest highland marsh, famous for its wildflowers. **p38**

08 Old Hakone Hwy
Go back in time with a trip down this centuries-old post road. **p42**

Explore

Tokyo, Mt Fuji & Around

The greater Tokyo area is fringed with mountains, lakes and marshes, offering myriad ways to commune with nature. There are big peaks, like Mt Fuji, and also easier, family-friendly outings. Advantages of walking around Japan's biggest city include easy trail access and plenty of English spoken on the ground.

Tokyo

All the walks in this chapter are accessible by public transport from Tokyo (東京), though many are best approached from a town closer to the trails. Easy day-trip destinations from Tokyo include Takao-san (p24), Ōtake-san (p26) and the Old Hakone Hwy (p42). Mt Fuji (p28) can be visited as an overnight trip from Tokyo.

Kawaguchi-ko

Kawaguchi-ko (河口湖), 110km west of Tokyo, is the largest town near Mt Fuji. It's on the lake of the same name, one of five caldera lakes that make up the resort area known as Fuji Five Lakes (富士五湖; Fuji Go-ko). Accommodation includes hostels, economy hotels and resorts. There are also plenty of restaurants; however, the town is quite spread out, so options within walking distance may be limited. Express buses connect Tokyo (Shinjuku) and Kawaguchi-ko (1¾ hours).

Nikkō

Nikkō (日光), 120km north of Tokyo, is a popular sightseeing destination with famous Shintō shrines and Buddhist temples. It's also the gateway to Nikkō National Park, which has mountains, lakes, waterfalls and hot springs; Oku-Nikkō Marsh (p36) is here. Lodging in the park is mostly small, family-run inns or large, expensive resorts. Many restaurants cater to day trippers and close early, but there are some options for after dark. Tōbu line Spacia limited-express trains travel to Nikkō (1½ hours) from Asakusa, on Tokyo's east side.

Hakone

Hakone (箱根) is the collective name for seven onsen resorts in the mountains 90km southwest of Tokyo. Of these, Hakone and Gōra are the most developed (and Hakone-Yumoto the easiest to access). There are some budget sleeping options; however, many visitors come specifically to splurge on ryokan (traditional inns), with meals and hot spring baths included. Note that many Hakone restaurants close by late afternoon. Odakyū line Romance Car limited-express trains run from Shinjuku Station to Hakone-Yumoto (80 minutes).

When to Go

Some walks in and around Tokyo can be done year-round, though snow is possible on mountain trails from mid-December to March. When planning ambitious day trips, also keep in mind that it gets dark early in winter. Mt Fuji has the narrowest walking season: 1 July to 10 September. To avoid the worst crowds, don't climb on

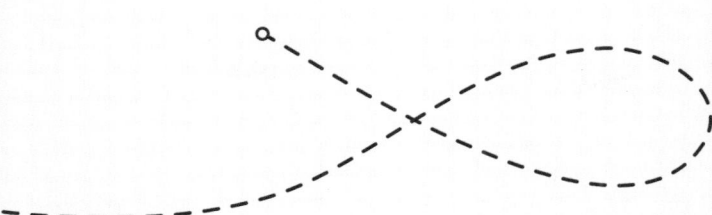

a Saturday or during the week of O-Bon (13 to 15 August). For Oze, the season is mid-May to mid-October; the trails are most crowded in June and July (when the wildflowers bloom). In general, the most popular time to walk is in autumn when the leaves change colour, which happens in October or November (depending on the altitude). Expect heavy traffic and limited vacancies at accommodation during this period (and especially on weekends).

 Transport

Shinjuku is a key transit hub on Tokyo's west side. Trains depart from Shinjuku Station for Takao-san, Mitake (for Ōtake-san) and Hakone-Yumoto. Express buses depart from Shinjuku Bus Terminal for Mt Fuji (1 July to 10 September), Kawaguchi-ko and Tokura (mid-May to mid-October), from where a shuttle bus runs to Oze. Seat reservations are required for express buses and limited-express trains. Only Takao-san has direct train access; otherwise a combination of trains and buses is required to reach the trails.

Local buses run more frequently in greater Tokyo than in remote areas, so you needn't be as mindful about return bus times (though, as everywhere, bus service can finish by late afternoon). Kawaguchi-ko (and all of Fuji Five Lakes) is an exception; local buses are less frequent than would be ideal, and most domestic travellers visit with a car. The access road to Mt Fuji's 5th station is closed to private vehicles during the climbing season, but is otherwise open mid-April to November, for visitors who want to see the mountain up close.

 Where to Stay

In Kawaguchi-ko, **K's House Mt Fuji** (kshouse.jp) is a great base for walkers. The English-speaking staff have lots of local tips and useful maps. There are dormitories and private rooms, plus a kitchen and laundry facilities. **Annex Turtle Hotori-An** (turtle-nikko.com) is a long-running traveller favourite in Nikkō.

Near Hakone-Yumoto, the ryokan **Fukuzumirō** (fukuzumiro.com), built in the late 19th century, has hot-spring baths and beautiful rooms with original woodwork overlooking the Tōno-sawa. In Gōra, **Hakone Tent** (hakonetent.com) is a fantastic budget choice: a hostel with a shared onsen bath and a bar.

 What's On

Hiwatari-sai On the second Sunday of March, Takao-san's Buddhist temple Yakuō-in holds its annual Fire Walking Festival, during which monks walk barefoot over smouldering coals.

Yoshida no Hi-matsuri The Yoshida Fire Festival takes place on 26 and 27 August, traditionally the last days of the Mt Fuji climbing season. At dusk on the first day, bonfires – said to pacify the mountain spirit – are lit on the main street in the town of Fuji-Yoshida, at the base of the mountain.

Resources

fujisan-climb.jp
Check news and weather updates for Mt Fuji.

Pick up English-language hiking maps and bus schedules for Fuji Five Lakes at the Kawaguchi-ko Tourist Information Center next to Kawaguchi-ko Station; staff speak English.

hakone-japan.com
The Hakone-Yumoto Tourist Information Center has English information on Hakone.

visitnikko.jp/en/
Info, hiking maps, itineraries and more for Nikkō.

01

Takao-san

DURATION	DIFFICULTY	DISTANCE	START/END
3-3½hrs	Easy-moderate	9km	Takao-san-guchi

TERRAIN	Paved and packed earth; some steps

Takao-san (高尾山; 599m) is the nearest mountain to central Tokyo and Tokyoites are very fond of it. It's never not full of people – families, young couples, groups of active seniors – as the ease of access can't be beaten. Still, parts of it feel wonderfully wild; it also has a historic Buddhist temple.

Getting Here

At Shinjuku Station, take a 'special express' (*jun-tokkyū*) Keiō line train to Takao-san-guchi (one hour). The line splits, so make sure to get a train bound for Takao-san-guchi (the terminus).

Starting Point

Exit right from the train station and walk 500m to the tourist village at the base, which has cafes and food stalls. **Takao 599 Museum** (takao599museum.jp) has displays on the creatures large and small that live on the mountain (pick up a map here). Seven trails run from the base (at 201m) to the summit. The loop described here goes up Trail 1 and returns via Trails 3 and 6; signs are in English. You can also opt to take either the cable car or the chairlift (adult/child one-way ¥490/250, return ¥950/470) halfway up the mountain.

01 Go straight up the paved path (to the right and before the cable car station). Takao-san is often dismissed as easy, but if you haven't hiked in a while you will feel this. Twenty minutes (and 1.3km) later, take a short detour to the lookout point, **Konpira-dai** (金比羅台; 387m), for views back over central Tokyo's skyscrapers.

02 Trail 1 is the Omote-sandō – the main approach to a shrine or temple – of the Buddhist temple, **Yakuō-in** (薬王院; takaosan.or.jp), established in the 8th century (long before

Gokuraku-yu

Hot-spring complex **Gokuraku-yu** (極楽湯; takaosan-onsen.jp; ⏲ 8am–11pm) is attached to the Takao-san-guchi Station building. It has indoor and outdoor baths, with naturally alkaline waters, and an infrared sauna. Unlike many onsen, the baths aren't kept very hot, ranging instead from 37.5°C to 41.5°C, which makes them appealing even after a hot day on the mountain. Towel rental costs extra (or bring your own); soap and shampoo are provided. Guests with tattoos are not permitted. If it's been a tough day, there's even a tatami room for 'napping' after your bath.

Best for

ESCAPING THE CITY

PICTURE CELLS/SHUTTERSTOCK ©

Tokyo). It belongs to the esoteric Shingon sect, and austerities are still performed on the mountain. At the fork, take either the 108 stone steps on the left or the easier slope on the right.

03 Take the stairs to the temple's Oku-no-in (inner sanctuary), from where it's a short push to the **summit**, usually crowded with picnickers. Beyond the visitor centre is a **viewing platform** from where you can see Mt Fuji on a clear day.

04 Returning from the summit, look to the right for the sign pointing to Trail 3, also known as the **Katsura Woods Trail** (*katsura* are Japanese Judas trees). It's a narrow, shady path on packed earth and is usually far quieter than Trail 1.

05 When Trail 3 ends, you can rejoin Trail 1 at the upper cable car station, or continue down the lower half of Trail 6 to the waterfall, **Biwa-taki** (びわ滝); mind the slippery parts on the latter. The 5m-tall falls is used in Yakuō-in's purification rituals. When Trail 6 ends, turn right onto the road to return to the base.

Take a Break

Fresh mountain air, scenic vistas and…all-you-can-drink beer. Takao-san's beer garden, **Beer Mount** (urban-inc.co.jp/tokyotakao/gourmet), is as much a destination as the mountain. There are (plastic) seats for hundreds at this outdoor terrace overlooking the greater Tokyo area from almost 500m. Admission (discounted for children) covers two hours of unlimited draught beer and food from the buffet. It's near the upper cable car station (in case you don't want to walk back down).

02

Ōtake-san

DURATION	DIFFICULTY	DISTANCE	START/END
4-5hrs	Moderate	12.5km	Mitake-san

TERRAIN	Packed earth and rocks; some steps

The round-trip walk from Mitake-san (御岳山; 929m) to Ōtake-san (大岳山; 1266m) is a classic Tokyo excursion: close enough for a day trip, but far enough to feel like a real mountain getaway (and with just enough climbing to feel like a workout). Highlights include an ancient Shintō shrine and forests of cedar and cypress. Season: April to November.

Getting Here
Take the JR Chūō line from Shinjuku Station, changing to the JR Ōme line at Tachikawa Station or Ōme Station (depending on the service) to Mitake (90 minutes). From stop 1 at Mitake Station take a bus to Takimoto (滝本; 10 minutes) from where a **cable car** (mitaketozan.co.jp; one-way/ return ¥600/1130; 7.30am-6.30pm) runs two to three times per hour most of the way up Mitake-san. You can skip the cable car and walk up the paved access road from Takimoto, which takes 1½ hours.

Starting Point
It's a 20-minute (1.5km) uphill walk from the upper cable car station (820m) to the trailhead at the shrine. Midway there, stop at the **Mitake Visitor Center** (御岳ビジターセンター; ces-net.jp/mitakevc/index.html; 9am-4.30pm, closed Mon) for English-language maps: it's on the right.

01 Pass under the gate and take the long flight of stairs to **Musashi Mitake-jinja** (武蔵御嶽神社; musashimitakejinja.jp). The trail starts from a point halfway up the stairs, but it's worth going all the way to the top to see the shrine. According to legend it was established 2000 years ago (the earliest written records of it are from 1000 years

Pilgrim Inns

Musashi Mitake-jinja was a popular pilgrimage destination during the Edo period (1603–1868) and the inns on the mountain were originally built to house religious visitors. **Komadori Sansō** (駒鳥山荘; komadori.com) has been run by the same family for 17 generations. All rooms have sweeping mountain views, and the owners speak English. In summer (and occasionally throughout the year) the innkeeper, a mountain priest, leads an early-morning ascetic practice (for an additional fee) that involves standing under a waterfall; inquire when booking.

Best for

ESCAPING THE CITY

ago); the current buildings are mostly from the 18th and 19th centuries. It's unique for its wolf imagery: there is an old tale of a lost pilgrim being led out of the fog on the mountain by a wolf. (The trail is well-signposted throughout, mostly in English; you won't get lost.)

02 A few hundred metres into the forest, the trail branches: both paths go to Ōtake-san. Take the upper one (on the right) that follows the ridge (you'll descend via the lower trail). An hour in, you'll reach **Oku-no-in** (奥の院; 1077m), a small, red sanctuary that's part of Musashi Mitake-jinja. In another 15 minutes, you'll crest the peak of **Nabewari-yama** (1084m).

03 It takes another hour to reach the summit of **Ōtake-san**, with some scrambling over rocks at the end. When it's extraordinarily clear, you can see Mt Fuji among the mountains to the west.

04 Head back down (2.2km) to the junction and take the path to the **Rock Garden** (ロックガーデン). A steady descent takes you to the waterfall, **Ayashiro-no-taki** (綾広の滝). It's considered a sacred spot, marked by a wooden *torii* (shrine entrance gate) and stone tablets (pictured) wrapped in *shimenawa* (hemp rope). From here follow signs back to Mitake-san.

 Take a Break

At the entrance to Musashi Mitake-jinja there is a small village with inns, shops and restaurants. **Momiji-ya** (紅葉屋; 10am-3pm, closed irregularly) serves noodle dishes, including a house special of chilled soba (buckwheat noodles) with a dipping sauce of crushed walnuts. The siphon-brewed coffee is made with local mountain-spring water.

03

Mt Fuji Yoshida Trail

DURATION	DIFFICULTY	DISTANCE	START/END
10-12hrs (1-2 days)	Hard	15km	Fuji-Subaru Line 5th Station

TERRAIN	Rocks and sand; steep grade

Mt Fuji (富士山; 3776m) is one of Japan's most enduring icons. Hundreds of thousands of people climb 'Fuji-san' every year, continuing a centuries-old tradition of pilgrimages up the sacred volcano. Of the four trails to the summit, the Yoshida Trail is the easiest and most popular. Reaching the top brings a great sense of achievement, but be aware that it's a gruelling climb up an often-crowded mountain and weather conditions can change in the blink of an eye. The trail is open from 1 July to 10 September; avoid weekends if you can.

Getting Here
The trail is broken into 10 'stations', with the climb starting from the Fuji-Subaru Line 5th Station.

During the season, there's direct bus service from Shinjuku Bus Terminal (2½ hours, 10 daily, reservations necessary) and from Kawaguchi-ko Station (one hour; every 30 to 60 minutes 6.30am to 7.10pm). Private vehicles are not allowed on the Fuji-Subaru line 5th station access road during the season. Drivers should use the **Mt Fuji Parking Lot** (富士山パーキング; ¥1000) at the base and take the shuttle bus to the 5th station (round trip ¥2500, 45 minutes, every 30 minutes 5.30am to 7pm).

Starting Point
The Fuji-Subaru line 5th station (2305m) has become like a small village, with shops, restaurants, vending machines and coin lockers. You're facing a 1470-vertical-metre climb and descent from here. Get up-to-the-minute weather forecasts and trail conditions at the **Fuji-Subaru Line 5th Station Management Center** (⏱7.30am-8.30pm 1 Jul-11 Sep, 9am-4.30pm May-Jun & 12 Sep-31 Oct; 📶).

Sunrise at the Summit

For many climbers the goal is to see *goraikō* (the rising sun) from the summit, which happens sometime between 4.30am and 5.30am. To do this, with new 2024 regulations, you'll need to stay in a mountain hut on your way to the top. It can be cold and windy at the summit and you may be inside a cloud with zero visibility; take appropriate gear. There may be clearer views and fewer crowds from the stations below. Weather permitting, sunrise is visible from anywhere on the Yoshida Trail above the 6th station. Check weather forecasts before you go; remember, you won't get that classic Mt Fuji view when you're actually on the mountain – only when viewing Mt Fuji from afar!

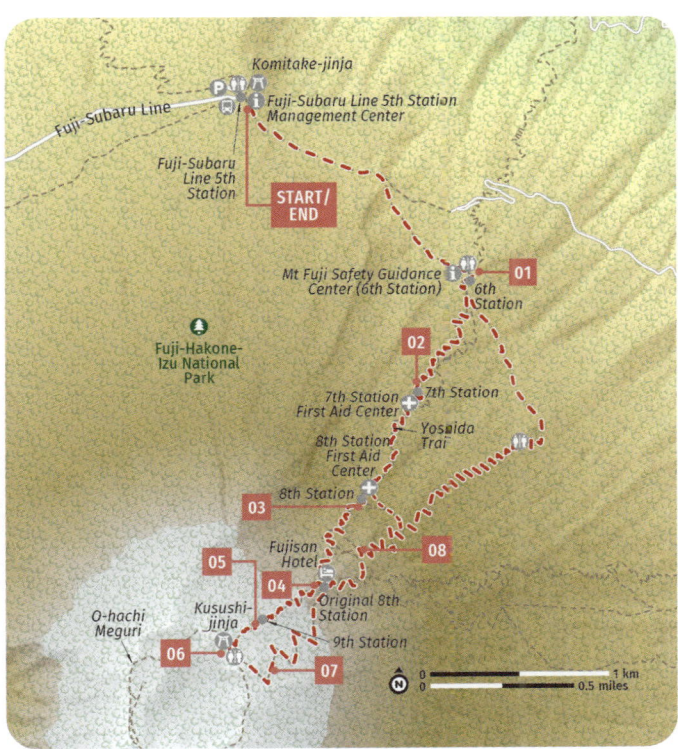

A gate at the 5th station bars access without the payment of a ¥2000-per-person fee, and a ¥1000-per-person donation is requested to cover maintenance. The gate limits hikers to 4000 daily during the climbing season. Book at fujisan-climb.jp up to a day before you climb; 3000 slots daily can be pre-booked and 1000 are open to climbers turning up on the day. The gate closes between 4pm and 3am to those without a booking at a mountain hut; climbers need to present proof of such a booking between these times. This prevents 'bullet climbing' – ascending and descending the mountain for sunrise without resting.

01 Keep in mind that before the advent of buses and cars, Mt Fuji climbers started at the base of the mountain, not at 2305m at the 5th station. These days, the climb begins with a nice warm-up to the **6th station** (六合目; 2390m). It's largely even, with some gentle ups and downs, taking about 30 minutes for the 1.8km stretch of trail.

02 From the 6th station, things start to pick up – this is when you really start to get the sense that you're climbing up the side of a massive volcano. The distance to the **7th station** (七合目; 2700m) is about the same as to the 6th station but takes twice as long. It's a zig-zag ascent that only gets steeper: just before the 7th station is the first rocky climb, where the route is marked with chains (though tempting, you're not supposed to use them to haul yourself up). There are first-aid stations at the 7th and 8th stations. If you feel any symptoms of altitude sickness (such as dizziness, nausea or listlessness), descend immediately. The descending trail is separate (but visible) from the ascending one, with connecting paths at points; but if you're sick, just go straight down.

03 The stretch between the 7th station and the **8th station** (八合目; 3100m) is the longest, taking approximately 100 minutes. This part of the trail is narrow, steep and rocky, often requiring hikers to proceed in single file. It's considered bad form to push the pace, so settle in for a slow and steady climb. From the 7th station, mountain huts are stacked pretty consistently every few hundred metres. It's free to rest on the benches in front of the huts (and it's recommended to rest often), but you need to order something to rest inside. Huts sell food and water (cash only); they also have toilets (¥200; toilet paper but no soap) and free wi-fi. Rubbish must be packed out. Take a moment to look back towards the Fuji Five Lakes (if you're walking in daylight); the big one is Yamanaka-ko. The 8th station is considered the halfway point.

04 As if to keep the goal posts coming, in about 80 minutes you'll reach what is called the **Original 8th Station** (本八合目; 3400m), or 'Hon-Hachigōme'. By now you're already higher than Japan's second-tallest mountain, Kita-dake (3193m), in the South Alps. The Yoshida and Subashiri ascending trails merge at this point. In another 20 minutes or so is the awkwardly named '8.5th Station' (八合五勺; 3450m). From here, it's an hour to the summit.

05 The **9th station** (九合目; 3600m) is marked with a plain wooden *torii*. On the other side is the most challenging part of the climb, a final push up crumbling rock. Watch your footing and for falling rock, which may be kicked down by someone above you. Just before the summit, there is a flight of stone steps and another *torii*, flanked by a pair of *komainu* (lion-dog guardian statues). Mt Fuji from the 8th station to the top is part of the precinct of the Shintō shrine, Fuji Sengen-jinja. The main shrine, located in the town of Fuji-Yoshida at the base, was established in the 8th century to pacify the mountain deity. Mt Fuji has erupted at points in Japan's recorded history (most recently in 1707), no doubt inspiring fear and awe.

06 Once you pass through the gate and round the corner, you're finally at the top! The first landmark is **Kusushi-jinja** (久須志神社), where many climbers perform a ritual greeting and offering. Past the shrine is 'Fuji Ginza', a string of huts (open 4am to 5pm) selling hot food and drink, such as *ton-jiru* (pork and vegetable soup), udon noodles and coffee, plus cold drinks including beer. Don't drink beer if you have any altitude sickness symptoms. There's an open area with benches, which is the gathering spot for sunrise. At the far end, climb up some rocks for a view of the crater. The summit of Mt Fuji is actually made up of eight peaks around a central crater, the highest of which is **Ken-ga-mine** (剣ヶ峰; 3776m), on the opposite side. A 2.6km trail, called the **O-hachi Meguri** (お鉢巡り), runs along the perimeter of the crater, connecting all the peaks,

New Fees & Rules

As of 1 July 2024, Yamanashi Prefecture has instigated a new set of rules to prevent 'overtourism' on Mt Fuji. The Yoshida Trail on the Yamanashi side of the mountain is the most crowded and popular trail, with the most bus services from Tokyo. The changes bring in a fee for climbing (¥2000), a daily limit of 4000 climbers, plus rules designed to increase safety. The new rules don't affect the other three trails on the Shizuoka Prefecture side (yet!). Mt Fuji is being viewed as a test case as Japan grapples with a massive increase in the number of international visitors.

 Take a Break

Mt Fuji's huts are very basic: they were originally built as emergency shelters. Expect tightly packed rows of futons in communal rooms, a hot meal, tea and an atmosphere of camaraderie. A stay in a Mt Fuji hut is a Japanese cultural experience in itself. The Original 8th Station, **Fujisan Hotel** (富士山ホテル; fujisanhotel.com), at 3400m, sets you up for a relatively short climb to the summit. It's very popular so book well in advance. Book other huts online at japanmountainhuts.com.

in about 90 minutes – though most climbers, save serious pilgrims, skip it.

07 Some hikers love descending Mt Fuji. Unlike the oft-times rocky and narrow ascent, the downward trail is gravelly and sandy and comparatively wide. It's mostly a series of neat tacks that you can jog – slide, really – down. Others find it troublesome: the long, unbroken descent gets monotonous and it can be hard on the knees. Unless you're confident that your joints can take the stress, hiking poles (and knee braces) are a big help. There are no huts on the descending trail below the 8th station, so stock up on any food and drinks you might want. The only toilets are the public ones at the 7th and 6th stations.

08 At the 8th station there is a junction, where the Yoshida Trail and the Subashiri Trail split; make sure to follow the yellow signs for the Yoshida Trail (it's well signposted but fog can make it easy to miss the signs). The trail is particularly steep between the 8th and 7th stations but evens out a bit on the way to the 6th, where it joins back up with the ascending trail to the 5th station. In total, it takes three to four hours to make it down the mountain. The last bus from the 5th station for Shinjuku departs at 5pm; for Kawaguchi-ko Station it's at 8.10pm (9.10pm Sunday to Thursday). Make sure to leave yourself plenty of time to get down by dark, unless you have a headlamp or torch.

04

Mitsu-tōge-yama

DURATION	DIFFICULTY	DISTANCE	START/END
4-5hrs	Moderate	8.6km	Mitsu-tōge Tozan-guchi/ Kawaguchi Asama-jinja
TERRAIN		Packed earth; some steps	

Mitsu-tōge-yama (三つ峠山; 1785m) is part of the Misaka mountain range, which forms a fan above the Fuji Five Lakes, north of Mt Fuji. It's a favourite among local walkers, of course, for its views of Mt Fuji and Kawaguchi-ko from the summit, but also because the trail passes through pretty native forest and descends via a waterfall.

Getting Here

One bus departs daily at 9.50am from stop 5 at Kawaguchi-ko Station for Mitsu-tōge Tozan-guchi (三つ峠登山口; 25 minutes). On weekends, there is an additional bus at 9.05am. Make sure to get off at Mitsu-tōge Tozan-guchi (not Mitsu-tōge Iri-guchi). A taxi costs around ¥6000. Snow can make the trail impassable between December and March; check ahead at the tourist information centre (p23).

Starting Point

The trailhead is on the access road 1km past the bus stop. The route is signposted in Japanese.

01 The trail climbs through **broadleaf woods** of *mizunara* (Mongolian oak), *buna* (Japanese beech), *keyaki* (Japanese zelkova) and *karamatsu* (Japanese larch) trees. The autumn foliage peaks in mid- to late October (this walk is very popular then; queue up early for the bus). In summer, wild orchids, irises and day lilies bloom here. After 90 minutes, there is a junction; follow the sign pointing to Mitsu-tōge Sansō (三つ峠山頂), the summit.

02 Walk along the ridge 10 minutes to the mountain hut, **Shiki Rakuen Sansō** (四季楽園山荘). There is a terrace here with picnic tables (¥100 per person) facing Mt Fuji. Payment is by the honour system, in the wooden box.

Fuji Spotting

Mt Fuji is notoriously shy, often hiding behind a curtain of clouds. The most reliable time of year to see it is winter (and especially winter mornings), when the days are crisp and the sky most likely to be clear. Still it can surprise you: one minute, nothing but haze and the next, there it is, in all its snow-capped glory (except for summer, when there's no snow). Mitsu-tōge-yama and Panorama-dai (p34) are two of the best viewpoints around Fuji Five Lakes; back on the ground, look for the mountain lording over the lakes Motosu-ko and Shōji-ko. In autumn, try your luck spotting Fuji framed with colourful foliage from Kōyō-dai (p45).

Best for

MOUNTAIN VIEWS

03 The final ascent to the highest of Mitsu-tōge-yama's three peaks, **Kaiun-san** (開運山; 1785m), is a climb up some newly built stairs. (Unfortunately, there's also a large communication tower here.) At the top, look south for Mt Fuji and Kawaguchi-ko and west over the Misaka mountains to the South Alps.

04 From the summit, backtrack to the junction, and this time take the other trail, which points to the waterfall, **Haha-no-shirataki** (母の白滝). Twenty minutes in there is another junction, and later an intersection with a logging road; be sure to keep following the signs to 母の白滝. After a gentle, 90-minute descent the waterfall appears on your left (don't mistake it for the dam above!). At the bottom there is a small Shintō shrine, **Shirataki-jinja** (白滝神社; pictured), where pilgrims headed for Mt Fuji once performed ablutions.

05 Past the waterfall, follow the road to another, much larger, Shintō shrine, **Kawaguchi Asama-jinja** (川口浅間神社), first built in the 9th century, following an eruption of Mt Fuji (the current building is a modern reconstruction). Exit through the front entrance and turn right to find the Kawaguchi Kyoku-mae (川口局前) bus stop, where buses run back to Kawaguchi-ko Station (10 minutes, seven daily).

Take a Break

Overlooking Kawaguchi-ko and Mt Fuji, long-running rest stop **Tenka-chaya** (天下茶屋; tenkachaya.jp) serves local specialities like *kinoko hōtō nabe* (hot pot with thick wheat noodles and mushrooms). Also fresh-brewed coffee and homemade *amazake* (non-alcoholic, fermented rice milk).

05

Panorama-dai

DURATION	DIFFICULTY	DISTANCE	START/END
2hrs	Easy-moderate	6km	Panorama-dai-shita

TERRAIN		Packed earth

This is a short and sweet walk with a big pay-off: when the weather is right, there's a dead-on view of Mt Fuji from the Panorama-dai (パノラマ台; 1328m) lookout point.

The trailhead is on the west shore of **Shōji-ko** (精進湖; 900m), the smallest of the Fuji Five Lakes and far less developed than Kawaguchi-ko. Take a bus from stop 4 at Kawaguchi-ko Station to Panorama-dai-shita (パノラマ台下; 35 minutes, seven daily). The bus stops right at the trailhead, which is marked with a big wooden sign that reads パノラマ台入り口 (Panorama-dai Iri-guchi). There's also a free car park nearby. The trail is easy to follow, signposted in Japanese and shaded by Japanese beech and Mongolian oak trees.

It's a steady, but not steep, climb to the lookout point. About an hour in you'll pass the first of two junctions; just follow the signs to パノラマ台 (Panorama-dai). Another 15 minutes takes you to a clearing, where wild grasses frame (hopefully!) a dramatic scene of Mt Fuji. Even if it's too cloudy to see the volcano, there are usually still good views of the Misaka mountain range to the northeast. There's enough room here for a couple of parties to picnic.

Return down the same route. If you have time before the return bus to Kawaguchi-ko, spend it on Shōji-ko's small sandy beach, **Tategō-hama** (他手合浜), across the street from the trailhead. Mt Fuji can be seen from here, too, across the lake. With a car, you can continue further to Motosu-ko (本栖湖), the deepest of the Fuji Five Lakes. There are only a few inns around these lakes, which are pretty sleepy outside of the peak summer season (so pack provisions). Panorama-dai can be walked year-round, though inquire at the tourist information centre (p23) about snow between December and February.

06

Oku-Nikkō Marsh

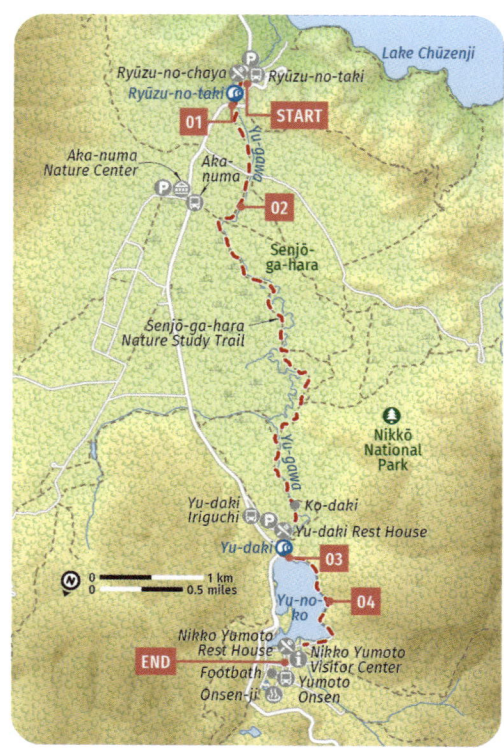

DURATION	DIFFICULTY	DISTANCE	START/END
3-4hrs	Easy-moderate	9km	Ryūzu-no-taki/Yumoto Onsen

TERRAIN	Packed earth, boardwalk and stairs

Oku-Nikkō Marsh (奥日光湿原) is a wetland preserved under the Ramsar Convention. The walk across it is flat, on boardwalks, making it popular with families. The marsh is bookended with two spectacular waterfalls tumbling over terraces of volcanic rock, which you can view up close. Season: April to November.

Getting Here

From stop 2A in front of Tōbu Nikkō Station, take a bus bound for Yumoto Onsen (湯本温泉) to Ryūzu-no-taki (竜頭ノ滝; one hour, twice hourly April to November). Stops are announced in English, but you'll need to signal the bus to stop. The Yumoto Onsen Free Pass (adult/child ¥3500/1750), available for purchase at the train station, covers bus travel between Nikkō and Yumoto Onsen for two days.

Starting Point

From the bus stop, walk back down the road and look for a narrow road on the left, which leads to the waterfall. To just do the boardwalk section (avoiding the stairs), stay on the bus two more stops to Aka-numa (赤沼) and get the return bus at Yu-daki Iriguchi (湯滝入り口), at the bottom of Yu-daki.

01 **Ryūzu-no-taki** (竜頭ノ滝) means 'dragon head falls': a diamond-shaped rock splits the roaring water into two streams, like smoke from a dragon's nostrils. There's a viewing platform (free) at the back of the teahouse, Ryūzu-no-chaya (龍頭之茶屋). To the right of the teahouse, take the path to the long, stone staircase that runs alongside the 210m-long falls.

02 When you reach the road, cross it, and pick up the **Senjō-ga-hara Nature Study**

Yumoto Onsen

Yumoto Onsen (湯元温泉) has several inns that open their baths to visitors (admission ¥500 to ¥1000). **Nikkō Yumoto Visitor Center** (9am-4.30pm, closed weekdays Dec-Jan & Wed Feb-Mar) has a list and a map. For a unique experience, visit the temple **Onsen-ji** (温泉寺), which is dedicated to Yakushi Nyorai (the Buddha of medicine and healing) and has a small bathhouse; the water comes in very hot, so use the tap to add cold water. There's also a **foot bath** near the Yumoto Onsen bus stop. At the back of the village, you can see the onsen's bubbling source.

Trail (戦場ヶ原自然研究路). This 6.3km wooden path traces the course of the **Yu-gawa** (湯川) across Senjō-ga-hara, a highland marsh seeded with hare's tail cotton grass, pink-flowered spiraea shrubs, white birch and Japanese larch trees. In June and July, many kinds of wildflowers bloom here, including Japanese water irises; in autumn, the grasses turn gold. The marsh is an important habitat for birds and a big draw for birdwatchers, who come to spot blue-and-white flycatchers and long-billed Latham's snipes (among others). It's also a habitat for Asian black bears, and most walkers wear bear bells, though the trail is usually sufficiently trafficked to keep sightings rare.

03 The nature trail ends at the foot of the 110m-long waterfall, **Yu-daki** (湯滝). There's a rest stop here that sells food and drink. Continue up another set of stone steps to the top of the falls.

04 Past the falls, pick up the path around the lake, **Yu-no-ko** (湯の湖). A left at the fork takes you on the longer, wooded route along the western shore to Yumoto Onsen. Return buses for Nikkō (1¼ hours) depart from the car park at Yumoto Onsen; the last one is at 7.30pm.

Take a Break

Back in Nikkō, treat yourself to an elegant course of *shōjin-ryōri*, Japanese Buddhist vegetarian cuisine, at **Gyōshintei** (尭心亭; meiji-yakata.com/en/gyoshin). Meals are made from locally sourced vegetables and bean curd and include Nikkō delicacy *yuba* (the thin skin that forms on the top of soy milk). While Gyōshintei looks like it requires reservations – the tatami-floored dining room overlooks a manicured garden – walk-ins are welcome.

07

Oze National Park

DURATION	DIFFICULTY	DISTANCE	START/END
10-12hrs (1-3 days)	Moderate	25km	Hatomachi-tōge/ Ichi-no-se

TERRAIN	Packed earth and boardwalk; some steps

Oze National Park (尾瀬国立公園) is an alpine wetland spanning the border of Gunma and Fukushima Prefectures. Highlights include Japan's largest highland marsh, Oze-ga-hara, and the pond, Oze-numa, both formed by prehistoric eruptions of the volcanoes that ring the park. It's among the most popular destinations in all of Japan, on account of its sheer natural beauty: glassy pools fringed with grasses and bright pops of wildflowers. What's also exceptional about Oze is that many of its trails are largely flat, allowing for long walks with little climbing.

Getting Here

Between mid-May and mid-October, there are three buses daily from Shinjuku Bus Terminal to Oze-Tokura (尾瀬戸倉; reservations required), on the Gunma side of the park. Two leave in the morning (4½ hours) and one leaves at 10pm and travels overnight (5½ hours). There is one bus daily from Yumoto Onsen (1½ hours) at 1.15pm. In Oze-Tokura, shuttle buses travel to Hatomachi-tōge (30 minutes, approximately hourly), the park's main gateway. The first one departs at 4.40am, so if you are diligent about time you can avoid overnighting in the park; however, for many, staying in one of Oze's mountain lodges is part of the experience (especially considering the journey to get here). Private vehicles are not allowed on the access road to Hatomachi-tōge; instead, park at Oze-Tokura (¥1000 per day).

Starting Point

A wooden signboard marks the entrance to the park at Hatomachi-tōge (鳩待峠; 1591m), 100m past the bus stop. Adjacent to the trailhead is **Hatomachi-tōge Rest House** (鳩待峠休憩所), a

Wildflowers

Oze's biggest draw is its wildflowers and particularly the white teardrop blooms of *mizu-bashō* (Asian skunk cabbage; pictured), which appear in late May and early June as the last snow melts. This is also the season for hooded purple *zazensō* (eastern skunk cabbage) and buttery *ryū-kinka* (marsh marigold). Late June sees white puffs of *watasuge* (tussock cottongrass) and blush pink *hime-shakunage* (bog rosemary). From late July to early August, the park's pools fill with sunny *oze-kohana* (East Asian yellow water lilies) and its fields with *nikkō-kisuge* (day lilies). The last to bloom are the bluish-purple *Ezo rindo* (clustered gentian) in September.

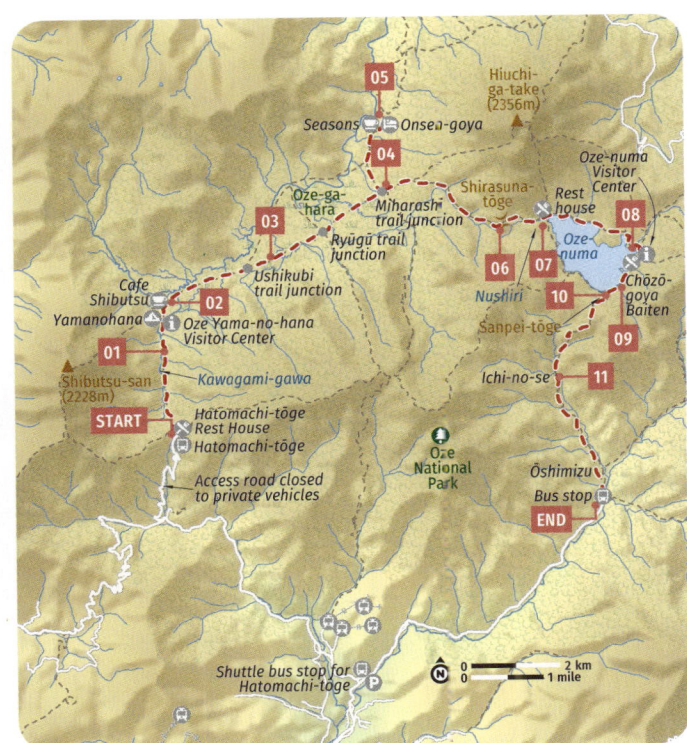

big wooden building with lots of benches out front and a huge gathering spot for pre- and post-walk meals. The restaurant is cafeteria-style; there's also a shop. This walk doesn't require any special equipment though most people carry a bear bell, which you can buy here (along with water and snacks). The trail is easy to follow and signposted in English. The best time to visit is between early June (after the snow melts) and early October. Bear in mind that the trail across Oze-ga-hara is often crowded, especially on weekends and during wildflower season. This isn't a place for solitude, but rather for joining Japan's community of nature lovers.

01 Take the trail marked 尾瀬ヶ原方面 ('for Oze-ga-hara'). It starts with a stone-paved path that descends (via steps, slippery when wet) through a forest of mostly broadleaf trees, including beech and Erman's birch. After the first kilometre, the path levels out and switches to boardwalks, crossing streams at several points, as it leads to the marsh.

02 The first landmark is the **Oze Yama-no-hana Visitor Center** (尾瀬沼ビジターセンター), which has displays on the park's flora and fauna, including details on what's blooming where (and also recent bear sightings; information is posted in Japanese, but there are pictures). You can pick up maps and brochures here in English, too. Adjacent to the visitor centre is the first of several rest spots located on the trails, **Cafe Shibutsu** (カフェ至仏; ⓘ 10am-2pm Mon-Fri, 6.30am-3pm Sat & Sun May-Oct). Look southwest to see **Shibutsu-san** (至仏山; 2228m). It's 3.3km from Hatomachi-tōge to Yama-no-hana (山の鼻; 1400m), which takes about an hour.

03 Beyond Yama-no-hana is wide-open skies and the marsh, **Oze-ga-hara** (尾瀬ヶ原). Oze's top attraction. It

takes about two hours to walk the 6km-long, level path across it, longer when it's crowded. It's also near impossible to resist the urge to stop and take photographs, so budget plenty of time. Ancient lava flows solidified into natural dams, creating oxbow lakes and swamps, and millennia of peat accumulation has resulted in the marsh that appears today. A rich variety of wild grasses, sedges and flowering shrubs grow here; it's also a habitat for dragonflies, damselflies, newts and frogs. (It's a fragile, protected ecosystem and under no circumstances should you stray from the boardwalk.)

04 Crossing Oze-ga-hara you will come to trail junctions at Ushikubi (牛首) and Ryūgū (竜宮); just keep going straight. At **Miharashi** (見晴), take the trail heading north to Aka-tashiro (赤田代). If you are here for a day trip, turn around at this point and return to Hatomachi-tōge; the last bus from Oze-Tokura to Shinjuku is at 3.30pm.

05 Going forward, it's a 30- to 40-minute walk (1.7km) to the mountain lodge, **Onsen-goya** (温泉小屋; oze-onsengoya.com), which is the perfect spot to overnight in the park. It has an onsen bath and a loyal following of repeat visitors. Most walkers are off the trails by 4pm, and you must check in before then. The earlier you arrive, the better: the lodge has an outdoor cafe, **Seasons** (10am-5pm mid-May-Aug, mid-Sep-Oct), with sun lounges and umbrellas facing the marsh. Frosty mugs of beer cost ¥800.

06 From Onsen-goya, return to the junction at Miharashi, and this time take the trail to Oze-numa (尾瀬沼). The 5km-long, wooded route (which takes two to 2½ hours) climbs from 1400m at Miharashi to 1680m at the pass, **Shirasuna-tōge** (白砂峠), before flattening out on the approach to the swamp. Because of the elevation change, the broadleaf forest gives way to one of conifers, including Maries' fir, northern Japanese hemlock and Japanese thuja.

07 Past Shirasuna-tōge is the wetland, **Nushiri** (沼尻), which means 'swamp bottom'. It's wetter than Oze-ga-hara, soaked in the run-off from Hiuchi-ga-take (燧ケ岳; 2356m), Oze National Park's tallest mountain, and is the source of the Nushiri-gawa, which flows down to Oze-ga-hara (and also forms the border between Gunma and Fukushima Prefectures). There's a solar-panelled rest house here that sells drinks and snacks.

08 At the junction, take the path towards **Oze-numa Visitor Center** (尾瀬沼ビジターセンター), which runs 2.7km on boardwalks along the north shore of **Oze-numa**, a large pond. Keep an eye out for mandarin ducks on the water, Asian house martins roosting in the eaves of the lodges and cute, white Japanese stoats dashing across the path. The visitor centre has similar information to the one in Yama-no-hana; it's convenient for checking return

bus times. Depending on your itinerary, you might choose to spend a second night in the park, in which case **Chōzō-goya** (長蔵小屋; chozogoya.com) is a good choice. It's the park's oldest lodge, built in 1910. There's a lounge with a wood stove, outdoor picnic area and, in the new building, a cafe and bar open in the evening.

09 Continue along the shore of Oze-numa, rounding south 1km towards Sanpei-shita (三平下). From this side, you should be able to see the jagged cone of Hiuchi-ga-take across the water.

10 At **Sanpei-shita**, take the trail away from the pond and back into the woods towards Ōshimizu (大清水).

There's a short climb up to the pass, **Sanpei-tōge** (三平峠; 1762m), followed by a descent to **Ichi-no-se** (一ノ瀬; 1420m). It takes 60 to 70 minutes to cover these 3km.

11 At Ichi-no-se, shuttle buses run to Ōshimizu (15 minutes) hourly from mid-June to mid-October; the last one departs at 3.30pm. Otherwise, it's a 3km walk on the level, gravel access road. At Ōshimizu, buses depart at 1.10pm and 3.10pm for Shinjuku Bus Terminal (4½ hours; reservations required) and seven times daily via Oze-Tokura (12 minutes) for Numata (1¾ hours), where you can connect to the JR rail network; the last one departs at 3.50pm.

Mountain Lodges

Oze National Park's lodges offer private or communal Japanese-style rooms with shared facilities, hot meals and a social atmosphere. Onsen-goya and Chōzō-goya are our top picks, but there are several others; a full list can be found at oze-hiking.com/lodge/select.html (in Japanese). Reservations are essential and rooms can fill up fast; during busy periods, single travellers may be asked to share rooms. Prices are comparable. Make sure to have enough cash to cover expenses and some warm clothes for after the sun goes down. Expect the lodges to be particularly busy on weekends over summer and during Japanese public holiday periods.

Take a Break

Mountain lodges, located at convenient intervals, have shops that sell bottled water (¥300 to ¥400) and other food and drinks and also have public toilets (¥100 to ¥200). Several also have cafes and restaurants open from early morning until mid-afternoon. **Chōzō-goya Baiten** (長蔵小屋売店; 7am-2.30pm May-Oct) sells delicious, brewed-to-order coffee (¥400) made with Oze spring water.

08

Old Hakone Hwy

DURATION	DIFFICULTY	DISTANCE	START/END
1½hrs	Easy-moderate	4km	Moto-Hakone/Hatajuku

TERRAIN	Cobbles and pavement; some steps

The Old Hakone Hwy (箱根旧街道; Hakone Kyū-kaidō) is a preserved section of the Tōkaidō, the feudal-era road that connected Tokyo (then called Edo) to Kyoto. Its cobbles have been worn smooth by centuries of foot traffic (the shōgun had banned the use of wheels). Unlike most of Hakone, this historic, wooded trail is usually uncrowded.

Getting Here

At Hakone-Yumoto Station, take either a Hakone-machi line (H; stop 2) or Hakone Kyū-kaidō line (K; stop 4) bus to Hakone-jinja-iriguchi (箱根神社入り口; 30 to 40 minutes), one stop before Moto-Hakone (元箱根), a tourist town on the eastern shore of the caldera lake, Ashi-no-ko (芦ノ湖). It's only a short walk between the two stops, and there's a pretty view from the lake of the red *torii* of Hakone-jinja (箱根神社) rising from the water (and if you're very lucky, Mt Fuji as well).

Starting Point

From the Hakone-jinja-iriguchi bus stop, take the road heading up from the main street (past a temple) a few hundred metres to the trail entrance, marked with a wooden sign. The route, which mostly runs gently downhill, is generally well marked in English; however, there are some tricky parts where the trail meets up with the road, and you'll have to keep a keen eye out for signs. It does snow occasionally in Hakone, but otherwise the trail is open year-round. One note of caution: the cobbles, which are uneven in places, can get very slippery; it's good to have shoes with some traction and to avoid walking during or the day after rain.

Hakone's Hot Springs

The main reason to visit Hakone is for its fantastic onsen. **Tenzan Tōji-kyō** (天山湯治郷; tenzan.jp) is an upscale day spa with indoor and outdoor baths, various saunas and tatami relaxation rooms. It's a perfect post-walk destination, as the Hakone Kyū-kaidō line bus from Harajuku stops right out front, at Oku-Yumoto-iriguchi (奥湯本温泉入り口). Part of the complex (not requiring admission) is the excellent soba restaurant, **Sukumo** (すくも), on the edge of the river. To return to Hakone-Yumoto, take the cheaper 'B' course shuttle bus, which departs from the same stop (or the regular bus if departing after 7pm).

Best for

ONSEN

PHOTONN/SHUTTERSTOCK ©

01 The first section of the trail is among the best preserved, leading through groves of cedar and bamboo. The style of **paving** is called *ishidatami* (石畳), combining the words for 'stone' (*ishi*) and 'tatami' (woven reed floor mats); it was laid down in the late 17th century.

02 The thatched-roof teahouse **Amazake-chaya** (甘酒茶屋; amazake-chaya.jp; 395-1 Futoko-yama; 7am-5.30pm) has been run by the same family for 13 generations. There were once many such teahouses serving as rest stops along the Tōkaidō, but now very few remain. The speciality here is the namesake *amazake* (¥400), a sweet, non-alcoholic, fermented rice milk that has long been considered a health tonic (providing stamina to the messengers and porters who travelled the old highways). The 2km walk here takes 30 to 40 minutes; it's the most popular section of the trail and many visitors only come this far. Hakone Kyū-kaidō line buses stop here.

03 Past the teahouse, you'll have to cross the road and pick up the trail on the other side. A later stretch requires walking a short distance along the winding mountain road (which is, unfortunately, narrow with no shoulder), until you see a staircase on the right, which takes you back to the trail. This final stretch is another beautifully old section of **mossy cobbles.**

04 The small settlement of **Hatajuku** is known for its marquetry craftsmanship and has a few shops. Buses return from here to Hakone-Yumoto (25 minutes, every 30 minutes).

 Take a Break

Start with a caffeine jolt at **Bakery & Table** (bthjapan.com; 9-1 Moto-Hakone), on the edge of Ashi-no-ko, in between the Moto-Hakone and Hakone-jinja-iriguchi bus stops. Head for the terrace seating and chill out, warming your feet in the *ashi-yu* (foot bath).

Also Try...

DOWRAIK/SHUTTERSTOCK ©

Mt Fuji Subashiri Trail

DURATION	DIFFICULTY	DISTANCE
10-12hrs	Hard	14km

This alternative route up Mt Fuji sees significantly fewer people than the Yoshida Trail (p28). The trade-off is that it has fewer amenities and is a little harder to access from Tokyo.

As the walk starts at a lower altitude, there are trees and wildflowers on the initial stretch. The other signature of the Subashiri Trail (pictured) is its *sunabashiri* ('sand run') descent from the 7th station (sunglasses and a scarf or bandanna to protect from dust recommended). Buses run 10 times daily (one hour, 7.30am to 6.30pm) between JR Gotemba Station and the Subashiri 5th station (2000m) during the climbing season (10 July to 10 September; note the later start date). The Subashiri Trail meets up with the Yoshida Trail at the 8th station, so you can go up one and down the other (just bear in mind that this means ending up on a different side of the mountain).

Nantai-san

DURATION	DIFFICULTY	DISTANCE
5-6hrs	Moderate-hard	8km

Nantai-san (男体山; 2486m), an extinct volcano in Nikkō National Park, is one of Japan's '100 Famous Mountains'. It's on the shore of the cobalt-blue caldera lake Chūzenji-ko (中禅寺湖).

A thousand years ago Nantai-san was a site of mountain worship, inspiring the construction of Nikkō's Shintō shrine, Futarasan-jinja. Another, smaller shrine, Futarasan-jinja Chūgūshi (二荒山神社中宮祠), marks the start of the trail and a third, Futarasan-jinja Okumiya (二荒山神社奥宮), simple and unadorned, stands on the summit. Some 1200 vertical metres divides the latter two, meaning this is a steep straight up and down a rocky track (be sure to bring plenty of water). There is a ¥500 fee, payable to Futarasan-jinja Chūgūshi, to climb. Nikkō–Yumoto Onsen buses stop at Futarasan-jinja (二荒山神社前). Walking season is 5 May to 25 October.

ANUJAK JAIMOOK/SHUTTERSTOCK ©

Kōyō-dai

DURATION	DIFF.	DISTANCE
4-5hrs	Moderate	12km

The *kōyō* in Kōyō-dai (紅葉台; 1165m) means 'coloured leaves': this Fuji Five Lakes lookout point is perfectly placed for autumn vistas.

From Kōyō-dai-iriguchi (紅葉台入り口) bus stop, it's a one-hour climb to Kōyō-dai for views of Mt Fuji (pictured), the forest, Aoki-ga-hara and the lake, Saiko. Return, or follow the trail as it undulates up and down over two more peaks, Sanko-dai (三湖台; 1202m) and Ashiwada-yama (足和田山; 1355m), to the Katsuyama (勝山) bus stop, on the southwest shore of Kawaguchi-ko (walkable from town).

Oku-Takao

DURATION	DIFF.	DISTANCE
5½hrs	Moderate	11.5km

Beyond Takao-san, trails continue to Oku-Takao (奥高尾; 'deep Takao').

Take any of the trails to the top of Takao-san (p24), then continue beyond the visitor centre (a useful resource). The packed-earth path (with some wooden steps) is pretty, lined with cedars and *sasa* (bamboo grass), travelling to Shiro-yama (城山; 670m) in about an hour. There are two teahouses at Shiro-yama with outdoor tables, and also one at Momiji-dai (モミジ台), the lookout point named for its maples (*momiji*). Further walks are possible, too.

Shibutsu-san

DURATION	DIFF.	DISTANCE
6hrs	Moderate-hard	11.5km

On the western edge of Oze National Park, Shibutsu-san (至仏山; 2228m) has rare alpine plants and a spectacular view over the marsh, Oze-ga-hara.

Most visitors to Oze National Park (p38) stick to the boardwalks; get away from the crowds with this climb up Shibutsu-san from Yama-no-hana. (You must ascend via Yama-no-hana and descend to Hatomachi-tōge; the trail is set up this way to lessen erosion.) The trail opens from 1 July. With an early start (and the night bus) you can do this walk in a day, or add it to a longer visit to the park.

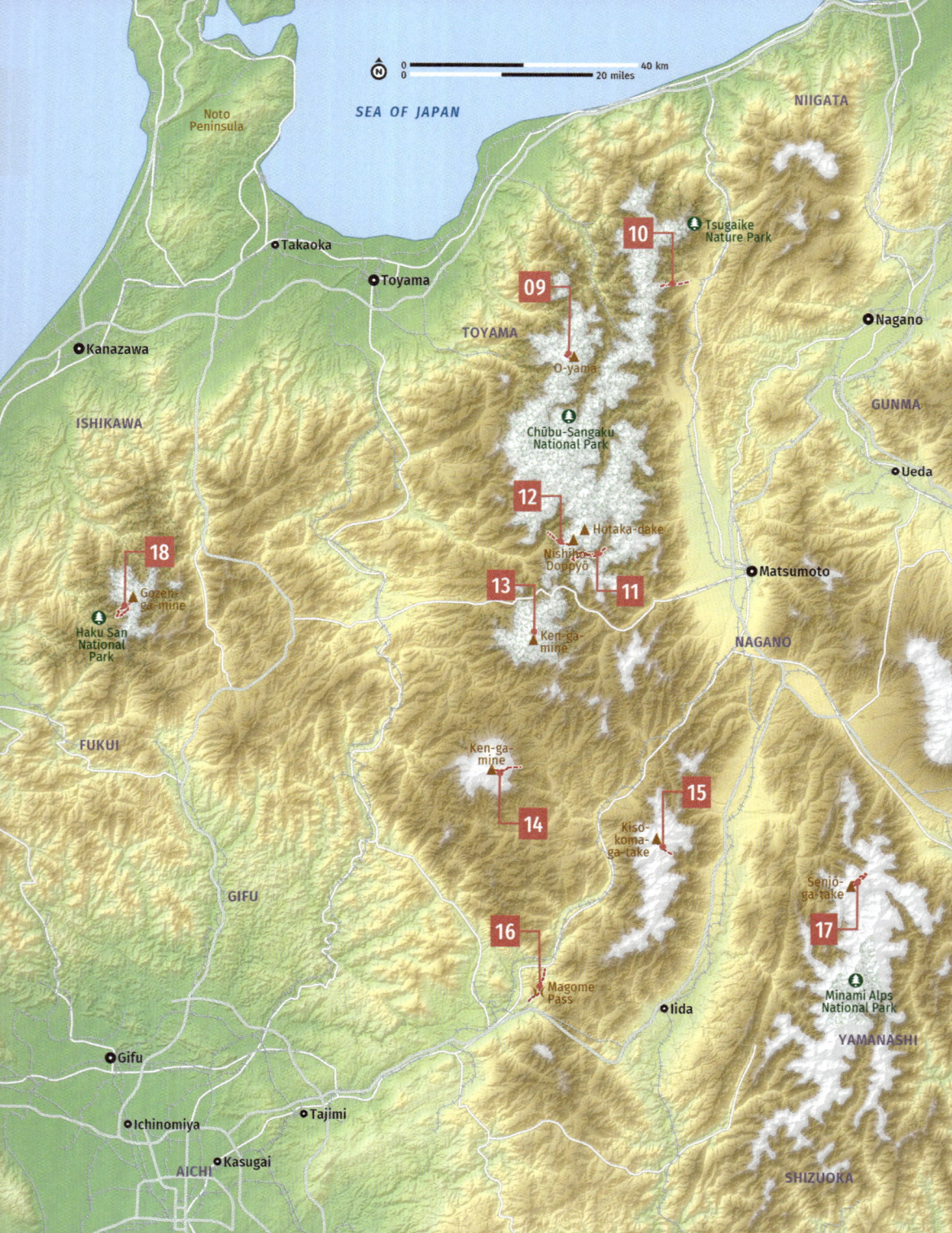

Happō-ike (p52)

Japan Alps & Central Honshū

09 Tateyama
Spectacular alpine scenery at one of Japan's three holiest mountains. **p50**

10 Hakuba Happō-ike
Stunning reflections in an alpine lake high above Hakuba. **p52**

11 Kamikōchi
Remote North Alps base for outdoor enthusiasts with unbelievable scenery. **p54**

12 Nishiho-Doppyō
Captivating views after walking from the top of the Shin-Hotaka Ropeway. **p58**

13 Norikura-dake
Relatively easy climb to the top of Japan's third-highest volcano. **p60**

14 Ontake-san
Deeply spiritual active volcano with its own religion. **p62**

15 Kiso-koma-ga-take
Climb the Central Alps' highest peak from the top of the ropeway. **p64**

16 Nakasendō
Atmospheric walk on the old post road from Magome to Tsumago. **p66**

17 Senjō-ga-take
A climb of the 3033m 'Queen of the South Alps'. **p68**

18 Hakusan
Climb to the shrine at the peak of this remote holy mountain. **p70**

Explore

Japan Alps & Central Honshū

Central Honshū, or Chūbu as it is known in Japanese, comprises the band of land extending from Kyoto in the west to Tokyo in the east and features the north, central and south regions of the Japan Alps. The highlights of walking in Japan are in this region: all 21 of Japan's 3000m-plus peaks, the three great spiritual mountains of Fuji-san, Tateyama and Hakusan, half of Japan's 100 Famous Mountains, and a stunning array of walking tracks, mountain huts, camping areas and hot springs. Thus Chūbu, and the North Alps in particular, is the most popular walking region in Japan.

Matsumoto

This vibrant city of 245,000 sits in a fertile valley, with the magnificent North Alps, in all their splendour, to the west. Matsumoto (松本) is an attractive, cosmopolitan place loved by both residents and admirers from around the globe, who come to enjoy its superb castle, pretty streets, galleries, cafes and endearing vistas. There seems to be some extra enthusiasm for life here, with a youngish population that includes those who have forsaken the massive cities for this regional beauty. The mountains are close, the air is fresh and the rivers are invigoratingly cold. Matsumoto makes a great stepping-stone on your way to the Alps and is easily accessed from Tokyo and points east.

Takayama

Officially known as Hida Takayama (飛騨高山), this city of 90,000 has one of Japan's most atmospheric townscapes, with Meiji-era inns, hillside shrines and a pretty riverside setting. The town's present layout dates from the late 17th century and incorporates a wealth of museums, galleries and temples for a place of its compact size. Excellent infrastructure and welcoming locals seal the deal. Takayama is easily explored on foot and is the perfect start or end point for walking trips into the North Alps. You'll likely pass through here if coming to the Alps from points west such as Nagoya, Kyoto or Osaka.

 ## When to Go

These are the high mountains in Japan and because of snow at altitude, most of the tracks in this chapter can only be walked from early July to mid-October. Places like Kamikōchi and Tateyama can get extremely crowded in midsummer and in autumn when the fall colours start to appear. Both places open up in time for the Golden Week holidays of late April, but the majority of walkers don't turn up until the start of July, at the earliest. Another reason the Chūbu mountains are popular in summer is that they are seen

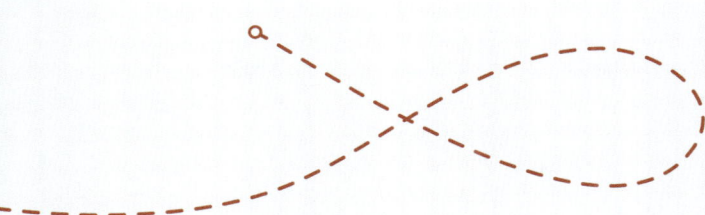

as an escape from the heat and humidity of the coastal cities.

 ## Transport

The best way to the hub cities for the walking regions of Central Honshū is by train or bus. Matsumoto is easily reached from Tokyo's Shinjuku Station by both train and bus. The shinkansen (bullet train) runs from Tokyo through Nagano (for Hakuba, p56), Toyama (for the Tateyama–Kurobe Alpine Route, p50) and on to Kanazawa (for Hakusan, p70). Takayama is reached by train from Nagoya with Kyoto and Osaka connections. The Nakasendō walk (p66) and Kiso-Fukushima (for Ontake; p62) are reached by the JR Chūō-Honsen line linking Nagoya and Matsumoto.

From the hub cities, buses will get you where you need to go, but there is a lot more freedom in having your own wheels. Most towns have rental-car offices. Cars are not allowed on some roads, such as on the Tateyama–Kurobe Alpine Route, into Kamikōchi, up the Norikura Skyline road and up to Kitazawa-tōge in the South Alps.

 ## Where to Stay

Some of Japan's finest *onsen ryokan* (traditional hot-spring inns) are found in the hollows of this densely forested alpine region or along the banks of its many rivers. In cities such as Matsumoto and Takayama, modern, practical hotels offer midrange comforts. A newish development throughout the region is guesthouses, which often offer the best value. And if you're willing to rough it a bit, there are mountain huts on nearly all the walks in this chapter.

 ## What's On

Many places will have mountain opening events such as Kamikōchi's festival on the first Sunday in June, the official opening of the walking season. Kamikōchi also has an opening of the mountain festival in late April to celebrate the reopening of the road into the valley after winter. In summer, all sorts of places host fireworks festivals and many ski resort areas attract visitors in summer with jazz festivals.

Resources

visitmatsumoto.com/en/
The official Matsumoto site has up-to-date visitor info.

hakuba-tourism.com
Accommodation listings for Hakuba.

kamikochi.org
Kamikōchi history, culture and tips on a user-friendly website.

minami-alpskankou.jp
Limited English-language resources, but a good resource for tours, events and links.

hakusan-guide.or.jp
News, weather and info for Hakusan.

Matsumoto Bonbon Matsumoto's biggest event is held on the first Saturday in August, when over 25,000 people of all ages perform the 'bonbon' dance through the streets.

Takayama Matsuri One of Japan's great festivals is in two parts. On 14 and 15 April there's the Sannō Matsuri, when decorated *yatai* (floats) are paraded through town. Hachiman Matsuri, on 9 and 10 October, is a slightly smaller version. In the evenings, the floats, with their carvings, dolls, colourful curtains and blinds, are decked out with lanterns.

09

Tateyama

DURATION	DIFFICULTY	DISTANCE	START/END
4-5hrs	Moderate	4km	Murodō
TERRAIN		Rough, rocky track, steep in parts	

The Tateyama (立山) caldera offers some of the most spectacular alpine scenery in Japan, easily accessed by the enthralling Tateyama–Kurobe Alpine Route. This is a special place. Tateyama is one of the three holiest mountains in Japan, along with Fuji and Hakusan, and it's easy to see why – towering peaks, a huge crater, gurgling hot springs – all reinforcing the idea of the mountains as the mother of all life.

Getting Here
Take the Tateyama–Kurobe Alpine Route (alpenroute.com) to Murodō (室堂) from Toyama (to the west) or Shinano-Ōmachi (to the east).

Starting Point
Murodō (2450m) is the highest point on the Tateyama–Kurobe Alpine Route.

01 Escape the crowds in the **Murodō complex** by heading up the stairs and outside to the huge rock with Tateyama (立山) written on it in *kanji*. If you stand in front of it, the line of high peaks directly behind are the Tateyama peaks. Follow signage and take the stone track that heads for the gap in the mountains slightly to the right of the peaks. It's a steady climb on an easy track to **Ichi-no-koshi** (一ノ越), a hut at 2705m, which should take an hour or so. That was the warm-up.

02 From here it is a steep, 300-vertical-metre climb to the shrine at the top. This is a popular route and there could be all sorts of people huffing and puffing up there – hundreds of

Tateyama–Kurobe Alpine Route

This famed route connects Toyama to the west of the North Alps with Shinano-Ōmachi to the east from mid-April to November. One of the top alpine draws in Japan, it is highly recommended. Travel is possible in either direction; take as long as you like at any of the stops. From Toyama Station, take the train, cable car, then bus up to Murodō, the start of the walk. Heading east from Murodō, take the tunnel trolley bus, ropeway, cable car, a walk over the Kurobe Dam, another tunnel trolley bus and, finally, a regular bus out to JR Shinano-Ōmachi Station. The route is extremely popular and can get insanely busy over holiday periods.

HIROI775/GETTY IMAGES ©

schoolkids on a school outing, middle-aged women smothered in sunblock – or, if it's windy and the cloud is in, you may be the only one there. It'll take an hour or so to the shrine at **O-yama** (雄山; 3003m), Tateyama's secondary peak and the target for most, which looks decidedly eerie in thick cloud.

03 If your target is **Ōnanji-yama** (大汝山), the highest point at 3015m, carry on along past the shrine. From O-yama is where you lose the crowds. To keep the unwary from venturing further than they should, there's a sign by the track stating that helicopter rescues past that point will cost the rescuee ¥3 million! It's a necessary scare tactic, because as you will have noticed on the way up, some walkers are seriously underprepared. The rocky track sticks close to the tops and 20 minutes past the shrine is Ōnanji-yama. **Tsurugi-dake** looks imposing off to the north and if you look east, over the top, **Kurobe Dam** and lake are below you. If you came from Ōgisawa on the Nagano side by the Tateyama–Kurobe Alpine Route, you will have walked over that dam in the morning.

04 Walk back over to the shrine at O-yama, then descend following the same track down to the Ichi-no-koshi hut and back to Murodō.

 Take a Break

A 15-minute walk from Murodō, you'll find Japan's highest natural onsen at 2410m, **Mikuri-ga-ike Onsen** (みくりが池温泉; mikuri.com). The hut here is a superb place to overnight, breaking up your journey on the Alpine Route into two days. The baths are open to the public (9am to 4pm), so after your walk, if you feel like a soak, head here.

10

Hakuba Happō-ike

DURATION	DIFFICULTY	DISTANCE	START/END
3-4hrs	Easy-moderate	4km	Happō-ike Sansō

TERRAIN	Rough rocky track, boardwalk and steepish sections

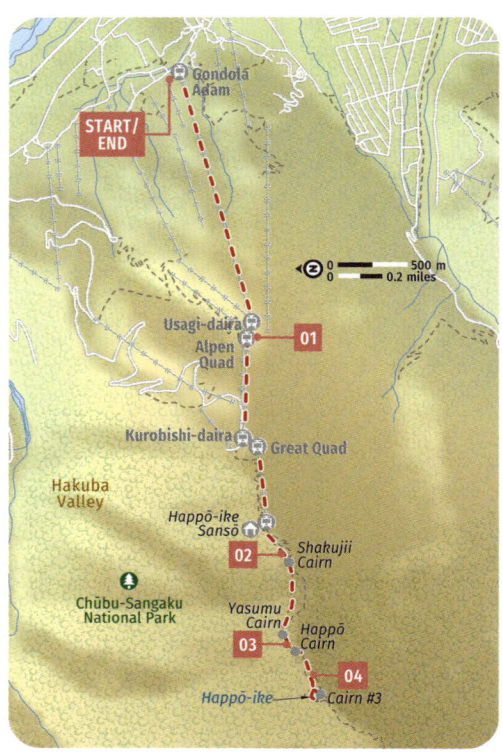

In a long north–south valley east of the northern Japan Alps, vibrant Hakuba (白馬), site of various skiing events at the 1998 Nagano Winter Olympics, is wholeheartedly embracing adventure tourism. It's long been a winter destination, but visitors now arrive in other seasons for walking, mountain biking, paragliding and other activities. This walk involves using three ski lifts up to an altitude of 1830m, from where it is a relatively easy walk up to Happō-ike (白馬八方池; 2060m), a small mountain lake renowned for its stunning reflections.

Getting Here
From JR Hakuba Station, take a bus to the bottom of Gondola Adam at the Happō-one ski area.

Starting Point
The track starts at Happō-ike Sansō, a hut at the top of the Great Quad chairlift. For the summer season, the lifts run from the start of June until the end of October and a return combined ticket for the three lifts costs adult/child ¥3300/2100 (happo-one.jp/en/trekking).

01 First up, take Gondola Adam from its lower station at 733m up to **Usagi-daira** (兎平; 1400m), where there's a **terrace with views and a cafe.** Next up is the Alpen Quad chairlift, which takes you up to **Kurobishi-daira** (黒菱平) at 1680m, followed by the Great Quad chairlift up to **Happō-ike Sansō** (1830m).

02 There are two ways to walk up from here. The track on the right is rough, rocky and has steep spots; the track on the left has lots of boardwalk, is less steep, but longer and may have

Two White Horses

Hakuba's legendary Shirouma-dake is one of Japan's 100 Famous Mountains. Shirouma means 'white horse' and the mountain supposedly got its name from the shape of the snow which lies on its side in spring. Hakuba (白馬) and Shirouma (白馬) are tricky for foreigners trying to learn *kanji* – they're different readings of the same characters. That is, in Japanese they're written the same way but pronounced differently. This is one of those quirky little things that you give up asking 'why' about and just accept – the town is called Hakuba and the mountain is called Shirouma – any Japanese you ask will have no idea why which is which and won't have given it a second's thought.

lingering snow if you're early in the season. Choose one for the way up, the other for the way down. The tracks come back together at your first target, **Shakujii Cairn** (石神井ケルン) at 1974m. Views out to the Hakuba Valley behind you and the peaks ahead are superb.

03 The track climbs gently up the ridge to **Yasumu Cairn** (ヤスムケルン; 2005m) and then to **Happō Cairn** (八方ケルン; 2035m), with alpine flowers and plants along the way. Carry on up the track to the less-eloquently named **Cairn #3** (第3ケルン) and take a break. If the weather is on your side, you'll get lovely views of Hakuba Sanzan (白馬三山; the three peaks of Hakuba) reflected in Happō-ike. This is the photo that most Japanese walkers have walked up here to take. The three peaks are, from north to south, Shirouma-dake (白馬岳; 2932m), Shakushi-dake (杓子岳; 2812m) and Hakuba Yari-ga-take (白馬鑓ヶ岳; 2903m).

04 Circumnavigate the **small lake** clockwise and the track will bring you back to the main track. Descend back to Happō-ike Sansō either on the rocky track or the boardwalk. If you opt for the boardwalk, remember you're in Japan and keep left! From Happō-ike Sansō hut, take the three lifts back down to Hakuba.

Take a Break

A long soak in an onsen after a day of action in the mountains is the perfect way to ease aching muscles and there are three public onsen nearby. **Mimizuku-no-yu** (みみずくの湯) is down towards JR Hakuba Station, **Happō-no-yu** (八方の湯) is near Happō Bus Station and **Sato-no-yu** (郷の湯) is not far from the Gondola Adam lower station.

11

Kamikōchi

DURATION	DIFFICULTY	DISTANCE	START/END
4-5hrs	Easy	14km	Kamikōchi bus station

TERRAIN	Easy, flat track in a river valley

Mention Kamikōchi (上高地) to Japanese outdoors enthusiasts and their eyes will light up. They'll tell you that this is where it's at and where you should be. Secluded in its own valley at the southern end of the North Alps, it's renowned for walking and climbing, whether that be summiting some of Japan's highest peaks, or enjoying the views in the magnificent Azusa River valley. It's feasible to visit as a day trip, but it's best to stay overnight and savour the snow-capped peaks, bubbling brooks, wild monkeys and ancient forests. Kamikōchi is closed from 15 November to 22 April.

Getting Here

Private vehicles are prohibited in the Kamikōchi valley. From Nakano-yu, on Rte 158 between Takayama and Matsumoto, access is only by bus or taxi. There are car parks en route to Naka-no-yu in the hamlet of Sawando with shuttle buses running into Kamikōchi from there. Buses from Shin-shimashima (by train from Matsumoto) and Hirayu Onsen (by bus from Takayama) run via Naka-no-yu to Kamikōchi's bus station.

Starting Point

This valley walk starts at Kamikōchi bus station. The **Kamikōchi Tourist Information Centre** (kamikochi.org) here is an invaluable resource, has English speakers on hand, provides information on walking and weather conditions and distributes the English-language *Kamikōchi Pocket Guide*, with a map of the main walking tracks. Be prepared

Up at Altitude

Serious mountaineers and climbers come to Kamikōchi with the peaks of Oku-hotaka-dake and Yari-ga-take in their sights. These are Japan's third- and fifth-highest mountains, and the three-day hike from Kamikōchi (1500m), climbing spear-like 'Yari' (3180m), traversing the Daikiretto (a legendary hole in the ridgeline), topping Oku-hotaka-dake (3190m) and then back into Kamikōchi, is the holy grail for Japanese hikers. Don't disrespect it! Be well prepared, do your homework and watch the weather forecasts if you're going to take this on. Kamikōchi is also the target for a week-long length-of-the-North Alps hike from Tateyama.

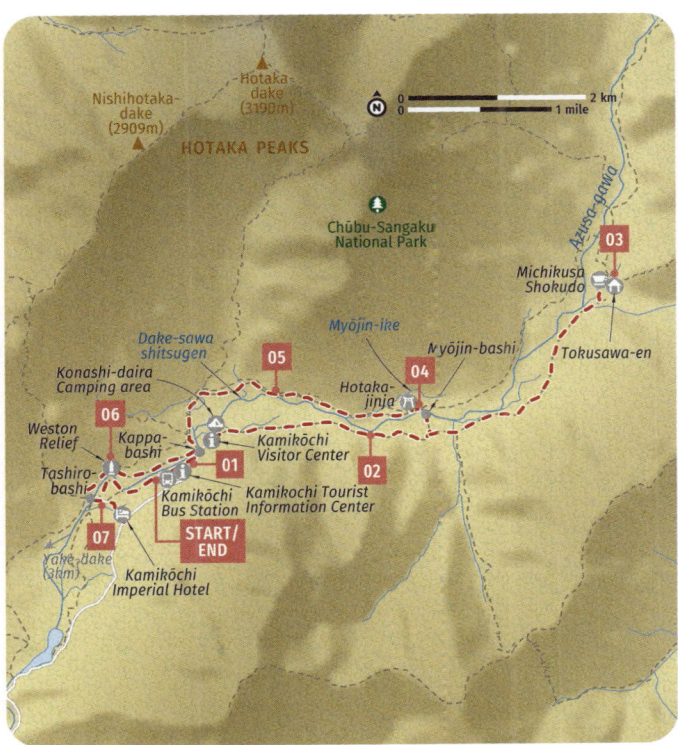

before you arrive in Kamikōchi: bring cash with you, as there's no ATM. There are souvenir shops, but no supermarket or convenience store; there's a baggage-storage counter at the bus station.

01 Visitors arrive at Kamikōchi's sprawling bus station and first stop should be the well-set-up tourist information centre. From here it's a 10-minute walk on either of two well-trodden tracks to **Kappa-bashi** (河童橋), a suspension bridge named after a legendary water sprite. If you're surprised by crowds of photo-taking visitors at Kamikōchi, especially at Kappa-bashi, keep in mind that 95% of visitors go no further than 500m from the bridge. The photo here of the bridge crossing the Azusa River with the Hotaka peaks in the background is *the* photo that everybody has to take at Kamikōchi. Watch out for tourists with selfie-sticks! From the bridge, if you look in the other direction, downriver, you'll get a fabulous view of the volcano, Yake-dake (焼岳; 2455m), often letting out smoke.

02 Without crossing the bridge, escape the crowds by heading up the track to the very worthwhile **Kamikōchi Visitor Center** (kamikochi-vc.or.jp/en), the place for information on Kamikōchi's flora, fauna, geology and history. There are fabulous photographs from all seasons. From here, the flat, well-used track wanders through the forested Konashi-daira camping area and finds its way out to the crystal-clear Azusa-gawa (梓川), the river that was flowing under the Kappa-bashi bridge. Within an hour, you'll have hit the **Myōjin** (明神) area, with a large bridge crossing the river on the left as you arrive. You'll be crossing that on your return leg. If you're happy with a shorter walk, cross it now and cut two hours off the walk.

55

03 Carry on up the east side of the Azusa River for an hour on an easy attractive trail to a wide, open area with two lodges and a camping area. Few get this far except climbers heading up to Yari-ga-take. **Tokusawa-en** (徳澤園) is the second of the lodges and a great place to take a break. Its cafe is open all day with a variety of refreshments. When you're ready, retrace your footsteps for an hour to the bridge, **Myōjin-bashi** (明神橋).

04 Cross the bridge and drop in to look over **Myōjin-ike** (明神池; pictured), a pond with the innermost shrine of **Hotaka-jinja** (穂高神社奥宮). Snowmelt from the Hotaka peaks produces crystal-clear waters here that flow out to the Matsumoto basin, irrigating the rice fields and linking this inner Hotaka-jinja with the main Hotaka-jinja in Azumino. There's a hub of lodges and shops here.

05 Walk downriver, now on the western side of the Azusa-gawa. After about 45 minutes you'll pass through the **Dake-sawa-shitsugen** (岳沢湿原; marsh area). This is where the Dake-sawa (Dake Creek) flows down from the Hotaka peaks high on your right to join the Azusa. Carry on and shortly you'll get back to the Kappa-bashi bridge, this time on its western side.

06 If this is the end for your walk, cross Kappa-bashi and head back to the bus station. If you're up for another 45 minutes of exploring, walk downriver past the set of

Walter Weston

In the late 19th century, British missionary Reverend Walter Weston toiled from peak to peak in the North Alps area and sparked Japanese interest in mountaineering as a sport accessible to all. This was a new idea in Japan, as the high mountains were seen as the realm of religious ascetics. Weston had a deep appreciation of Japanese culture and natural landscapes, and he is honoured to this day with an annual festival in Kamikōchi on the first Sunday in June, held at the Weston Relief monument on the west side of the Azusa-gawa.

four lodges and hotels and on for another 10 minutes to the **Weston Relief** (ウェストン碑), a small monument in honour of Walter Weston (1861–1940), the English missionary who introduced Western-style mountain climbing to Japan. Carry on past another couple of hotels before crossing the Azusa River on the **Tashiro-bashi** (田代橋).

07 Once over the river, turn a sharp left and follow the eastern riverbank back upriver. If visiting the **Kamikōchi Imperial Hotel** (上高地帝国ホテル) appeals, once you've crossed the Tashiro bridge don't turn left but head straight up the road for five minutes. Built in 1933, this historic red-roofed beauty is an outpost of Tokyo's Imperial Hotel and requires very early pre-booking (and deep pockets!) if you want to stay. If you turned left once over the bridge, follow the riverbank for 15 minutes back to the bus station.

Take a Break

While there are a few places to get a bite and refreshments at Kamikōchi bus station and by Kappa-bashi bridge, two hours into the walk, at **Tokusawa-en** (tokusawaen.com) mountain lodge, you'll find the very cute little Michikusa Shokudo (みちくさ食堂). It's open for coffee, tea, beer, ice cream and desserts like blueberry cheesecake all day long, while you can also get curry, soba and udon noodles to 3pm. Take a break with whatever takes your fancy out on the terrace.

12

Nishiho-Doppyō

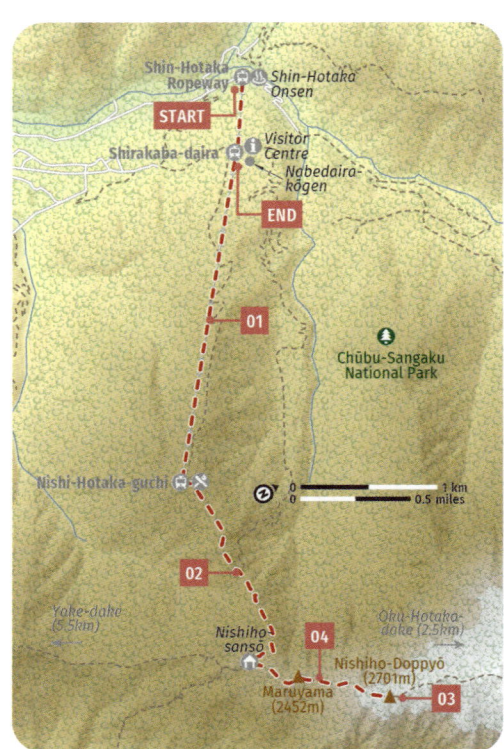

DURATION	DIFFICULTY	DISTANCE	START/END
4-5hrs	Moderate-hard	8km	Nishi-Hotaka-guchi upper ropeway station

TERRAIN	Rough, rocky track with some steep sections

The climb to Nishiho-Doppyō (西穂独標; 2701m), on the main line of peaks at the southern end of the North Alps, will reveal stunning views of the surrounding mountains and is relatively easy thanks to the Shin-Hotaka Ropeway carrying you up to 2156m, eliminating most of the climb. For those who are after a shorter walk, there's a 2.3km nature trail at Nabedaira-kōgen, where you change ropeway cars.

Getting Here

Shin-Hotaka Onsen (新穂高温泉) is 40 minutes by bus from Hirayu Onsen (平湯温泉), which in turn can be reached by bus from Takayama and Matsumoto. If you come by car, drive up to Nabedaira-kōgen (鍋平高原), at the top of the first ropeway, and park there.

Starting Point

The track starts at the upper station of Shin-Hotaka Ropeway's second ropeway (shinhotaka-ropeway.jp). A combined return ropeway ticket for both lifts from the bottom costs adult/child ¥3300/1650.

01 Ride the first ropeway from Shin-Hotaka Onsen (1117m) up to **Nabedaira-kōgen** (1300m), where you'll find a **visitor centre**, a **nature trail** and an **onsen.** The second ropeway is known for having Japan's first double-decker gondola cars and will take you up to **Nishi-Hotaka-guchi station** (西穂高口; 2156m), where there is a cafe, restaurant and observation deck.

02 Head out the back of the ropeway station's 4th floor and follow the *tozandō* (登山道; mountain track) for a gentle start. Things will steepen and get rocky as you climb up to **Nishiho-sansō** (西穂山荘), a hut on the ridge at 2367m.

Onsen Ryokan

Shin-Hotaka Onsen boasts some lovely *onsen ryokan*, where you can stay, eat, bathe and relax in a traditional setting. A top choice is the wonderful riverside **Yarimikan** (槍見舘; yarimikan.com), with two indoor baths, eight riverside *rotemburo* (outdoor bath) and 16 rooms. Guests can bathe 24 hours a day and day visitors (¥600) are accepted between 10am and 2pm. Cuisine features local Hida beef and grilled freshwater fish. There are a number of small, atmospheric onsen villages in the region and you could also consider staying at Hirayu Onsen, Fukuji Onsen or Shirahone Onsen.

Best for

ONSEN

CRAIG MCLACHLAN/LONELY PLANET ©

You'll have been walking an hour or so in forest. The hut is at the confluence of a number of trails. South is Yake-dake; a trail drops down to the east to Kamikōchi and the one you'll be taking heads north to Nishiho-Doppyō (西穂独標) and on to the high Hotaka peaks, including Oku-hotaka-dake (奥穂高岳; 3190m), the third-highest peak in Japan. After Nishiho-Doppyō though, the track gets difficult and is only for the experienced and well prepared.

03 From the hut, head northeast on the track signposted to Nishi-Hotaka-dake (西穂高岳). You'll pass over Maruyama (円山; 2452m), descend to a saddle, then climb steadily up to the target for the day, **Nishiho-Doppyō**. The final section requires a bit of scrambling following the white painted arrows and markings on the rocks. If it's a good day, you won't need them, but if you're in the middle of a cloud you'll find the paint markings extremely useful! From the peak at 2701m, there are excellent views in all directions. It will have taken 1½ hours or so from the hut.

04 When you're ready, head back down the track you came up, enjoying the **views south** as you go, to Nishiho-sansō and back down to the upper ropeway station. You'll have climbed and descended 550 vertical metres for the day and thoroughly deserve refreshments.

Take a Break

Shirakaba-daira Station is the lower ropeway station for the double-decker gondola car and a good spot to take a break after your walk. You'll find **Take-out Panorama**, selling snacks, drinks and ice cream, **Alpine Baker** with popular croissants and, possibly best of all, an *ashi-yu* (foot bath) outside where you can take off shoes and socks and relax your feet in the soothing hot waters.

13

Norikura-dake

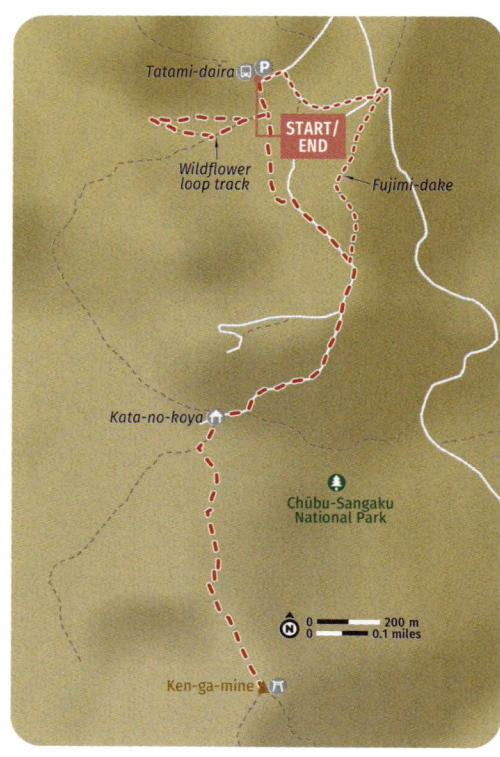

DURATION	DIFFICULTY	DISTANCE	START/END
3hrs	Moderate	6km	Tatami-daira

TERRAIN	Easy trail changing to rough and rocky

Sitting just south of the North Alps, Norikura-dake (乗鞍岳) is Japan's third-highest volcano, at 3026m. This mighty mountain is relatively easily climbed thanks to the Norikura Skyline road (closed to private cars; norikuradake.jp), whereby a bus can deliver you to Noriku-ra Tatami-daira terminal at 2700m.

The characters for Norikura (乗鞍) mean 'riding saddle', referring to the mountain's resemblance to a horse's saddle, and there is often residual snow on north-facing slopes, even in midsummer. Start out at the Tatami-daira (畳平) bus terminal by following signage for the high point of Ken-ga-mine (剣ヶ峰). In the flat meadow below Tatami-daira you'll find a great little **wildflower loop track** which is worth walking.

Back on the main track, it's a relatively easy 30 minutes to the mountain hut **Kata-no-koya** (肩の小屋) at 2800m. Allow another hour from there to the peak on a rocky, steepening, easy-to-follow trail. Remember, you're up at altitude and the air is thin. Take your time. Just before the top you'll find a small hut selling snacks and souvenirs, and at **Ken-ga-mine** there's a Shintō shrine and spectacular views in all directions. Directly north are the North Alps; Ontake-san is directly south; Hakusan is away to the west, and the Central and South Alps are to the southeast. This is **one of the best 360-degree panoramas in Japan.** Follow the same track back to Tatami-daira, or if you're up for more, take the **Fujimi-dake** (富士見岳) optional sidetrack, which will add 20 minutes on to the return. Fujimi-dake means 'the peak from which you can see Fuji-san' and on a good day you'll be rewarded with a peek of Japan's highest mountain.

Best for

MOUNTAIN VIEWS

14

Ontake-san

DURATION	DIFFICULTY	DISTANCE	START/END
5-6hrs	Moderate	7km	Iimori-kōgen-eki

TERRAIN	Rough, rocky track, steep in sections

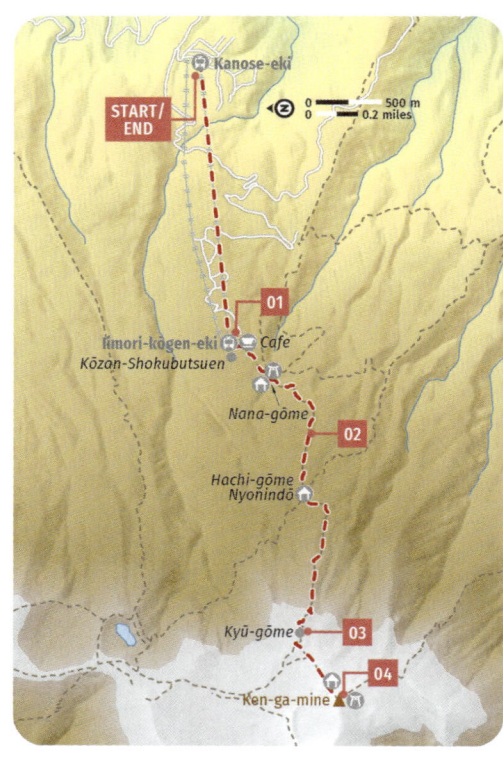

About 20km west of the Kiso Valley is Japan's second-highest volcano (after Fuji-san), the massive Ontake-san (御岳山; 3067m) with five crater lakes. With its own religion (Ontake-kyō) and small shrines, Shintō gates and religious statues along the walk, Ontake-san is an unforgettable experience. Ontake-san is an active volcano. Sixty-three walkers lost their lives in 2014 when it erupted, covering the mountain in ash. In 2019, Ontake's activity level was given the lowest possible rating for an active volcano, and the route to the peak from the top of Ontake Ropeway (ontake-rope2150.jp) was reopened.

Getting Here

Having your own wheels would be very useful, but there are also buses from Kiso-Fukushima (on the JR Chūō-Honsen line linking Nagoya and Matsumoto) to the lower ropeway station, Kanose-eki (鹿ノ瀬駅; 1570m). There is lots of free parking here.

Starting Point

Ride the Ontake Ropeway to the upper station, Iimori-kōgen-eki (飯森高原駅), where the track begins.

01 At Iimori-kōgen-eki you'll find a **Kōzan-Shokubutsuen** (高山植物園; alpine plant garden), where you can check out the Ontake region's alpine plants and flowers before getting going.

02 The track starts off with an easy 10-minute warm-up to **Nana-gōme** (七合目; the 7th station), where there is a small **shrine** and a moun-

Ontake-kyō: Mountain Religion

Ontake-san boasts its own religion, Ontake-kyō. A 'mountain religion', it can be considered as similar to Shugendō, but while Shugendō mixes Buddhist and Shintō beliefs, Ontake-kyō is a Shintō offshoot that guides the practitioner to overcome evil and get closer to nature. It incorporates ascetic practice and harsh physical training, and Ontake-kyō's version of *yamabushi* (mountain priests) in years past held positions of great respect for the powers they attained. Of course, *yamabushi* these days are mostly weekend practitioners and after talking to some you'll get the impression that their biggest hardship is the long car trip from the big city to Ontake-san.

tain hut. From there, an hour or so of steady climbing, initially through trees and bamboo grass, then sparser landscape, will get you to **Hachi-gōme Nyonindō** (八合目女人堂; 8th station Women's Hall). This is where female pilgrims, who were not allowed to climb to the peak until the mid-1870s, waited and prayed while the men carried on climbing. You might start to get a whiff of volcanic sulphur from here.

03 Another 1½ hours of steady, then steepish climbing will get you to **Kyū-gōme** (九合目) and you'll be in a bare, rocky volcanic landscape, feeling a little bit like being on the moon, having left all hints of vegetation behind.

04 From there it will take around 25 minutes of climbing through more bare rocks to get to three concrete emergency shelters built post-2014 eruption just below the summit. The mountain hut that was here pre-eruption was virtually destroyed and was torn down. Climb the final set of 80 steps that take you up to the **shrine** at the top (3067m). The high point is known as **Ken-ga-mine** (剣ヶ峰) and offers spectacular **views of volcanic lakes** and the surrounding landscape.

05 Follow your tracks back down to the upper ropeway station in two to 2½ hours and descend on the ropeway back to Kanose-eki.

 **Take a Break**

There are not a lot of places to eat, buy supplies or get information once you've left Kiso-Fukushima and headed west towards Ontake-san. Get the info you need at **Kiso's tourist information centre** (en.visitkiso.com) opposite JR Kiso-Fukushima Station. For a break after the walk, there's a cafe with spectacular views at the upper ropeway station open until 4pm.

15

Kiso-koma-ga-take

DURATION	DIFFICULTY	DISTANCE	START/END
4hrs	Moderate	4km	Shirabidaira lower ropeway station

TERRAIN	Rough mountain track, steep in some sections

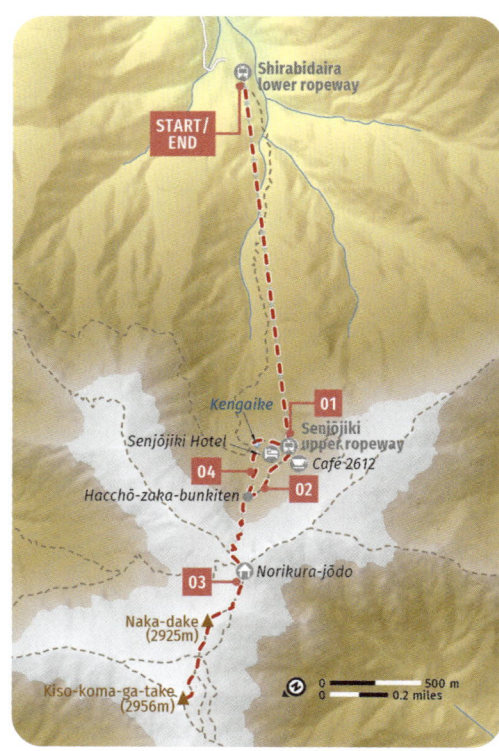

Officially called Kiso Sanmyaku (木曽山脈), the range of mountains east of the Kiso Valley is better known to the Japanese as the Chūō (Central; 中央) Alps. They may not be as high as the North and South Alps, but the Central Alps present a brilliant opportunity for just about anyone to climb 2956m Kiso-koma-ga-take (木曽駒ケ岳), one of Japan's 100 Famous Mountains, thanks to the Komagatake Ropeway, which lifts visitors up to 2612m in the Senjōjiki cirque.

Getting Here

The Komagatake Ropeway is on the eastern side of the Central Alps. Make your way to Komagane (駒ヶ根), on the JR Iida line in the Tenryū river valley.

Starting Point

Private cars are not allowed up to Shirabidaira (しらび平), the bottom ropeway station. Take the bus from Komagane Station if you came by train, from the Suga-no-dai car park if you came by car, then ride the **Komagatake Ropeway** (駒ヶ岳ロープウェ; chuo-alps.com; return adult/child from ¥4390/2190 incl bus).

01 The ropeway from Shirabidaira (1662m) takes eight minutes to get to Senjōjiki, almost 1km higher at 2612m. This is reputedly the highest station in Japan, and even if you only make it this far, you're in for a thrill: on a good day you can see virtually all the South Alps and even Fuji-san. At the top of the ropeway, where there is food and refreshments as well as the **Senjōjiki Hotel** (千畳敷ホテル), you're surrounded by the cliffs of **Senjōjiki** (千畳敷), a towering glacial cirque. A very good 45-minute nature walk has been set up

Less of a Mouthful

The 'koma' (駒) of koma-ga-take (駒ヶ岳) means horse or pony, so Kiso-koma-ga-take means 'the horse peak of the Kiso area'. There are 'horse peaks' all over Japan – Akita-koma-ga-take, Eizo-koma-ga-take, Uonuma-koma-ga-take and, just across the Tenryū valley from Kiso-koma-ga-take and visible on a good day, Kai-koma-ga-take. These names are all a bit of a mouthful to say, and it's perfectly acceptable in a conversation to drop the '-ga-take' off the end once everyone knows which one you're talking about. This doesn't only apply to the koma-ga-takes: Yari-ga-take is known as Yari, Oku-hotaka-dake as Oku-hotaka, Utsugi-dake as Utsugi, and so on.

CRAIG MCLACHLAN / LONELY PLANET ©

within the confines of the cirque and can clearly be seen from the starting point.

02 Head out of the ropeway station and follow the nature walk track for about 20 minutes to **Hacchō-zaka-bunkiten** (八丁坂分岐点), where the road forks. Take the left path. On your way back down, you'll be taking the bit of the nature walk you haven't walked back to the upper ropeway station from here.

03 From Hacchō-zaka-bunkiten to **Norikura-jōdo** (乗鞍浄土), at 2850m, on the main ridge at the top of the cirque, the track climbs reasonably steeply, but this is the steepest bit you'll face all day. From Norikura-jōdo, where there are two mountain huts, it takes around an hour, passing over Naka-dake (2925m), to the **summit of Kiso-koma-ga-take** (2956m) with its bare rock, stone cairns and shrines. The summit is more like a rounded hillock than a sharp peak and on a good day the views are breathtaking of Fuji-san and the South Alps to the east, Ontake to the west, and Norikura and the North Alps to the north. There's a hut near the peak where you can take refuge if it's blowing.

04 Return back down the way you came, and at Hacchō-zaka-bunkiten stay to the left and take the nature walk via **Kengaike** (剣ヶ池), a pond surrounded by wildflowers, back to the upper ropeway station.

Take a Break

Café 2612 is in the upper ropeway station and claims to be the highest cafe in Japan – its name comes from the altitude, 2612m. Have a meal, soup, beer, coffee or ice cream while enjoying the views. Coffees are made with snowmelt water!

16

Nakasendō

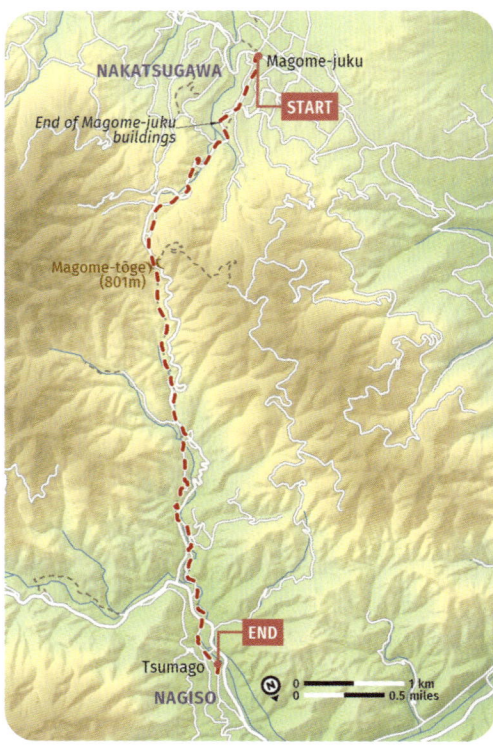

DURATION	DIFFICULTY	DISTANCE	START/END
3-4hrs	Easy-moderate	8km	Magome/Tsumago

TERRAIN	Mostly paved, some well-worn track, steepish sections

The Nakasendō (中仙道) was one of the two great roads of the Edo period connecting Edo (now Tokyo) with Kyoto. This was the inland mountainous route, preferred by many to the Tōkaidō, which went around the coast and required many river crossings. Much of the route is now followed by national roads; however, in the thickly forested Kiso Valley there exist several sections of twisty, craggy post road that have been carefully restored. Most impressive is the 8km stretch between Magome and Tsumago.

Pretty **Magome-juku** (馬篭宿; 600m), in Nakatsugawa, Gifu Prefecture, is the furthest south of the Kiso Valley post villages. Its buildings line a steep, cobblestone pedestrian road, with rustic shopfronts and mountain views that will keep your finger on the shutter. After climbing through the village, the walk to Tsumago follows a steepish, largely paved road until it reaches its peak at the top of **Magome-tōge** (a pass at elevation 801m). After the pass, the trail meanders by **waterfalls**, **forest** and **farmland** to **Tsumago** (妻籠; 420m), which is about 15 minutes' walk from end to end and feels like an open-air museum. Part of Nagiso town in Nagano Prefecture, it has been designated a protected area for the preservation of traditional buildings. The dark-wood glory of its lattice-front buildings is particularly beautiful at dawn and dusk.

The route is easiest in this direction and is clearly signposted in English; allow three to four hours to enjoy it. The towns offer a handy baggage-forwarding service between tourist information centres. Deposit your bags between 8.30am and 11.30am for pick up at the other end between 1pm and 5pm. This service costs ¥1000 per item.

17

Senjō-ga-take

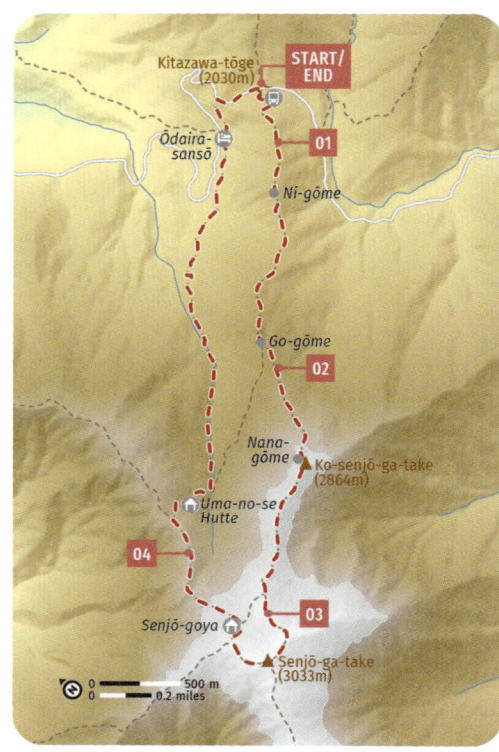

DURATION	DIFFICULTY	DISTANCE	START/END
7-8hrs	Hard	9km	Kitazawa-tōge

TERRAIN	Rough, rocky and steep in places

The South Alps is the highest range of mountains in Japan. With much of the 100km-long range remote and difficult to access, the South Alps are less popular than walking hotspots in the North Alps. This, they say, is where you go if you want to get away from it all. With 10 of Japan's 100 Famous Mountains though, popularity is on the rise, especially at the northern end of the range. At 3033m Senjō-ga-take (仙丈ヶ岳), known as 'the Queen of the South Alps', is the easiest to access and climb of the South Alps' great peaks.

Getting Here

The trailhead is at Kitazawa-tōge, a pass at the northern end of the South Alps, accessed by bus (late June to early November) from Hirogawara to the east or from Senryūsō to the west. These towns can be reached by bus from JR Kōfu Station and JR Chino Station, respectively, on the JR Chūō-honsen line. Having your own wheels is preferable.

Starting Point

The trail starts at Kitazawa-tōge (北沢峠; 2030m), the pass between two great peaks, Senjō-ga-take (仙丈ヶ岳; 3033m) and Kai-koma-ga-take (甲斐駒ケ岳; 2966m). Many hikers come to climb both over two days, staying in one of the three huts at the pass.

01 Starting at 2030m and climbing to 3033m, you have 1000 vertical metres to ascend along a well-marked trail to the peak, taking around four hours – you'll be rounding the top of a cirque to the high point, then descending the same number of vertical metres on a different track, taking about 3½ hours back to the pass. Initially, follow signage

Length of the South Alps

For the experienced, fit and hardy hiker, a six-day, 80km length-of-the-South Alps trek is one of the most adventurous trips possible in Japan and includes all the major peaks. While it's a long hike through very remote and challenging mountain country, you take a well-used, easy-to-follow track with plenty of mountain huts, emergency shelters and camping areas along the way. The route starts at Hirogawara (広河原; 1530m), climbs Kita-dake (北岳; 3192m), then heads south along the range's spine before descending to Sawara-jima (椹島; 1100m) on day six. Be well prepared if taking this on!

from Kitazawa-tōge for Senjō-ga-take and spend your first hour in **forest** to **Ni-gōme** (二合目; the second stage point). The track to the peak is marked with 10 stage points, so it's easy to see how you're doing.

02 Another hour of ascent in forest will bring you to **Go-gōme** (五合目; 5th stage), where a track that you don't want to take splits off to the right. Continue heading up the ridge to **Ko-senjō-ga-take** (小仙丈ヶ岳; 2864m). You'll pass above the treeline and get excellent views of what's ahead from this secondary peak, that is also Nana-gōme (七合目; 7th stage).

03 A final hour of climbing and you'll be rounding the top of a large cirque to the high point of **Senjō-ga-take** (3033m). Views are truly spectacular, though you'll be thankful for the red paint marks on rocks to guide you if the cloud is in.

04 Drop down the other side of the peak from which you came and walk down to the hut, **Senjō-goya** (仙丈小屋) in about 15 minutes. From here, following signage for Kitazawa-tōge (北沢峠), you'll get to the attractive mountain hut of **Uma-no-se Hutte** (馬ノ背ヒュッテ) in about an hour.

It will take two more hours to descend to **Ōdaira-sansō** (大平山荘) and a well-earned beer! From there it's an easy 15-minute walk back up to Kitazawa-tōge and the bus stop.

 **Take a Break**

Below Kitazawa-tōge on its western side, **Ōdaira-sansō** is a perfect spot to take a break after the walk and is on the track on which you'll descend from Senjō-ga-take. This friendly family-run mountain hut provides overnight accommodation but is happy to have day visitors drop in for refreshments. Make sure to peruse the terrific collection of photos that adorn the walls of the main building.

18

Hakusan

DURATION	DIFFICULTY	DISTANCE	START/END
8-9hrs	Hard	11km	Bettōdeai

TERRAIN	Rough, rocky, steep mountain tracks

Rugged and remote Hakusan (白山; White Mountain) is the highest mountain in Japan west of the Alps. It stands exposed to frigid northwest winds in winter, which whip across the Japan Sea and dump oodles of snow, giving the mountain its name. Areas near the peak can have snow year-round and the first snow usually falls in October.

Getting Here

If driving, during the July to October season you'll have to park at Ichinose (free) and take a shuttle bus to Bettōdeai. Limited Hokutetsu Kankō (hokutetsu.co.jp) buses run from Kanazawa Station (on the shinkansen line from Tokyo) to Bettōdeai in summer.

Starting Point

Bettōdeai sits to the southwest of Hakusan. You are required to fill out a 'climbing notification' (*tozantodoke*) and put it in the box at the trailhead.

01 From **Bettōdeai** (1200m) take the track that crosses the river and heads straight up the valley. This track is called Sabō Shindō (砂防新道) and makes for an easier climb than the Kankō Shindō (観光新道) track, heading up the ridgeline on your left. After an hour or so of climbing, the track will cross a road before climbing steeply to an emergency hut, reached after another 1½ hours.

02 About 15 minutes later, turn left at the track intersection and head for **Mida-ga-hara** (弥陀ヶ原), with a final steep climb to get up to the wide plain in an hour. At the plain, the Kankō Shindō track will join up from the left – take note, as that's your way down. That's the end of the hard stuff. From here the Murodō cluster of

Holy Hakusan

Hakusan is a mountain of profound religious significance and it is said that priests and pilgrims have been climbing it since 717 CE. Along with Fuji-san and Tateyama, Hakusan is one of Japan's 'Big Three' holy mountains. One of the reasons is because heavy winter snows disappear to be replaced by spectacular flowers in spring. Traditional worship of the power of nature and the fact that Hakusan provides such a perfect environment for ascetic training have made the peak's reputation as a religious mountain. Its remoteness and the effort it takes to get there have also meant that only the most dedicated have made it this far over the centuries.

Best for

OFF THE BEATEN PATH

YAGI STUDIO/GETTY IMAGES ©

buildings and Gozen-ga-mine, the high point of Hakusan, are dead ahead. It's 30 minutes of gentle climbing to **Murodō** (室堂; 2450m). The ascent will have taken four to 4½ hours. If you've opted to make this a two-day trip, make sure you've reserved your Murodō accommodation before coming to Hakusan.

03 Continue to **Gozen-ga-mine** (御前峰; 2702m) in another 40 minutes. It's surprisingly easy after all the early hard work to get up the Sabō Shindō. At the peak you'll find the Shirayama Hime-jinja Oku-miya (白山比咩神社奥宮) **shrine** and incredible views on a good day. Looking east, the North Alps from Tateyama all the way down to Norikura-dake and Ontake stand supreme. (Walkers in the North Alps can see Hakusan too. One of the best-known images of the mountain is that of Hakusan as an island sticking out above the clouds, as seen from Tateyama.)

04 There are various options for getting back to **Murodō**, including dropping off to the north among the **crater lakes** and peaks before rounding back to the south. It's all fairly self-explanatory when you're there. If you're inside a cloud, head back down to Murodō on the track on which you climbed.

05 From Murodō, head back across the plain and take the **Kankō Shindō** (観光新道) track back down to Bettōdeai. The descent will take three to 3½ hours from Murodō.

Take a Break

Hakusan is a big day walk and you might want to consider overnighting at **Hakusan Murodō** (白山室堂; hakusan-guide.or.jp; from ¥8200; May-Nov), which is more like a village than a lonely mountain hut. There's a visitors centre, a shrine, dining facilities and dorm accommodation. Reservations are a must. A bonus of overnighting is that you can be at the peak for sunrise.

Also Try...

AMSTK/SHUTTERSTOCK ©

Myōkō-san

DURATION	DIFFICULTY	DISTANCE
8hrs	Hard	9km

Almost directly north of Nagano city, the Myōkō mountain range is a popular destination among both walkers and skiers.

In the warmer months, the lush, verdant forests of Myōkō Kōgen draw hikers and strollers alike to wander their many sunlit paths – the area is a certified 'forest therapy base', where walkers can practise the art of *shinrin-yoku* (forest relaxation). For an extended walk, the climb of Myōkō-san (妙高; 2454m), one of Japan's 100 Famous Mountains, from Tsubame Onsen (1200m) is a highlight. Allow 4½ hours for the climb, with some scrambling and chains to help near the top. On a good day, you'll be able to spot Fuji-san, almost directly south. Allow 3½ hours for the descent. It's a big day, but waiting are the milky white waters of Tsubame Onsen, including Kawara-no-yu, a free, mixed gender *rotemburo* by the river.

Yatsu-ga-take

DURATION	DIFFICULTY	DISTANCE
7-8hrs	Hard	10km (starting at Minōdo)

Southeast of Matsumoto, with ease of access from Tokyo, Yatsu-ga-take (八ヶ岳) is a popular playground with walking, onsen, resort villages and craft shops.

Yatsu-ga-take means 'eight peaks' as there are eight major peaks along the main ridge, which runs from north to south. The story goes that Yatsu-ga-take used to be the highest volcano – higher even than Fuji – but in a fight for supremacy Fuji knocked Yatsu-ga-take down, forming eight lower peaks in the process. The highest is Aka-dake (赤岳; 2899m), climbable from Minōdo-guchi (美濃戸口) bus stop (1500m) in a day. Take the unsealed road up to Minōdo (美濃戸; 1800m). If you've got your own wheels, you can drive up this far. Allow four hours for the climb to Aka-dake (pictured), one of Japan's 100 Famous Mountains. There are a number of options for the descent; allow another three hours.

RAYINTS/SHUTTERSTOCK ©

Tsugaike Nature Park

DURATION	DIFF.	DISTANCE
2-3hrs	Easy	5.5km

Sitting at 1900m at the top of the Tsugaike ski gondola and ropeway at Hakuba is an excellent loop walking course.

Open from mid-May to early October, the walk through Tsugaike Nature Park (栂池自然園; pictured) features wetlands, spectacular views of the Hakuba Sanzan (Hakuba three peaks) and a changing progression of alpine plants through the seasons. The track is 80% boardwalk. Round-trip tickets for the gondola, ropeway and park entrance cost adult/child ¥3700/2100. See tsugaike.gr.jp.

Bijodaira

DURATION	DIFF.	DISTANCE
2½hrs	Easy	4km

At the top of the Tateyama cable car on the Tateyama–Kurobe Alpine Route are four loop walking track options taking from 30 minutes to 2½ hours.

This is one of Japan's top 100 'forest relaxation' spots and features massive Tateyama cedar and beech trees as well as over 60 species of birds. Bijodaira (美女平; 677m) is a major draw for birdwatchers and you may spot the Japanese robin or the blue-and-white flycatcher. It's a good place to bring the kids and an easy stop on the full Alpine Route.

Jōnen-dake

DURATION	DIFF.	DISTANCE
8hrs	Hard	10km

Views from the peak of Jōnen-dake (常念岳; 2857m) out over the Matsumoto basin make this big climb worthwhile.

This is a summer-only hike with a 1500m climb, so walkers must be fit and properly prepared. From JR Hotaka Station, 30 minutes north from Matsumoto on the JR Ōito line, it's a 30-minute taxi ride to the Ichi-no-sawa trailhead. Maps are available at the tourist information centre outside the station. There are many options for hikes extending over several days, such as descending to the west into Kamikōchi (but you must be suitably prepared).

Fushimi Inari (p78)

Kansai

19 **Fushimi Inari**
A maze of paths through over 10,000 vermillion shrine gates. **p78**

20 **Daimonji-yama**
Stunning views of Kyoto from high above Ginkaku-ji. **p80**

21 **Kurama to Kibune**
The quieter side of Kyoto at the end of the train line. **p82**

22 **Rokku Gaaden**
Fun 'urban hike' with views, peaceful forest and unusual rock formations. **p84**

23 **Kasuga-yama**
Walk through the 'Forest of the Gods', virtually untouched for 1000 years. **p86**

24 **Yama-no-be-no-michi**
Enjoy this rural, historical ramble through the Nara countryside. **p88**

25 **Kōya-san**
Climb to Kōbō Daishi's mountaintop monastery complex and mausoleum. **p90**

26 **Kumano Kodō**
Walk along the ancient network of trails on the Kii Peninsula. **p92**

Explore

Kansai

Kansai offers some outstanding walks within easy reach of the region's major cities – Kyoto, Osaka, Nara and Kōbe. Surrounded by mountains on three sides, the Kyoto area is particularly rich in walkable terrain. Since many of Kyoto's walks start or finish at mountainside temples, it's easy to combine physical and cultural pursuits in one outing. Likewise, walks around Nara are rich in history, and many of them follow ancient trade routes and pilgrimage trails. Both Kyoto and Nara are peppered with World Heritage Sites, while further south Kōya-san and the Kumano Kodō are part of the Kii Peninsula's World Heritage–listed Sacred Sites and Pilgrimage Routes in the Kii Mountain Range.

Kyoto

Kyoto (京都) is old Japan writ large: quiet temples, sublime gardens, colourful shrines and geisha scurrying to exclusive engagements. With more than 1000 Buddhist temples and over 400 Shintō shrines, it is one of the world's most culturally rich cities and on the 'go to' list of most visitors to Japan. It's also surrounded by forested mountains and has great spots to take a break on well-worn trails to get that magnificent view out over the city.

Osaka

If Kyoto was historically the city of the courtly nobility and Tokyo the city of the samurai, then Osaka (大阪) was the city of the merchant class. Osakans take pride in shedding the conservatism found elsewhere in Japan, and this spirited city is a place where people are a bit brasher – the city's unofficial slogan is *kuidaore* ('eat until you drop') and it seems that everyone is always out for a good meal – and a good time. It's relatively easy to get to all the walks in this chapter from Osaka.

Nara

History in Nara Prefecture goes back further even than Kyoto's, as it was here in the Yamato basin that the forerunners of Japan's ruling Yamato dynasty consolidated power. They chose Nara (奈良), but while its time as capital was short, Nara's cultural legacy was enormous. It was here that Buddhism first flourished in Japan, and the city's fantastic repository of temples and Buddhist art attests to that fact. Fascinating historic trails await those willing to go for a walk.

Kōbe

Perched on a hillside sloping down to the sea, backed by the very walkable Rokkō range of mountains, Kōbe (神戸) is one of Japan's most attractive and cosmopolitan cities. It was a maritime gateway from the earliest days of trade with China and home to one of the first foreign settlements after Japan reopened to the world in the mid-19th century. Kōbe is compact, designed for walking, and easily visited as a day trip from

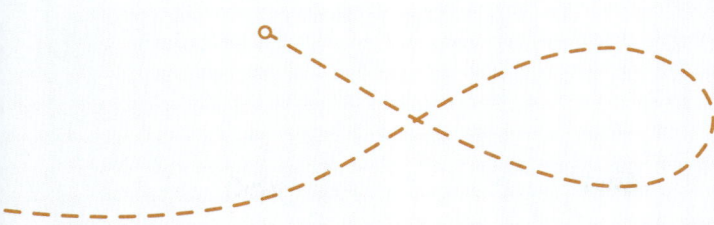

Resources

kyoto.travel/en/
osaka-info.jp
visitnara.jp
feel-kobe.jp/en/
Official tourism websites for Kyoto, Osaka, Nara and Kōbe.

rokkosan.com
See news, events and weather updates for Kōbe/Rokkō-san.

kasugataisha.or.jp
History and culture of Kasuga Taisha shrine.

koyasan.net
Info on World Heritage-listed Kōya-san.

Osaka or Kyoto, or as a stopover en route to points west.

When to Go

Most of the walks in this chapter can be walked year-round, although the mild weather of spring and autumn is ideal. Winters are cold but the low-lying areas of Kansai see very little snow. The heaviest snowfalls are found on the mountains and the areas near the Sea of Japan coast. Summer can be oppressively hot on the plains, but marginally less so in the mountains.

Transport

Kansai International Airport (KIX) is the main international point of entry for the region. There are also domestic airports, including Osaka Itami Airport and Kōbe Airport. Kyoto, Osaka (Shin-Osaka Station) and Kōbe (Shin-Kōbe Station) are on the shinkansen (bullet train) network, easily accessed from points east (such as Tokyo) or west (such as Hiroshima or Fukuoka).

The walks around Kyoto are easily accessed by train or bus, as are those around Nara and Kōbe. Kōya-san (p90) is reached by train from Osaka, while the Kumano Kodō area (p92) is accessed by train from Osaka to JR Kii-Tanabe Station, then by bus.

Where to Stay

The big Kansai cities offer a huge variety of places to sleep, from bunk beds in dorm rooms at hostels, to family-run *minshuku* (guesthouses), ryokan (traditional Japanese inns), business hotels and even 'love hotels'. Kōya-san offers *shukubō* (temple lodgings), while there are *onsen ryokan* (traditional hot-spring inns) on the Kii Peninsula.

What's On

Barely a week goes by without a festival taking place somewhere in one of the main cities or out in the Kansai countryside. Here are some festivals connected to walks in this chapter:

Daimon-ji Gozan Okuribi (Daimonji-yaki Festival) Enormous fires are lit on five mountains around Kyoto on 16 August. The largest fire, in the shape of the kanji 大 (*dai*), is burned on Daimon-ji-yama.

Kurama-no-hi Matsuri (Kurama Fire Festival) Huge flaming torches are carried through the streets of Kurama, north of Kyoto, by men in loincloths on 22 October.

Mantōrō (Lantern Festival) Held at Kasuga Taisha in Nara on 3 February, featuring lights in each of its 3000 stone and bronze lanterns. The festival is held again in August for O-Bon.

Kōya-san Rōsoku Matsuri (Candle Festival) Thousands of people come to light some 100,000 candles along the approaches to Oku-no-in on 13 August in remembrance of departed souls.

Nachi-no-Ōgi Matsuri (Nachi Fire Festival) One of Japan's three biggest fire festivals, held on 14 July. *Mikoshi* (portable shrines) are brought down from Kumano Nachi Taisha to Nachi-no-taki, Japan's highest single-drop waterfall, where they're met by groups bearing flaming torches.

19

Fushimi Inari

DURATION	DIFFICULTY	DISTANCE	START/END
2-3hrs	Easy	6km	Inari Station

TERRAIN	Both paved and unpaved track, steepish in sections

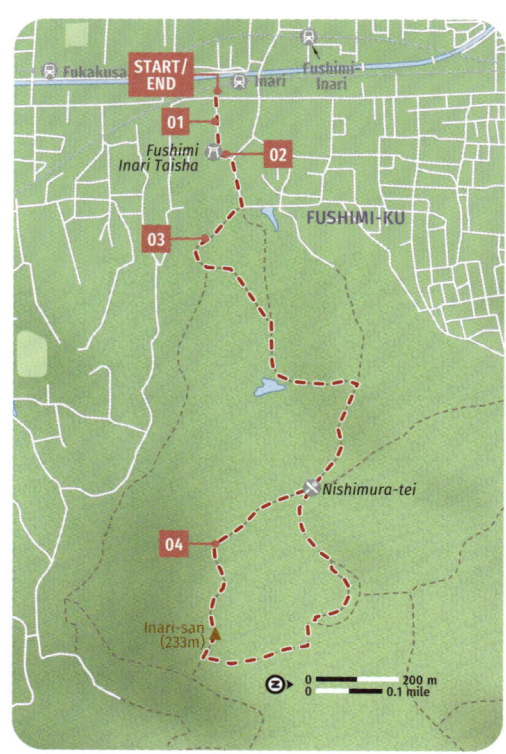

With seemingly endless arcades of vermilion *torii* (shrine gates), the vast shrine complex of Fushimi Inari (伏見稲荷) is a world unto its own. It is, quite simply, one of the most impressive and memorable sights in all Japan. The entire complex, consisting of five shrines, sprawls across the wooded slopes of Inari-san, while a pathway wanders up the mountain, makes a loop at the top and is lined with dozens of atmospheric sub-shrines.

Getting Here
JR Inari Station is on the JR Nara line, the third stop from Kyoto Station. You can also take the Keihan line to Fushimi-Inari Station.

Starting Point
Head out of the JR station and look slightly left for the huge vermilion *torii* at the entrance to the shrine.

01 Pass through the large *torii* just over the street from the JR station and head up towards the shrine buildings. There's a **cobbled street** lined with souvenir shops and teahouses ahead to the left that's worth a stroll. An unusual speciality of the area is *yakitori* (grilled sparrow), not to be confused with the *yakitori* (grilled chicken) found in restaurants. Not really the most succulent of morsels, sparrows are considered a nuisance by farmers, who roast them as a warning to the ones still flying free.

02 Visit the main **Fushimi Inari Taisha** (伏見稲荷大社) building, then go up the

Fushimi Inari Taisha

Fushimi Inari was dedicated to the gods of rice and sake by the Hata family in the 8th century. As the role of agriculture diminished, deities were enrolled to ensure prosperity in business. Nowadays, it is the head shrine for some 40,000 Inari shrines scattered the length and breadth of the country. The tens of thousands of *torii* you see have been donated, mostly by individuals or companies hoping for success in business. Names and date of donation are printed in black on the gates. You'll also come across thousands of stone foxes. The fox is considered the messenger of Inari and the key often seen in the fox's mouth is for the rice granary.

stairs behind the shrine to where the first colonnade of red *torii* begins. From here you'll spend most of the next hour on stone paths passing through countless *torii* on the forested mountain. The contrasting colours are pleasing to the eye, although even in the middle of the day it can seem quite dark due to the thick forest canopy.

03 Early on, the row of gates splits in two. Take either path, as they merge again further on. You will then come to a small **shrine** and another set of *torii* leading to the left. This path, with plenty of stairs, gradually winds its way up the mountain, turning north until it arrives at a T-junction. Turn right and continue uphill to a saddle where there are a couple of teahouses and a four-way intersection. You'll be making a loop from here.

04 Turn right at the junction, climbing steps and passing through more *torii*, and follow the ridge over the peak of **Inari-san** (稲荷山; 233m). Veering left and dropping into a valley on the north side of the mountain, the path winds its way past more evocative small **shrines** until it eventually comes back to the junction where you turned right on the way up. Take a break at the **Nishimura-tei** rest stop before carrying on back down the way you came up and out to the main Fushimi Inari shrine.

 **Take a Break**

At the junction where you start the loop around the top of the mountain you'll find **Nishimura-tei** (にしむら亭), a good spot for a break and refreshments. Open daily 10am to 4pm, this relatively informal little place serves noodles, local sweets, ice cream and drinks and has a good area to sit and take a rest.

20

Daimonji-yama

DURATION	DIFFICULTY	DISTANCE	START/END
3-4hrs	Moderate	7km	Ginkaku-ji

TERRAIN	Unpaved forest path with some steepish sections

A great way to see a lot of Kyoto in a short time, this walk combines temples, enjoyable walking and outstanding views of Kyoto on a well-used, easy-to-follow track. Visit one of the city's premier sites, the Ginkaku-ji, climb Daimonji-yama (大文字山) behind it, descend to one of Kyoto's more relaxing temples, Nanzen-ji, and then return to where you started on the Philosopher's Path.

Getting Here
Take Kyoto City bus 100 to the Ginkaku-ji-michi stop.

Starting Point
From the bus stop, cross the bridge and walk up to the Ginkaku-ji entrance. A visit to the temple is highly recommended before commencing the walk.

01 Before the temple entrance, take a left, turn right at the stone *torii* and walk uphill past a car park to enter the forest on a wide, gravel path. Ten minutes from the start, take a right up a flight of stairs and cross a metal bridge onto the well-used track. Steep climbing on steps soon eases off and you arrive at a clearing marked by a small stone Jizō (guardian statue). Take a left here to pass directly under the lift used to transport the firewood for the Daimonji-yaki Festival. Next come two flights of steep stone steps, and 30 minutes from the start, you'll be at a small **shrine** in the middle of the festival's *dai* (大) with stunning views out over Kyoto.

02 Climb the concrete steps behind the small shrine, then head straight up the ridgeline. After the trail enters the forest, walk along the ridge to the 466m summit of **Daimonji-yama**. There are great views from here too.

Daimonji-yaki Festival

Officially known as the Gozan-no-Okuribi, this festival, held on 16 August at the end of O-Bon, has been going since the early Tokugawa period. Fires are lit on five mountains around Kyoto to guide the souls of the departed to their final resting place. The 'dai' (大) on Daimonji-yama is the largest fire, stretching 89m from side to side, 160m from top to bottom, and consuming 9000kg of wood in 75 separate fire pits. On the walk, you'll pass under the small ropeway used to transport firewood for the festival and stand at the mid-point of the 大, with magnificent views out over Kyoto.

Best for

MOUNTAIN VIEWS

03 Descend the trail on the opposite side of the peak. Take a right at the trail junction five minutes down from the summit and continue on the main track, following signage to **Shichifuku-shiandokoro** (七福思案処; seven fortune thinking place). It will take close to an hour from the peak. Take the track marked to Nanzen-ji heading down to the right. First up you'll reach the **Oku-no-in** (inner sanctuary) of Kōtoku-an, a sub-temple of Nanzen-ji. Here hardy pilgrims sometimes pray while standing beneath the waterfall. Back on the main track, carry on down to the main precinct of **Kōtoku-an** and its adjoining graveyard.

04 Just past Kōtoku-an you pass under a most un-Japanese piece of architecture – the **Suirō-kaku aqueduct**, built in the early Meiji period to bring water from Biwa-ko to Kyoto. Walk under this and enter the main precinct of **Nanzen-ji**. After looking around, exit the grounds by the main gate. Walk past Higashiyama high school and continue straight, passing the Buddhist temple of **Eikan-dō** (永観堂) on your right.

05 Signage will take you to the **Philosopher's Path** (哲学の道; Tetsugaku-no-michi), named after a philosophy professor at Kyoto University who would contemplate life on the walk. The lovely 1.8km canal-side strolling path back to Ginkaku-ji features art galleries, boutiques and coffee shops along the way.

 **Take a Break**

Once you're on the Philosopher's Path, an extremely popular stroll for visitors to Kyoto, you'll find cafes, restaurants, sweet vendors and dessert shops.

21

Kurama to Kibune

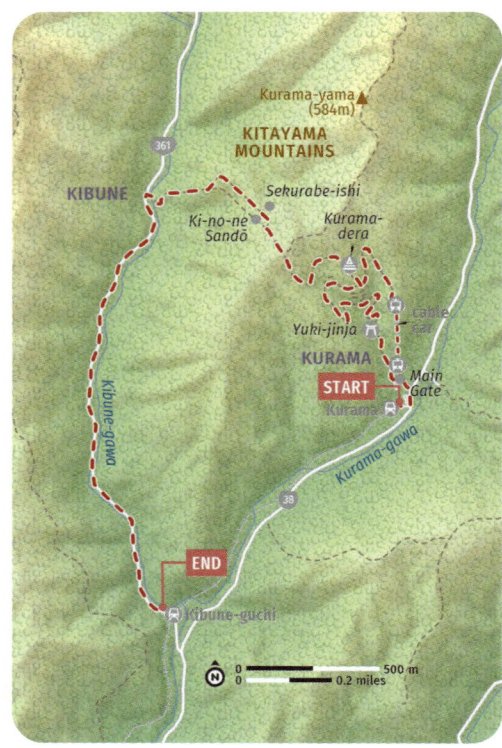

DURATION	DIFFICULTY	DISTANCE	START/END
2-3hrs	Easy-moderate	4.5km	Kurama/Kibune-guchi

TERRAIN	Paved and unpaved track, steps with steepish sections

Only a 30-minute train ride north from Kyoto, Kurama (鞍馬) and Kibune (貴船), in neighbouring valleys, feel worlds away. Tucked into the Kitayama mountains, these two tiny villages have long served as rural retreats from the heat and congestion of the city.

Walk straight out of Kurama Station, last stop on the Eizan line from Kyoto's Demachiyanagi Station, past the big-nosed red goblin, and head up to the main gate of Kurama-dera (鞍馬寺). Entrance to the temple and mountain costs ¥500. This walk is easy to follow as it goes up through the temple, over the mountain and descends to Kibune in the next valley.

From the gate, either walk via **Yuki-jinja** (由岐神社) or take the cable car (¥200) up to the final stone steps to the *honden* (main hall) of **Kurama-dera**. Continue climbing and at the high point you'll find **Sekurabe-ishi** (背比べ石; height-comparing rock), which the young Minamoto Yoshitsune used to measure his height before heading off to join the powerful Minamoto clan. On the left is **Ki-no-ne Sandō** (木の根参道), a short walk covered with the tangled, exposed roots of old *sugi* trees.

Take the trail down the west side of the mountain through cedar forest, past two sub-temples and down to **Kibune.** The quaint village is set along a narrow river valley with a single road. In summer, Kibune's restaurants and inns construct *yuka* (dining platforms) over the river to take advantage of the natural cooling effect of the water. When you're ready to return to Kyoto, take a bus or walk down the road for 2km to Kibune-guchi Station.

Best for
ESCAPING THE CITY

22

Rokku Gaaden

DURATION	DIFFICULTY	DISTANCE	START/END
3-4hrs	Moderate	7km	Ashiyagawa Station/ Okamoto Station

TERRAIN	Rough track with steep sections

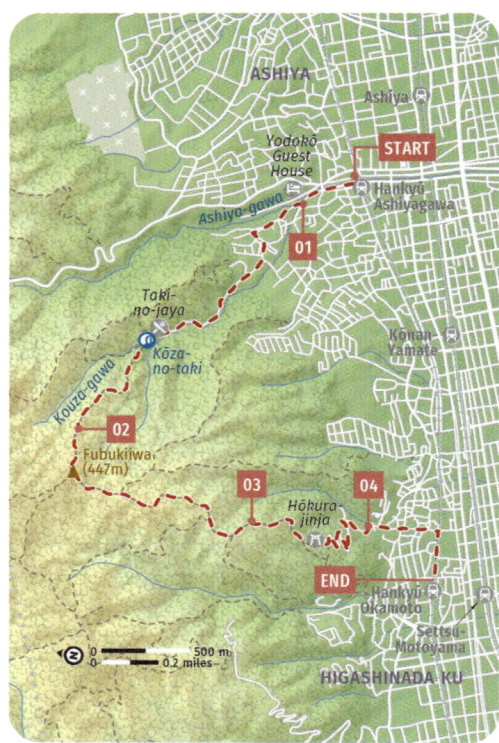

This 'urban hike', convenient to both Osaka and Kōbe, is perfect for a quick escape from the city. Hike through one of Kansai's most affluent neighbourhoods, over some unusual rock formations and through peaceful forest. Highlights include spectacular views of the Kansai metropolis and some fun rock scrambling.

Getting Here
Use either the Hankyū Kōbe line to Ashiyagawa Station or the JR Kōbe line to Ashiya Station. Both lines have trains from Osaka and Kōbe.

Starting Point
Begin the walk at the exit of Ashiyagawa Station. If you came on the JR line, walk west from Ashiya Station to the river, then head up to Ashiyagawa Station.

01 From Ashiyagawa Station, head up and into the hills! Follow the river to the bridge at the traffic lights. Architecture buffs will want to pick out **Yodokō Guest House** on the hill on the far side of the river. This is the only surviving Frank Lloyd Wright–designed residence in Japan, completed in 1924. Continuing up beside the river, you'll start to see signs (in Japanese) for Kōza-no-taki (高座の滝) and **Rokku Gaaden** (ロックガーデン). Take a left fork to enter one of Kansai's most exclusive residential neighbourhoods and follow the signage for Kōza-no-taki. Before long the road enters forest with the Kōza-gawa visible down to your left. About 30 minutes' walk from Ashiyagawa Station, you'll get to two well-weathered **teahouses**, Taki-no-jaya (滝の茶屋) and Ōtani-jaya (大谷茶屋). Just past these is the attractive little waterfall **Kōza-no-taki.**

02 Cross the bridge in front of the waterfall, pass the small shrine and climb up steep rock steps. It's a bit of a scramble up an exposed,

Great for Families

This walk is great for family fun. It's also popular with school groups and if you turn up on the right day, you might share the fun with 100 school kids on an outing. Take a *bentō* (boxed meal) for a picnic lunch at Fubukiiwa, the highest point on the track. Food and drinks are available at convenience stores at both Ashiyagawa and Ashiya stations at the start of the walk. Make sure that children have good footwear as there's a fair bit of scrambling on the way up and don't get too close to *inoshishi* (wild boar) if you meet any along the way.

Best for

ESCAPING THE CITY

TORU KIMURA/SHUTTERSTOCK ©

rocky ridge to a clearing where *inoshishi* can often be seen. Use the chains to help with the steeper bits until the climb levels off and the trail works northwest. Don't forget to look back at the growing views. Eventually, you'll arrive at the exposed sandstone outcrops of the summit of **Fubukiiwa** (風吹岩; 447m) and an electrical tower. Enjoy the tremendous views over Osaka, Kōbe and Osaka Bay with a picnic.

03 Leaving the summit, skirt around the base of the rocks and walk downhill towards Kōbe through the forest. At a track junction, head left for Hōkura-jinja (保久良神社). The trail continues through peaceful forest to a junction with Totoya-michi (魚屋道). This track heads back to the starting-point of this walk in about 45 minutes. To continue to Okamoto Station (岡本駅) take a right, following the signs to Hōkura-jinja. Part way through the descent is a clearing with magnificent views out over Kōbe city. Carry on down a long set of stone stairs to the **Hōkura-jinja** complex (pictured).

04 After checking out the shrine, head straight out under the *torii*, turn left, and after descending steep switchbacks you will come to the outskirts of Okamoto. Take a right at the first major road junction, then follow your nose to Hankyū Okamoto (阪急岡本駅) Station, only a few minutes' away. If the JR Kōbe line suits you better, JR Settsu-Motoyama station is only another five-minute walk towards the water, on the far side of the major road Yamate Kansen.

 Take a Break

The street immediately to the south side of Hankyū Okamoto Station at the end of the walk is very cute with a number of restaurants and cafes, a bakery, chocolate shop and a tea and antique shop. Cross the tracks at the eastern end of the station and turn right.

23

Kasuga-yama

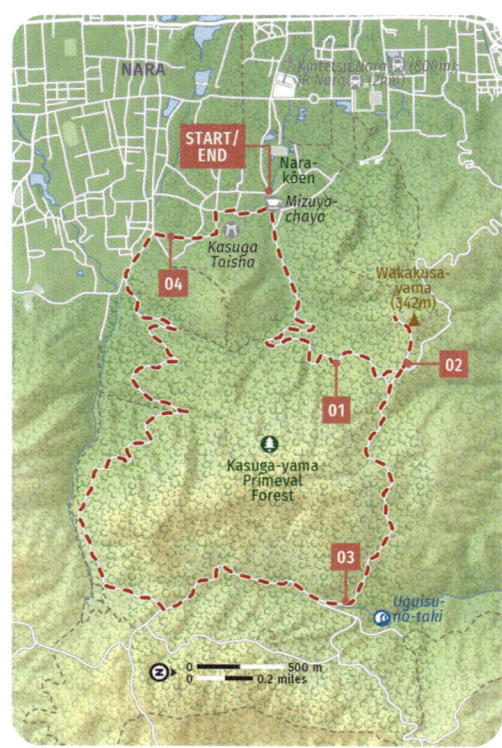

DURATION	DIFFICULTY	DISTANCE	START/END
3-4hrs	Easy-moderate	12km	Mizuya-chaya

TERRAIN	Unsealed road with gentle slopes

Behind Kasuga Taisha, Nara's principal shrine, is Kasuga-yama (春日山), with its 'Forest of the Gods' and a lovely walk through virtually untouched forest – hunting and logging were prohibited in 841 CE, preserving much of the area's flora and fauna. Kasuga-yama Primeval Forest is part of the Historic Monuments of Ancient Nara World Heritage Site.

Getting Here

Nara has both JR and Kintetsu train stations and is easily accessed from both Osaka and Kyoto. Both Nara stations have a good tourist information office; pick up a map.

Starting Point

Mizuya-chaya (水谷茶屋) is just north of Kasuga Taisha (春日大社). Walk or take a bus from either train station bound for Kasuga Taisha-honden. At the final stop, alight and backtrack 200m, cross the small bridge and immediately turn right. Up the road 100m, Mizuya-chaya is the thatch-roofed building on your right.

01 From Mizuya-chaya carry on up the sealed road for 100m to a hairpin curve; the track is the unsealed trail heading up the valley. It's a steady 3km climb on this winding road under thick forest canopy until you hit the ridgeline and a sealed road coming up from the other side of the mountain. Make sure to stay on the main track until you reach the road.

02 Turn left and only 400m away, past the car park, is the high point of **Wakakusa-**

Great Buddha

Don't leave Nara without checking out the Daibutsu (Great Buddha) at **Tōdai-ji** (東大寺; todaiji.or.jp), one of the world's largest bronze statues. Unveiled in 752 CE, it lives in the Daibutsu-den, the largest wooden building in the world. The Daibutsu is 16m high and consists of 437 tonnes of bronze and 130kg of gold. As you circle the statue towards the back, you'll see a wooden column with a hole through its base. Popular belief maintains that those who can squeeze through the hole, which is exactly the same size as one of the Great Buddha's nostrils, are assured of enlightenment. Helpful pushing and pulling is allowed.

MATTMANAGED/SHUTTERSTOCK ©

yama (若草山; 342m), offering supreme views out over Nara city and the Nara plain. There'll likely be a number of tame deer here asking for handouts.

03 Head back to where you reached the road and carry on straight ahead on a carless, mostly unsealed road for 30 minutes to a red bridge on the left. This turn-off leads to **Uguisu-no-taki** (鶯の滝), a cute little waterfall, that makes a good 30-minute return extension of the walk. At the bridge is a monument stating Kasuga-yama Primeval Forest's World Heritage status.

04 Carry on, climbing up the unsealed road now for 30 minutes until you reach a small building by the roadside. Turn right here and it's all downhill on a gentle track for an hour or so through the impressive old-growth trees until you reach a sealed road. A few minutes later, turn right into **Kasuga Taisha** (pictured). Founded in the 8th century, this sprawling shrine was created to protect the new capital, Nara. It was ritually rebuilt every 20 years, according to Shintō tradition, until the late 19th century and is still kept in pristine condition.

After exploring Kasuga Taisha, find your way out its northern side to Mizuya-chaya, where you started the walk, and take a break.

Take a Break

The quaint thatched-roof teahouse **Mizuya-chaya** (水谷茶屋), the starting and finishing point for this walk, is in a brookside clearing. It's one of Nara's most atmospheric spots. Stop by after coming down off the walk for a cup of *matcha* (powdered green tea), *onigiri* (rice balls) or a bowl of udon noodles. In warm seasons, sit outside and enjoy *kakigōri* (shaved ice with toppings of condensed milk, sweet red beans or fruit syrups).

24

Yama-no-be-no-michi

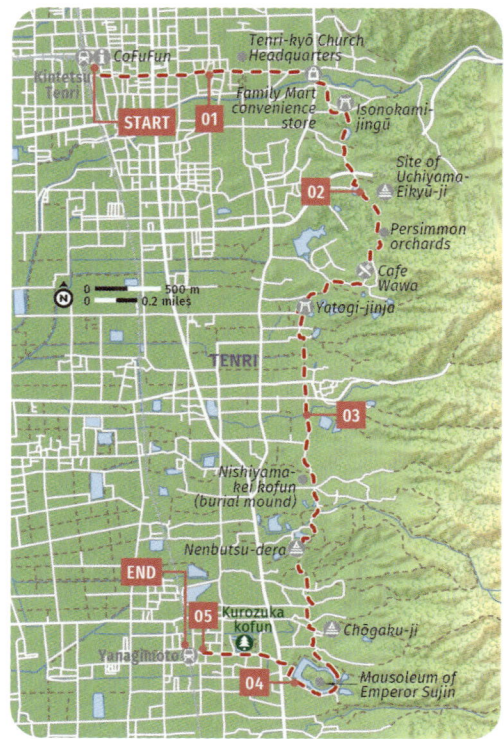

DURATION	DIFFICULTY	DISTANCE	START/END
4hrs	Easy	9km	Tenri Station/ Yanagimoto Station

TERRAIN	Mostly paved paths; gentle up and down

A fascinating ramble through the Nara countryside: expect farming villages, 1400-year-old emperors' tombs, shrines and temples, family grave sites, stalls selling fruit and vegetables, persimmon orchards, rice paddies, barking dogs and a rich mix of aromas that make this walk an extremely pleasant way to immerse yourself in historical and rural Japan.

Getting Here
Tenri Station is served by both JR and Kintetsu trains and is easy to access from Kansai's major cities.

Starting Point
Outside Tenri Station, you'll find CoFuFun (cofufun. com), a community building designed to look like a *kofun* (burial mound). Pick up a map labelled in English here.

01 Head east towards the mountains through the Tenri shopping arcade to the surprisingly large **Tenri-kyō Church Headquarters**. The crowds of people in black *happi*-coats are Tenri-kyō believers. Carry straight on up the road, turn right at Family Mart, cross the river, take the first left and you've started the treasure hunt. From here you'll find excellent signage for Yama-no-be-no-michi (山辺道) every time you need to make a turn. First up is **Isonokami-jingū** (石上神宮), a shrine with roosters and chickens running around.

02 Walk south through the **forest** before coming out on a paved road. Turn left and wander through a housing area, under an overpass, past a large pond and on your left is the site of **Uchiyama-Eikyū-ji** (内山永久寺), a temple built in 1114 that was so large it was called the Nikkō of

Kofun Burial Mounds

The origins of the Japanese imperial line and the Japanese people are shrouded in mystery, but much of what we know comes from large, earthen burial mounds called *kofun* (古墳) that served as tombs for members of Japan's early nobility and imperial household. The practice of building these mounds started in the 3rd century. They were often constructed on hilltops overlooking fertile land, usually in a keyhole shape, and along with the corpse, a variety of military and ceremonial objects were buried. Buddhism, however, favoured cremation over burial, and the building of *kofun* died out in the 7th century. You can see a number of *kofun* on this walk and around Nara.

Kansai. It was torn down in the Meiji period and only the pond remains. The trail then winds through **persimmon orchards** until you come out at a citrus orchard complex. Take a break at **Café** わわ (Café Wawa).

03 After passing vegetable fields and honesty stalls, **Yatogi-jinja** (夜都伎神社) is a good example of a small working shrine. After a long, straight stretch, you'll pass between ponds and the **Nishiyama-kei** *kofun* is on your right. Signage in Japanese includes a photo taken from directly above. Pass countless *ohaka* (family burial sites) before arriving at **Nenbutsu-dera** (念仏寺), a local Buddhist temple. Fifteen minutes on, **Chōga-ku-ji** (長岳寺) is a larger temple known for its *sōmen* (thin white noodles).

04 Soon, the massive **Mausoleum of Emperor Sujin** appears dead ahead. Follow the track up and around the back of the mausoleum, then down the south side of the moats and out towards the main road. The keyhole shape of the moats and raised 'island' burial mound are incredibly impressive, especially considering that the mausoleum is thought to have been built between 250 and 350 CE.

05 Cross the main road at the traffic lights and head straight down past **Kurozuka** (黒塚古墳) *kofun*, which has become Yanagimoto Park, and on to JR Yanagimoto Station, two stops south of Tenri, where the walk started.

Take a Break

An hour or so into the walk, you'll find cute little **Café** わわ (Café Wawa) at the Tenri Citrus Orchard complex. Stop for refreshments such as fresh juices, coffee, ice cream and shaved ice (*kakigōri*) or for something more substantial such as pizza or curried rice. Generally open 10am to 3pm each day.

25

Kōya-san

DURATION	DIFFICULTY	DISTANCE	START/END
3-4hrs	Easy-moderate	7km	Gokuraku-bashi Station/ Oku-no-in bus stop

TERRAIN	Mostly paved; steep sections at the start

Thickly forested Kōya-san (高野山), nestled in the mountains of northern Wakayama Prefecture, is home to a large monastic complex founded in the 9th century by Kōbō Daishi, the founder of the Shingon sect of Buddhism and the 88 Sacred Temples of Shikoku Pilgrimage. This is one of the most intensely spiritual places in Japan and part of the Sacred Sites and Pilgrimage Routes in the Kii Mountain Range World Heritage Site.

Getting Here
Nankai Railway trains from Osaka's Nankai-Namba Station terminate at Gokuraku-bashi, at the bottom of the Kōya-san cable car.

Starting Point
Exit Gokuraku-bashi Station and follow signage and the small road to Gokuraku-bashi, the red bridge about 200m down the valley. Cross the bridge and start walking up the Fudozaka (風土坂) trail.

01 The **Fudozaka trail** is a steep, paved 2.5km path up through the forest that most visitors dodge by using the cable car. This atmospheric trail is one of the approaches used by female pilgrims in centuries past and it ends at **Fudozaka-guchi Nyonindō** (風土坂口女人堂), the sole survivor of seven *nyonindō* (women's halls) built around Kōya-san's perimeter that catered to female visitors, who were banned from entering the temple town until 1872.

02 Take the walking track to the left of Fudozaka-guchi Nyonindō for 20 minutes until you hit a sealed road. Turn right to take you

Staying at a Temple

Kōya-san presents a brilliant opportunity to stay at a Buddhist temple. The simplest *shukubō* (temple lodging) rooms are very basic, though some temples offer a private bathroom and others have gorgeous rooms with garden views. *Shukubō* have a fairly set routine. Check in by 5pm; most temples have evening prayers that guests can attend, followed by a *shōjin-ryōri* (vegetarian Buddhist cuisine) dinner. Communal bathing facilities are usually available until 10pm, and guests are expected to retire early. Monks perform their daily morning prayers, which guests can observe, usually at 5am or 6am. A *shōjin-ryōri* breakfast follows, then an early checkout.

past Kōya-san Hospital and down into town. At the main road, turn right to visit **Kongō-bu-ji** (金剛峯寺), the headquarters of the Shingon sect and residence of Kōya-san's abbot.

03 As you come out the front gate of Kongōbu-ji, turn left and enjoy a 20-minute stroll through town. Take the left option when the road forks, to **Ichi-no-hashi** (一の橋), the bridge that marks the entrance to the temple complex of **Oku-no-in** (奥の院; pictured), the 'inner sanctuary'. It's a fascinating 2km walk through Japan's largest cemetery, with thickly forested grounds and some 200,000 tombs of those who wanted their remains interred close to the legendary saint, Kōbō Daishi.

04 At the end of the path, **Gobyō-bashi** (御廟橋), the final bridge, crosses the Tama-gawa, which flows down from Yōryū-san, the mountain behind the crypt. Enter the **Tōrōdō** (燈籠堂), a large hall full of lanterns, then head out the back to the wooden, thatched-roof gate – humble by contrast – that marks the entry to **Gobyō**, **Kōbō Daishi's mausoleum**. This is as far as anyone can go. Pilgrims, in a constant stream, pause here to light incense, candles and chant sutras.

05 Walk back out over the bridge, then keeping left, cross back over the Tama-gawa (river) and stroll out towards the main road through more tombs, some sure to bring a smile to your face. Spot UCC Coffee's eye-catching company tomb along the way, topped off with a massive stone coffee cup! The bus stop is at the road exit.

 Take a Break

Bononsha (梵恩舎) is a chilled little cafe on the main street of town; you'll pass it on your left as you head to Oku-no-in. It's generally open 7am to 5pm, serves a daily set-menu lunch, vegetarian dishes like tofu cheesecake, plus coffee and chai.

26

Kumano Kodō

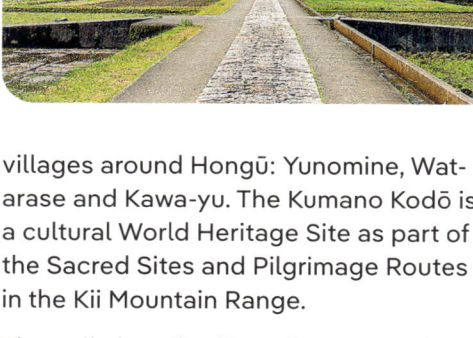

Best for
ONSEN

DURATION	DIFFICULTY	DISTANCE	START/END
3-4hrs	Easy-moderate	7.5km	Hosshinmon-ōji/Kumano Hongū Taisha

TERRAIN | Paved and unpaved track; nothing too steep

The Kumano Kodō (熊野古道) is an ancient network of roads – dating back more than 1000 years – running through the mountainous interior of the Kii Peninsula. These are pilgrim trails, connecting historic shrines and temples of deep spiritual significance. The most accessible and most popular route is the Nakahechi, also known as the Imperial Route (several emperors of old travelled along it), which crosses the width of the peninsula from Tanabe, a town on the western coast, to the towns of Shingū and Nachi-Katsuura on the eastern coast. There are walks for all levels, quiet mountain hamlets and some excellent onsen in the villages around Hongū: Yunomine, Watarase and Kawa-yu. The Kumano Kodō is a cultural World Heritage Site as part of the Sacred Sites and Pilgrimage Routes in the Kii Mountain Range.

The walk described here features a mixture of forest trails, remote mountain roads, isolated villages and impressive panoramas on the last 7.5km of the Nakahechi route from the west into the great shrine of Kumano Hongū Taisha.

Getting Here

Most travellers access the Kumano Kodō (tb-kumano.jp) via Kii-Tanabe Station, on the western side of the Kii Peninsula, connected by JR trains to

A Bit of History

From the earliest times the Japanese believed the wilds of the Kii Peninsula to be inhabited by *kami*, the deities of its native Shintō belief system rooted in nature worship. When Buddhism arrived in the 6th century, it didn't wipe out the *kami*; instead, it enveloped them, transforming them into *gongen* – manifestations of the Buddha or a Bodhisattva. A syncretic religion evolved which was long practised in the mountains of Kii. Each of the Kumano Sanzan (three great shrines of Kumano) is rich in natural, Shintō and Buddhist significance. It's believed that mountain ascetics called *yamabushi* established the first trails here as they engaged in acts of endurance, hiking and climbing for days on end.

Wakayama and Osaka. Having a set of rental wheels will make it a lot easier to explore this fascinating region.

Starting Point

The track we outline here is just a 'taster'; you can spend anywhere from a day to a week on the trails. For details of what's available on the Kumano Kodō, visit tb-kumano.jp. For this walk, take a bus from Kumano Hongū Taisha to Hosshinmon-ōji bus stop. Get bus details online or at Tanabe Tourism Information Center (田辺市観光センター), beside Kii-Tanabe Station, with English-speaking staff and lots of info. You'll need to take a bus from Kii-Tanabe Station to Kumano Hongū Taisha first, in order to catch the bus to the trailhead.

01 From the bus stop, head a few minutes further up the road to **Hosshinmon-ōji** (発心門王子), the last of the five major *ōji* (smaller shrines along the Kumano Kodō) before Kumano Hongū Taisha. Hosshinmon-ōji marks the outer limits of the grand shrine's precincts and literally means 'gate of awakening of the aspiration to enlightenment'. It's a small building, painted red, with a stone *torii*. Pilgrims who have walked from points further west get to Hosshinmon-ōji by climbing the steep track on the left that comes up from the south.

02 It's a 1.7km walk on paved road through isolated farming areas to **Mizunomi-ōji** (水呑王子). Look out for roadside folk-art wooden carvings on the way. Mizunomi-ōji is a tiny shrine with a spring; make sure to sip the water. The small Jizō statue on the right of the spring is split horizontally in the middle; people put coins in the crack and pray for relief from backache. The run-down white building here is an old school.

03 The next kilometre of walking is on mountain track, followed by another kilometre on road through the Fushiogami settlement to **Fushiogami-ōji** (伏し拝み王子). Along the road are a number of small mountaintop plantations and terraced fields producing local tea known as Otonashi-cha and Fushiogami-cha. Most of the tea is harvested in May and can be purchased at roadside stalls. Fushiogami-ōji is the first point where pilgrims can see Kumano Hongū Taisha. Fushiogami literally means 'kneel and worship' as this is what pilgrims would do on seeing their goal. There's a covered rest area with toilets here and locals serve snacks and drinks to walkers.

04 After a kilometre of walking on forested mountain track, you'll reach **Sangen-jaya** (三軒茶屋), at the point where the Kumano Kodō's Nakahechi and Kohechi routes meet. The Kohechi route links Kumano Hongū Taisha with Kōbō Daishi's mountaintop monastery complex at Kōya-san, 78km to the north. It's the track coming in at right angles to the Nakahechi from the left. Sangen-jaya means 'three teahouses' and, as the name implies, three teahouses stood at this spot in centuries past. These days you'll find a replica of an Edo-period *sekishō,* a barrier gate for controlling the movement of people and collecting tolls.

05 After a short climb from Sangen-jaya, you'll reach a sidetrack to a **lookout point** from where you can see Oyunohara, the holy sandbank in the Kumano River where Kumano Hongū Taisha was originally located until a flood destroyed it in 1889. The salvaged remains were used to rebuild the

For a Longer Walk

A popular multi-day walk starts at **Takijiri-ōji** (滝尻王子), which serves as the trailhead for the Nakahechi route to Hongū. Accessed by bus from Kii-Tanabe, it's a two-day trek, usually including an overnight stop in the village of **Chikatsuyu** (近露). For more walking, from Hongū continue on foot southeast for two days along the Kogumatori-goe and Ōgumatori-goe routes to **Kumano Nachi Taisha** (熊野那智大社), another of the three sacred shrines of Kumano, built on the side of a mountain facing Nachi-no-taki (133m), Japan's highest single-drop waterfall. Alternatively, take the Kumano River Boat out to Kumano Hayatama Taisha, the third of the Kumano Sanzan, in Shingū. This is also a traditional way to end a Kumano Kodō pilgrimage.

shrine on higher ground at its present location in 1891. The world's largest *torii*, 34m tall and 42m wide, made of steel and erected in 2000, marks the place where Kumano Hongū Taisha used to stand. It's easy to spot from the lookout.

06 A further 1.5km of descent will bring you to **Kumano Hongū Taisha** (熊野本宮大社; hongutaisha.jp) itself, one of the Kumano Sanzan (three great shrines of Kumano) and a major goal for pilgrims through the ages. Though the shrine has been rebuilt many times over the years, it remains an excellent example of Japanese shrine architecture, made of unpainted wood using traditional carpentry techniques with few nails, intricate joint work, cypress bark roof and the signature *chigi* (cross-hatched beams) on the roof. From here, a bus will get you back to Kii-Tanabe Station, but if you have some time up your sleeve, consider staying close by. There are good accommodation options in the onsen villages of Yunomine, Watarase and Kawa-yu Onsen.

Take a Break

While there are other excellent onsen options in Yunomine and Watarase, **Kawa-yu Onsen** is a natural wonder: geothermally heated water percolates up through the gravel banks of the river. In winter, the riverside is turned into a giant *rotemburo* known as **Sennin-buro** (仙人風呂, literally 'thousand-person bath'. The rest of the year you can make your own bath by digging out some of the stones and letting the hole fill with hot water. It's free; bring a bathing suit year-round.

Also Try...

SEAN PAVONE/SHUTTERSTOCK ©

BEIBAOKE/SHUTTERSTOCK ©

Yoshino-yama

DURATION	DIFFICULTY	DISTANCE
2-3hrs	Easy	6km

In Nara Prefecture, Yoshino-yama (吉野山) is famous throughout Japan for its cherry blossoms, with some 30,000 trees covering its slopes.

Start at Yoshino Station, take the ropeway, then walk up on mainly sealed roads past temples, shrines and parks to Hanayagura Tenbōdai (花矢倉展望台), a viewpoint for that classic photo. As the trees are staggered in elevation, a 'blossom front' moves up the mountain over a number of days, usually starting in late March or early April. Expect crowds in blossom season, and a sleepy little village outside of that. Along with Kōya-san and the Kumano Kodō, Yoshino is a cultural World Heritage Site as part of the Sacred Sites and Pilgrimage Routes in the Kii Mountain Range. While Yoshino makes a great day walk, it is also the start of the 80km Omine-Okugake pilgrimage trail to Kumano Hongū Taisha.

Atago-san

DURATION	DIFFICULTY	DISTANCE
5hrs	Moderate	8km

This day walk in western Kyoto offers abundant nature, good city views, a clear river, quaint villages and famous temples.

According to ancient beliefs, Kyoto is protected by the mountain sentinels Hiei-zan and Atago-san (愛宕山). The latter is home to Kagutsuchi-no-Mikoto, the fire deity, and many people climb to the peak to buy paper charms to protect their homes against fire. From the Kiyotaki bus stop, cross the red bridge spanning the Kiyotaki-gawa, pass through the red *torii* and take the traditional route up Atago-san. It's a solid climb and will take a couple of hours to Atago-jinja, the shrine by the peak (924m). Descend on a different trail via Gatsurin-ji (月輪時) to the Kiyotaki-gawa, known for its picnic spots, bathing holes, *hotaru* (lightning bugs) and *ōsanshō-uo* (giant salamanders). Follow the river northeast to Takao and its bus stop.

MASANORI SARAI/SHUTTERSTOCK ©

NU SNIPER/SHUTTERSTOCK ©

VISUN KHANKASEM/SHUTTERSTOCK ©

Ōdai-ga-hara

DURATION	DIFF.	DISTANCE
2-3hrs	Easy	9km

The remote alpine plateau of Ōdai-ga-hara (大台ヶ原) is famous for its mossy forests, abundant wildlife and high rainfall.

A feature of the eastern section of Yoshino-Kumano National Park, mountain walls drop away into deep gorges on all sides of the Ōdai-ga-hara plateau. On a good day there are superb views in all directions from various points. The high point is Hide-ga-take (日出ヶ岳; 1695m) and since you'll be driving up to the car park at 1580m, this is an easy walk.

Minō Falls

DURATION	DIFF.	DISTANCE
2hrs	Easy	6km

This city escape starts at Minō Station at the end of the Hankyū-Minō line, only 35 minutes north of Osaka Station.

Officially, this attractive nature park is Meiji-no-mori Minō Quasi-National Park at the western end of the Tōkai Nature Trail, linking Osaka and Tokyo. There are lots of interesting things on the well-signposted 3km path to the 33m-high waterfall, Minō-taki (箕面大滝), such as Minō Insect Museum (箕面公園昆虫館), Minō-yama Ryūan-ji (箕面山 瀧安寺) temple and places to get refreshments. The track is paved all the way to the waterfall.

Maya-san

DURATION	DIFF.	DISTANCE
3-4hrs	Moderate	5km

Prepare for sensational views of Kōbe on this walk up Maya-san (摩耶山; 699m) in the Rokkō range of mountains.

The track starts on the mountain side of Shin-Kōbe Station; pick up a map at the tourist information office. It first takes you past the set of four Nunobiki Falls (布引滝), then up through the forest. You can take a short detour to the Nunobiki Herb Garden (布引ハーブ園; pictured), then head to the Kikuseidai (掬星台) viewpoint just before the historic Maya upper ropeway station. Use the ropeway and cable car (koberope.jp) for the descent.

Akiyoshidō (p112)

Hiroshima & Western Honshū

27 Daisen
Majestic mountain with stunning water views. **p102**

28 Sandan-kyō
Lushly forested riverside walk with waterfalls. **p106**

29 Miyajima
'Floating temple', ropeway, observatory and deer. **p108**

30 Sanbe-san
Beautiful forest walking and panoramic views. **p110**

31 Akiyoshidō
Japan's longest cave with amazing limestone formations. **p112**

Explore

Hiroshima & Western Honshū

All too often overshadowed by the history surrounding WWII, the Hiroshima and Western Honshū region offers a wealth of fantastic day walking opportunities that include temples in the mountains, grand vistas of water and pine forests, unique rock formations and one of Asia's largest caves. The diversity of experiences here rivals anywhere else in Japan, and most walks are just a few hours away from Hiroshima, meaning they're doable as self-contained day trips or as overnight excursions.

Hiroshima City

Hiroshima (広島市) is the largest city in the area and one that has easy connections to many international destinations as well as airports all over Japan. It's also a key stop on the shinkansen. This makes it a great spot to base your walks from. Its history extends far beyond the tragic events of WWII, and its museums, sights and restaurants offer a wealth of options for your off days or when waiting out rainy weather. You can also stock up at excellent hiking stores and supermarkets if you're low on supplies.

Misasa Onsen

The tiny onsen town of Misasa Onsen (三朝温泉), along with nearby Misasa, makes a good hub for Daisen-area walks. It's known for the healing powers of its radium-rich waters, as well as excellent seafood. Together, the town and village are large enough to have conveyor-belt sushi shops, bookshops and supermarkets, yet are still small enough to feel like you've got away from it all. Most inns will have their own in-house baths; however, there's a lovely mixed-gender bath by the river, as well as several foot onsens.

Yonago City

Though not nearly as atmospheric as the quaint onsen villages nearby, the city of Yonago (米子市) offers more in the way of budget accommodation, as well as a wide range of restaurants, with dining options in Japanese and many Western cuisines. Shoppers will find it easy to stock up on supplies here. It's also next to the ocean, a plus should there be any beachcombers in the group who want to check the shores after the walking's done.

Shimonoseki

At the western tip of Honshū, Shimonoseki (下関) is an interesting city, a transport hub known for its seafood, especially *fugu* (pufferfish), poisonous if not prepared in the correct manner. The Kanmon Straits separate Honshū from Kyūshū here, and for a different kind of short walk, stroll through the 780m underwater pedestrian tunnel linking these two main islands.

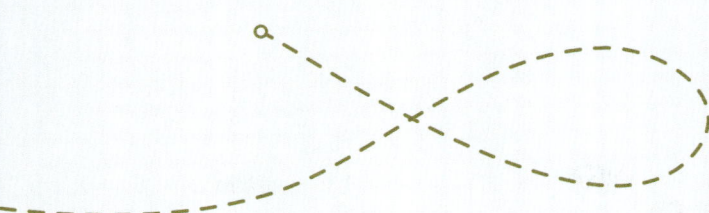

Resources

visithiroshima.net
The official Hiroshima tourism website has lots of current info, events and more.

akiooota-navi.jp
The official tourism page for the Sandan-kyō Gorge area, with maps and other info with which to plan your visit.

tourismdaisen.com/en
Tourism guide to Daisen, the tallest mountain in Western Honshū.

 ## When to Go

Though winter in the Hiroshima region is warmer than, say, Hokkaidō, walking is at its best in the spring or autumn, when the temps are moderate and it's not too hot (summer) or cold (winter). Some walks are even closed in the winter, so make careful preparations beforehand if you're planning a winter excursion. Even in summer, weather can change on a dime, so pay attention to forecasts and bring protective layers just in case.

 ## Transport

Japan's public transport is wonderful to a point, but for doing serious walking or hiking, it's nice to have the flexibility to arrive when you need to (often before buses have started for the day) and leave when you finish the walk, so the optimal way to get around is by rental car. All the major rental agencies have booths in **Hiroshima Airport** (hij.airport.jp), with rates around ¥7000 a day. You can sometimes get a deal by renting outside of the airport, as you don't have to pay an airport fee. In Japan, almost all companies require you to pick up and drop off at the same location, so do not count on a one-way unless you wish to pay an exorbitant additional fee.

Many buses depart from the **Hiroshima Bus Center** (広島バスセンター; h-buscenter.com).

Train and bus combos are doable for some of the walks, though the trick is often to catch the absolute earliest option; otherwise, one is stuck midway up the mountain at sunset. You will probably not be able to do day trips out of Hiroshima for most of these, but some walks have hotels nearby, so it may make sense to arrive the night before and then be ready to walk the next day.

Some of the more popular walks, such as Daisen (p102), have transport that has walkers in mind, with early morning links from the train station to the start of the trail.

 ## Where to Stay

You'll be missing out on one of Japan's best walking luxuries if you don't stay in either an *onsen ryokan* (inn with in-house public bath) or an onsen village, giving you the chance to soak your sore muscles in the soothing warmth of an onsen bath. **Misasa Onsen** is a cute and quiet town with a host of Japanese-style inns. For Daisen-bound walkers, a near-trailhead option is the simple **Daisen Guesthouse Juan** (daisen-guesthouse-juan.com).

What's On

Hanayu Festival Misasa's celebration of the birth of Buddha happens in early May and includes a giant tug-of-war with ropes made of wisteria vines. The outcome determines if the town will reap a good harvest or have good business success in the coming year.

Tōrō Nagashi Hiroshima City's haunting Lantern Floating Festival happens in early August each year, when thousands of lanterns are lit, then set on the river to pray for peace.

27

Daisen

DURATION	DIFFICULTY	DISTANCE	START/END
4-6hrs	Moderate-hard	9km	Daisen trailhead

TERRAIN	Steps, dirt, roots, walkways

The highest mountain in the Chūgoku region, Daisen (大山) rises dramatically above the surrounding landscape of rice fields, bamboo groves and villages, commanding the respect of anyone nearby. It's a beautiful mountain, despite its asymmetry (one side was blown out in an eruption that left ash as far away as Tōhoku). Not surprisingly, it is one of Japan's 100 Famous Mountains.

Several factors affect the summit. Earthquakes have made the highest peak unsafe to climb due to risk of landslides; Mt Misen is undergoing major erosion control, so some areas are closed.

Getting Here

Daisen is well-served by buses from Yonago, the nearest city, where a loop bus departs seasonally from Yonago Station.

Starting Point

This trailhead is located just to the right of the parking area near Daisen-ji Bridge.

01 Begin at the **Daisen National Park Center**, near the trailhead, where you can get current conditions and pick up info on proper waste disposal (you are not allowed to heed nature's call without proper carry-out bags and disposal). The centre has maps, information and lots of interesting photos about the flora and fauna, but be sure to stop here first, as conditions change.

02 The **trailhead** car park is nearby, and it's important to fill out the hiking register

This Little Piggy Went to Daisen...

Among the fauna you'll possibly see in the Daisen area are *inoshishi*, or wild pigs. In Daisen-Oki National Park, like all wildlife within the park grounds, they're protected. After humans (who rank number one in environmental degradation), pigs are the most destructive species – uprooting plants, scraping bark off trees and eating anything they can get their snouts on. They've become such a problem that park rangers have requested that you report any sightings of them, so that they're able to keep track of where the populations are and respond, if necessary, to protect trees and other wildlife.

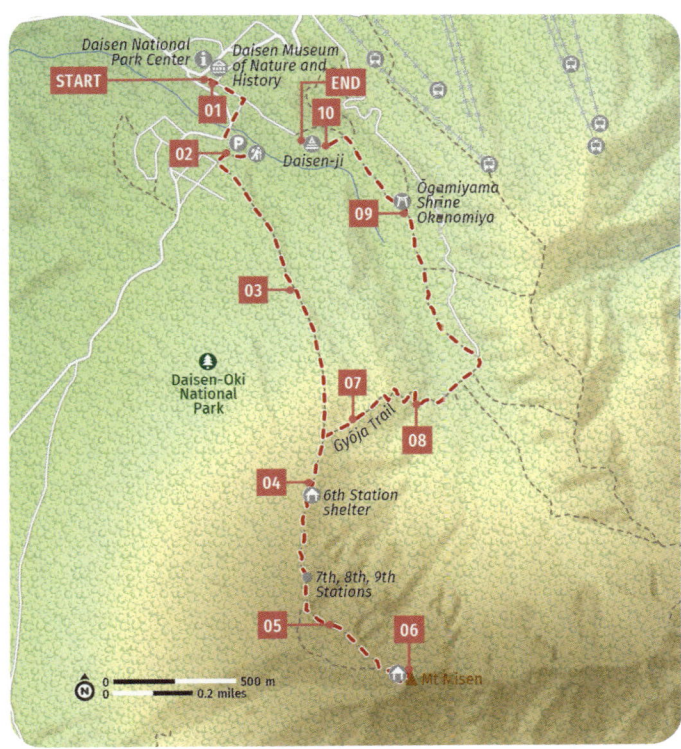

with your departure day and time and expected return. The trail starts with a long, straight, cypress-lined stairway that goes up and up and up, intersecting with the path and continuing. It's all moss-covered stones, attractive leaf litter and the occasional wood frog. In summer, expect plenty of cicadas to be humming in the trees.

03 The walk continues, a seemingly never-ending succession of steps, some formed by roots, some human-made with sandbags or stones, others natural rock formations. Around you is verdant woodland forest, a mix of oaks and hemlocks, rings of red pine, cypress groves and brushy undergrowth. Chances are high of seeing birds, wood frogs, insects of a variety of sizes and shapes, and (watch your step!) snakes. Fox, *inoshishi* or *tanuki* (raccoon dog) sightings are also common.

04 At the **6th station** there's a small shelter hut in case of sudden inclement weather, which hopefully you'll have avoided by checking with the park centre first. There's also a pack-out-only toilet, so if you're feeling the need, now's a good time to use the facility, since the next chance is all the way at the top. This is also where you'll get your first views above the treetops of the landscape below. But before you get too excited, know that better views are coming. Alpine flowers and low-growing plants are all that can survive here, being able to withstand the bitter cold and winds of winter.

05 Going upwards, you'll pass the **7th, 8th and 9th stations** before reaching Mt Misen. You'll navigate a sturdy wooden walkway to get there. From the 7th station onward, you're above the treeline, so the panoramic views of Japan's Inland Sea, the town of Yonago and the coastline are spectacular. It may be significantly more windy here, so if you've brought your layers, now may be a great time to don them.

06 **Mt Misen**, the de facto summit, is where you'll see a shelter, have additional pack-out toilets, and – until restoration is complete – have to avoid the marked areas and stay strictly to marked trails. While not as scenic as some peaks, it's a grand vista and reaching it is an achievement – your thighs will feel it in a day or two.

07 Retrace your steps to the 6th station and turn right, following the signs for Ōgamiyama Shrine Okunomiya (大神山神社奥宮), 1.6km away.

08 The trail now curves into the concavity of the crater, known as the **Gyōja Trail**. It runs into the centre then turns and heads downhill until you reach the shrine.

09 **Okunomiya** was Daisen's original temple since the Heian era and is the oldest building in all of Tottori Prefecture. It's a stunning edifice with intricate woodwork, beautiful sloped roofs and the dramatic vista of Mt Daisen behind. Set at the top of a long stairway, it was so difficult to access in wintertime that the monks constructed an easier-to-get-to building further downhill. Over time, this new temple complex became the most used one, and Okunomiya was termed the 'summer temple' rather than the *honkan* (main building). But the quirky history doesn't end there: in 1868, with the Meiji government coming to power, Buddhism and Shintō, previously merged, were separated – the Buddhist items once contained in this building were removed,

Too Much of a Good Thing

Daisen is one of Japan's most popular walks. School trips, walking clubs and tourists all come and with the crowds come some serious environmental problems. As in many national parks, human waste in Daisen must be carried out – the visitors centre has disposable, high-strength zip-top bags for sale, which are required in the various trail toilets. Instructions for proper use are inside the stalls.

Foot traffic also has an impact. Walkers are required to use plastic caps for walking poles, and even a few footsteps can destroy important vegetation, so always walk on existing paths, and – when possible – step on rock or gravel rather than plants.

and since then it has been a Shintō-only shrine. It's possible to access the building simply by walking up to it (without a Daisen summit detour), but the chance to see it on the way down is a popular walking choice.

10 End the walk by continuing down the steps to the incredible main building of **Daisen-ji** (大山寺; daisenji.jp). This Buddhist temple dating from 718, long considered a sacred mountain, seems eternally tranquil. In reality, from the 8th to the 14th century the Daisen-ji shrine complex was a hub of power, where armed priests exerted control over the area, protecting its 100 shrines. Over 3000 monks lived in and around the grounds. Having survived a tumultuous history of anti-Buddhist sentiment with closure in 1875 and a fire in 1928, the complex of four wooden worship halls you see today is an image of serenity among the trees. In addition to the building, nearby there's a small museum where you can view some of the artefacts the complex owns.

Take a Break

The friendly **Daisen Museum of Nature and History** (daisen-museum.jp) has two floors and offers naturalists or the curious a peek at flora, fauna and geology they might not see otherwise. The bird exhibits are especially colourful, and there are displays of butterflies, insects and animals, as well. The seasons of Daisen are brought to life in large screen displays, and overall, it's an excellent – if small – museum, perfect for waiting out a rain cloud before walking or for meeting at afterwards.

28

Sandan-kyō

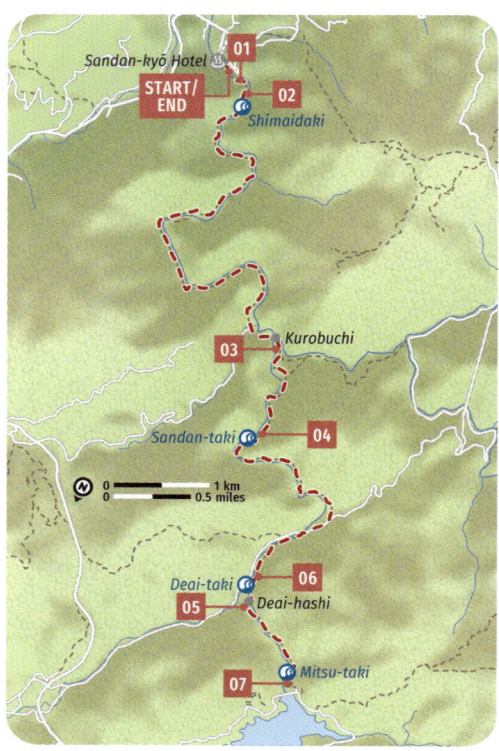

DURATION	DIFFICULTY	DISTANCE	START/END
6hrs	Easy-moderate	32km	Entrance gate

TERRAIN	Paved pathway, stairs, small slopes

'Forest bathing' is why many Japanese come here – the chance to meander in the healing peacefulness of pristine forest, the gurgling beauty of Shibaki River, the refreshing mist of waterfalls. Moss grows thick here and that's a good thing: indeed, every surface not in motion seems to be bright, vibrant green. Sandan-kyō (三段峡) can take as long as you want it to, as the trail goes for 16km along a river gorge. Whether there are hordes of people here or you're the only one wandering the trails, you'll be basking in beauty moments after starting your walk. It's that beautiful.

Getting Here

While Sandan-kyō can be reached by bus from the Hiroshima Bus Center, you'll appreciate the freedom of some rental wheels to explore around here. If you're using trains, take the JR Kabe Line from Hiroshima Station and transfer to a bus at Kabe Station.

Starting Point

Sandan-kyō entrance gate is about 30m from the bus stop, with car parks aplenty for self-drivers nearby.

01 From the entrance gate, follow the path over **Nagabuchi Bridge**. Even 5m along you'll swear you've left civilisation far behind. The trees seem to beckon you to shed the day's troubles and relax.

02 Impossible to miss, the first of many beautiful waterfalls is across the river on your left: **Shimaidaki**. It's enough to just stop there,

The Giant Pepper Fish

The Japanese giant salamander (*ōsanshōuo*, 'giant pepper fish') is one of the world's great marvels, and – if you're lucky! – you might catch a glimpse of one in Sandan-kyō. These mammoth amphibians can grow up to 1.5m in length and weigh up to 25kg, although they are typically much smaller than that. They're nocturnal though, and it's truly rare to see one. You might *smell* one, however, if your nostrils are in the right place at the right time. The Japanese name comes from their unique defensive spray, an odd, pepper-like odour, which the animal releases when threatened.

Best for

ESCAPING THE CITY

HERLOCK_00/SHUTTERSTOCK ©

and turn around if you want to make this a truly easy walk or you're pressed to catch public transport.

03 At **Kurobuchi**, the main trail climbs to the right. To the left is a landing where you can take a boat ride for 300m through a scenic section of the gorge. If you are lucky you might catch a glimpse of the giant Japanese salamander, though this is rare as they are generally nocturnal. There is a toilet and a small restaurant across the bridge.

04 Next, you'll want to find **Sandan-taki**, the 'Three-Tiered Waterfall'.

There's a viewing area where the waterfall empties into a nice emerald pool. Considered one of the prettiest spots on the walk, this is worth seeking if you're up for a longer meander.

05 If you continue upstream, the trail crosses two suspension bridges before reaching a third bridge at the 5.7km mark, called **Deai-hashi**.

06 The waterfall on the far side of the river is called **Deai-taki**, and 10 minutes further on the river pushes through a narrow rock channel called **Ryūmon (Dragon Gate)**.

07 **Mitsu-taki** (pictured), the last waterfall to be reached, is also incredibly beautiful. Return by retracing your steps through the gorge to the entrance gate.

 Take a Break

Right at the entrance gate there's a lovely onsen, the **Sandan-kyō Hotel** (sandankyo.co.jp), which offers a perfect soak for those post-walk aches and pains. Be aware that this is a radon (radioactive) onsen; you bathe at your own risk. The baths are lovely, and the outdoor ones overlook the now placid, quiet Shibaki River – in contrast to the rushing, roaring scenery upstream.

29

Miyajima

DURATION	DIFFICULTY	DISTANCE	START/END
4hrs	Easy-moderate	6.4km	Ferry terminal

TERRAIN	Pavement, rocky paths, ropeway

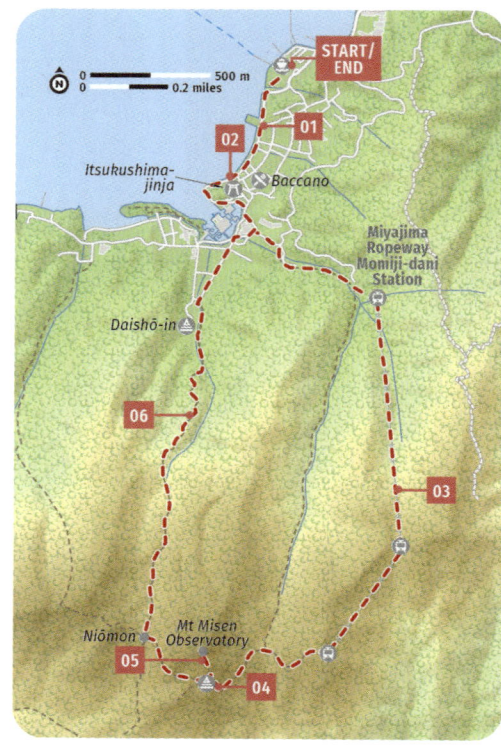

Miyajima (宮島) is a picturesque island well known for its parks, deer, temples and shrines. The island itself has been worshipped as a god in its own right. The Shintō shrine of Itsukushima-jinja and its floating *torii*, one of the three famous views of Japan, is crowded with tourists and children on school trips, but the forest-clad mountains behind it are comparatively peaceful. Both were designated a World Heritage Site in 1996, and a climb to the summit gives an eagle's view of the panorama below.

Getting Here

You have to arrive on Miyajima by ferry from Miyajimaguchi on the mainland (trains depart regularly from Hiroshima Station for Miyajimaguchi). Vessels run frequently throughout the day, starting around 6.30am and finishing after 10.30pm.

Starting Point

This walk begins at the ferry terminal.

01 From the **ferry terminal**, head towards Itsukushima-jinja and the famous floating *torii* gate, taking the required 'me with a deer' selfies along the way. (Note: While often deceptively docile, the deer are wild animals and thus unpredictable, especially if they think you have food. Use appropriate caution around them.)

02 After a stop at or near **Itsukushima-jinja**, head uphill towards the ropeway. This is a gentle, paved slope, with some lovely spots for photographs, especially if the leaves are changing colours. You'll likely see plenty of deer here too.

Itsukushima-jinja

This incredible 6th-century 'floating' **shrine** (厳島神社) is one of Japan's most prized and most visited. The shrine's unique and attractive pier-like construction is a result of the island's sacred status: commoners were not allowed to set foot on the island and had to approach by boat through the *torii* (shrine gate; pictured) in the bay. On one side of the shrine is a floating stage, built by local lord Asano Tsunanaga in 1680 and still used for *nō* (stylised dance-drama) performances each year from 16 to 18 April, as part of the Toka-sai Festival.

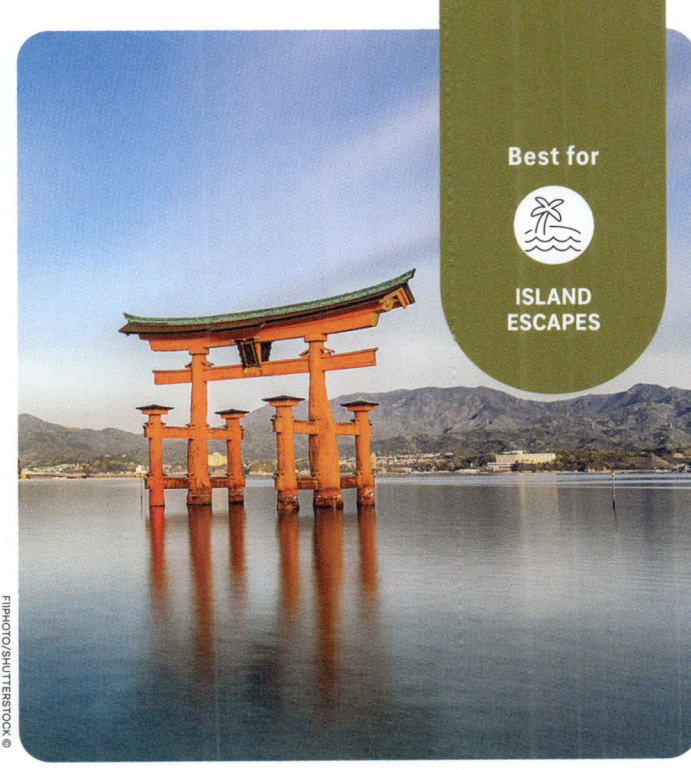

Best for

ISLAND ESCAPES

03 Take the **ropeway** (one-way ¥1100) to the upper end, looking out over the treetops at the pine and maple forests, the deep blue water and the deer. Did we mention the deer? *The deer!*

04 At the ropeway's end, follow the trail to the peak, passing some truly unique **rock formations** that make you feel as if you've entered a giant's garden. Next to the **main temple** hall is a flame that's been burning continually since Kōbō Daishi lit it 1200 years ago.

05 The **observatory** is in many ways what you'd expect, with an unbroken, 360-degree view of mainland Honshū, the Inland Sea and the island's lush greenery. Conveniently, there are also toilets and a vending machine.

06 The less daring will opt to return via the ropeway, and there's nothing wrong with that. The brave will take the slow route, which winds down the mountainside in a series of twists and turns, passing under the beautiful, twin-demon-guarded gate of **Niōmon** (仁王門) before arriving at the **Daishō-in** (大聖院) temple complex at the edge of town. From either it's a short walk back to the ferry terminal.

Take a Break

On a hot day nothing beats a nice creamy gelato or a shaved ice, and as luck would have it, there are plenty of options in the tourist-filled streets. A Japanese 'soft cream' (soft-serve in a cone or cup) will set you back ¥300, but if you want the real deal – gelato on par with something you'd find in Italy – you'll want to head for **Baccano** (バッカーノ; 435 Miyajima-chō; ⏱10am-6pm): you'll get creamy cones in a variety of flavours, including non-dairy options (such as fig). It's a luxury, but one that will seem oh so worth it after you return from the walk in the hot afternoon sun.

30

Sanbe-san

DURATION	DIFFICULTY	DISTANCE	START/END
4-5hrs	Moderate	6km	Ukinunoike trailhead

TERRAIN	Rough path, stairs, roots, rocks

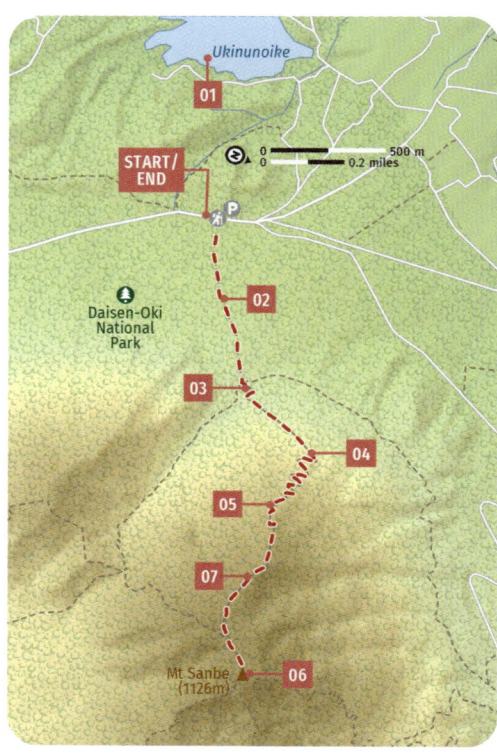

Sanbe-san (三瓶山) is a popular, relatively short walk with a big pay-off: lovely 360-degree views of the surrounding area, much of it national park. There are forests, alpine meadows, crater rims and a few small lakes to see from the summit, assuming the weather is clear. The trail primarily tracks through lush deciduous forest, with a chance to see wild pigs, foxes, deer, wood frogs and birds. The walk is popular, so don't expect to be the only one on the trail, but in off-times there's some solitude to be had, and with or without other walkers, it's a rewarding way to spend an afternoon.

Getting Here

A car will give you the most flexibility, especially if you want to see the buried forest before or afterwards, but buses run between Ōda-shi Station (in the town of Ōda, 120km north of Hiroshima city and accessible by bus and train) and Sanbe Onsen (40 minutes); you'll need to get off at the Sada-no-Matsu stop.

Starting Point

There are several routes, one of which starts at Sanbe Onsen (bus users may want to use that one). However, the route described here begins and ends at the Ukinunoike trailhead.

01 If you want to detour before beginning the walk, take a peek at **Ukinunoike** (浮布池), the lovely pond for which this route is named. Once you start walking you won't see it except from above, so stop in here. If the conditions are right

The Buried Forest

Sanbe-san may seem docile now, but it has erupted repeatedly over Japan's geologic history. The **Sanbe Azukihara Buried Forest Museum** (nature-sanbe.jp/buried_forest) has real trees that were buried in their entirety by an ancient eruption and were discovered in 1983. The trees take up most of the museum; one of them is over 12m high. Some have complete root systems, preserved exactly as they were thousands of years ago. It's bizarre, yet wonderful, and an interesting diversion if you're tired of the trails.

RAY BARTLETT/LONELY PLANET ©

you can view Sanbe-san in the water's reflection, but even if there's wind it's very scenic.

02 The first part of the trail is a mix of roots, steps and dirt, with **pretty deciduous forest** and lots of verdant green.

03 About 15 minutes in, the trail opens on a small clearing with a covered **picnic area** and some benches. This is a nice spot for a break, though you may not be needing it yet.

04 Continuing onward, the trail gets noticeably steeper, with a series of **switchbacks**. Rocks, roots, loose dirt and mud make the going slippery at times.

05 As you ascend further, the trees get lower and thinner, and you'll have your first glimpses of the **view** around the 700m mark.

06 The view only gets better as you reach the **summit** (1126m), where it all becomes worth it: a beautiful panorama of the surrounding forest, park and villages, with the lake visible far below you and another small lake in the crater depression.

07 Return the way you came, being careful to stay on the trail to Ukinunoike and not to detour on the Chūgoku Nature Trail.

 Take a Break

Sanbe-san isn't only known for its beautiful peaks. **The Sanbe Burger** (sanbe-bg.com) is a famous local speciality with devoted followers worldwide. Made with Shimane beef, these juicy patties aren't known for being giant (you're in Japan, after all), but when you've added on Japanese-style extras (like a fried egg, for instance) the burgers are filling. The Sanbe-san branch is a log-cabin-style spot, clean and bright and cheery, and a stop here will certainly satisfy.

31

Akiyoshidō

DURATION	DIFFICULTY	DISTANCE	START/END
1-2hrs	Easy	2km	Akiyoshidō car park

TERRAIN	Wet cement, gravel, stairs

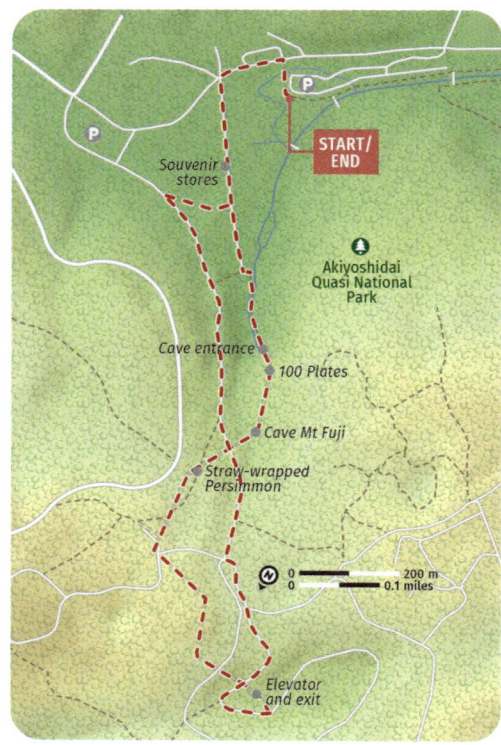

Akiyoshidō (秋芳洞) is Japan's longest cave, and while the walkway only traverses a small 1km portion of it you'll easily be able to see how impressive it is. A subterranean river marks the entry, where you'll step into a grotto the size of an auditorium. The walkway is not exactly slippery, but it is damp or wet in places, and those with mobility issues may want to use particular care on the few sections of steps. The reward is seeing a number of limestone formations up close and personal, some with humorous names.

Park at one of the cave lots and walk through the gauntlet of souvenir shops and ice-cream stands to the entry of the cave. A **river** (with fish!) flows out, and the path turns into a raised walkway that brings you right to the entrance.

Once inside, it's only dimly lit, preserving both the limestone formations and the sense that you're in a real, honest-to-goodness cave system. The entry is enormous, impressive in itself, but as you meander through you'll appreciate some of the beautiful formations as well. Stops have only minimal English signage, but include the **Straw-Wrapped Persimmon**, **Cave Mt Fuji** and **100 Plates**, among others. The walk has a few short stairways and winds to an exit point, which requires either a one-hour walk back to the entry outside or a 45-minute walk back through the cave.

If neither of those options is feasible, you can also take a taxi, several of which wait at the upper exit near where the elevators are. It's only a 10-minute zip back around to the parking area.

Also Try...

IZZARD/SHUTTERSTOCK ©

Mitoku-san

DURATION	DIFFICULTY	DISTANCE
2hrs	Hard	900km

Sanbutsu-ji is a temple perched high on a sheer cliff face on Mt Mitoku (三徳山), in Tottori Prefecture.

Getting here is hard: it requires near-vertical climbing, using roots and chains and whatever else you can hold onto. It's closed when rainy due to the increased chance of slipping, but when sunny, it's a challenging, yet one-of-a-kind experience to clamber and scramble up, up, up, to the temple (pictured) – which seems to float, almost, on the cliff, suspended there by thin wooden beams.

Hyōnosen

DURATION	DIFFICULTY	DISTANCE
4-6hrs	Hard	8km

Hyōnosen (氷ノ山) is a long, beautiful trek that will take you to the highest peak in Hyōgo.

Winter views can be stunning, with snow-covered trees similar to those seen in Tōhoku, but winter ascents can be very slippery and some of the exposed trails have sheer drops. Autumn walking brings front-row seats to the Japanese *kōyō* (changing leaves). Be cautious even in the summer and spring. But the rewards are worth it – spectacular views over the prefecture, and a challenging walk with lots of altitude gain.

YMZK-PHOTO/SHUTTERSTOCK ©

Hibayama

DURATION	DIFF.	DISTANCE
4hrs	Moderate	8km

Hibayama (比婆山) is in Hiba-Dogo-Taishaku Quasi-National Park. It's known for its alleged sightings of the Japanese yeti, a primate-like creature known in Japanese as Hibagon.

While you probably won't get a selfie with a yeti, you will see gorgeous beech trees, protected here as part of Japan's official natural treasures. The hike is a challenging one, with lots of inclines and some tricky spots, especially in winter.

Akiyoshidai

DURATION	DIFF.	DISTANCE
2hrs	Easy	5km

The Akiyoshidai (秋吉台) plateau's karst-strewn fields are about a 15-minute drive away from the Akiyoshidō cave system.

Originally part of a coral reef millions of years ago, the landscape is now steep hills dotted with thousands of boulder-like limestone karsts (pictured). The karsts vary in size from football to small car, and no matter what the season, walking among them is a unique experience.

Kogorōyama Loop

DURATION	DIFF.	DISTANCE
4hrs	Easy-moderate	11.5km

The Kogorōyama Loop (小五郎山ループ) is a great walk because while it doesn't summit grand peaks, you get a nice range of scenery and something very unique: the chance to detour into an abandoned copper mine with hand-dug shafts.

If you're lucky, you may still find pieces of copper ore among the other stones. In the autumn, this walk is particularly pretty with the changing leaves.

Akita Koma-ga-take (p126)

Tōhoku

32 **Zaō-san**
Trek through an otherworldly volcanic landscape with deep spiritual significance. **p120**

33 **Dewa Sanzan**
Follow in the footsteps of Tōhoku's famous *yamabushi* (mountain ascetics). **p122**

34 **Akita Koma-ga-take**
Alpine wildflowers in summer and bronzed foliage in autumn. **p126**

35 **Hakkōda-san**
A perfect Tōhoku day: mountain vistas and onsen in the deep north. **p128**

36 **Tsuta-numa**
Crystal-clear ponds in a beech forest and a haven for birds. **p130**

37 **Oirase Keiryū**
Trace the path of this mountain stream over waterfalls. **p132**

38 **Tanesashi Kaigan**
Explore northern Tōhoku's spectacular Pacific coast. **p134**

39 **Tōno**
A storybook village of rice paddies, farmhouses and folk tales. **p136**

Explore

Tōhoku

Tōhoku (東北) is the northern reach of Japan's mainland, Honshū (Tōhoku means 'northeast'). The volcanic, 500km-long Ōu mountain range, the longest in Japan, forms a spine down the centre. It has also historically kept Tōhoku isolated, and even today the region is considered remote, which means few people, Japanese included, visit (though like anywhere in modern Japan it's easy enough to access). The mountains promise sweeping alpine meadows and high-drama volcanic landscapes; there are also scenic coasts and pastoral villages.

Sendai

Sendai (仙台), the capital of Miyagi Prefecture, is Tōhoku's largest city (with a population of just over one million) and the gateway to the region. It's still pretty far south, but makes for an attractive stopover – thanks to its eating and drinking scene. There's a bus service connecting Tokyo's Narita Airport with Sendai.

Yamagata

The capital of Yamagata Prefecture, Yamagata (山形) is in Tōhoku's mountainous interior ('Yamagata' means 'mountain shape'). It's lively and developed for a small city. Buses depart here for Zaō Onsen.

Tsuruoka

Tsuruoka (鶴岡) is Yamagata Prefecture's second-largest city, near the Sea of Japan coast, and the departure point for the Dewa Sanzan trek (p122). It's pretty sleepy, but there are some basic hotels, restaurants and convenience stores near the train station.

Aomori

Aomori (青森) is the capital of the prefecture of the same name, the northernmost one on Honshū, and the nearest transport hub for Hakkōda-san (p128), Tsuta-numa (p130) and Oirase Keiryū (p132). The town centre, unexciting but with plenty of amenities, is closest to Aomori Station, which requires a transfer from the shinkansen station, Shin-Aomori.

Hachinohe

Hachinohe (八戸) is a small, scrappy port city on the Pacific coast of Aomori Prefecture, from where it's a short trip to Tanesashi Kaigan (p134). The compact downtown, with hotels, restaurants and a very fun bar strip, is located about 1km south of Hon-Hachinohe Station (the shinkansen stops at Hachinohe Station).

When to Go

The best time to visit Tōhoku is between the end of the rainy season, sometime in July, and early to mid-autumn. Summers are mild in the mountains (but generally not in the cities), with wildflowers peaking in alpine meadows in mid- to late July. Tōhoku isn't typically as affected by early-autumn typhoons as other parts of Honshū. Depending on the altitude, autumn foliage can be seen between late September and late October. This is the most popular time of year to visit for domestic travellers, and accommodation often fills up (and may cost more). Snow can fall at higher elevations as early as October and some mountain roads close

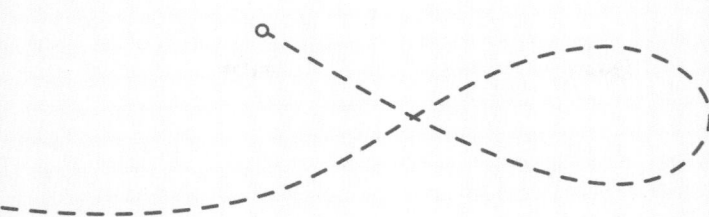

Resources

tohokukanko.jp
Travel to Tōhoku, the region's official tourism page.

dewasanzan.jp/en
Learn more about Dewa Sanzan.

Publisher Yama-to-Kōgen's *Hakkōda & Iwaki-san* (八甲田・岩木山) and *Iwate-san & Hachimantai* (岩手山・八幡平) editions include detailed trail maps for many of the hikes included here (in Japanese).

between November and April; if you're driving during the shoulder season, run your intended route by staff at a local tourist information centre or your accommodation.

 ## Transport

Tōhoku's remoteness is more a state of mind than an actual reflection of its transport situation. The Tōhoku Shinkansen runs frequently from Tokyo via Sendai (1½ to two hours), Shin-Hanamaki (2½ hours; slower trains only), Morioka (2¼ hours) and Hachinohe (three hours) to Aomori (Shin-Aomori Station; 3½ hours). The Akita Shinkansen travels the same route until Morioka, then heads west for Tazawa-ko (three hours). The Yamagata Shinkansen travels to Yamagata (2¼ hours). For Tsuruoka, take the Jōetsu Shinkansen to Niigata (2¼ hours) and transfer to a JR limited express Inaho train (1¾ hours). Long-distance buses (including night service) are a cheaper option.

A network of JR trains and buses (JR and regional) connect the shinkansen stations to town centres and trailheads. Note that buses outside the cities typically run seasonally and infrequently; check schedules at the nearest tourist information centre and plan ahead.

For extensive travel around the area, the JR East Tōhoku Pass (jreast.co.jp/multi/en) gives you five days of unlimited travel (including the shinkansen to/from Tokyo) within a 14-day period.

You can pack more into an itinerary with a car. Expressways (requiring tolls) connect the same hubs that the shinkansen does, and traffic in Tōhoku is light compared to more populated areas. Even up here, road signs are generally in English. Many mountain roads are breathtaking, but they are also often steep and narrow, with hairpin turns.

 ## Where to Stay

Tōhoku has several destination-worthy *onsen ryokan* (traditional inns with hot-spring baths). Many people in Japan feel that they would like to stay once in their lives at Sukayu Onsen Ryokan (p129) or Tsuru-no-yu Onsen (p127). Tōno's B&Bs and farm stays are ideal places to sample Japanese country life.

Cities have outposts of the usual economy chain hotels, but nothing fancy (and 'nicer' properties are often dated). Outside the cities, accommodation is largely independent inns with Japanese-style bedding. It's always best to book ahead; some inns may offer free pick-up service from the nearest train station if you ask in advance.

 ## What's On

Tōhoku is famous for its summer festivals. The biggest is Aomori's **Nebuta Matsuri**, held 2 to 7 August. It has parades of spectacular illuminated floats, accompanied by thousands of rowdy, chanting dancers. Nearby Hirosaki holds its own version, the **Neputa Matsuri**, from 1 to 7 August. The same week (6 to 8 August), Sendai celebrates **Tanabata** (Star Festival) with colourful streamers hung from the streets, parades, performances and fireworks.

32

Zaō-san

DURATION	DIFFICULTY	DISTANCE	START/END
3-4hrs	Moderate	9km	Zaō Jizō-son

TERRAIN	Gravel and rock; some scrambling

Zaō-san (蔵王山) is a hulking compound volcano straddling the border of Yamagata and Miyagi Prefectures. It's long been a destination for religious pilgrims and it's easy to imagine why: Zaō-san's peaks and ridges are a rocky, barren moonscape, intermittently blanketed in thick mist. Its most famous feature, however, is a shockingly teal crater lake, Okama. The season runs June to mid-October.

Getting Here

Buses run hourly from stop 1 at Yamagata Station for Zaō Onsen (45 minutes). There's a **tourist information centre** (zao-spa.or.jp) inside the bus terminal. Walk back along the road five minutes to the **Zaō Ropeway** (zaoropeway.co.jp), which takes you up to **Zaō Jizō-son** (蔵王地蔵尊; 1660m) in about 20 minutes (a transfer between two cable cars is required). It is also possible to drive to Okama via the Zaō Highline (蔵王ハイライン; ¥550 per vehicle; late April to early November) and do the walk in reverse. This is laid out as a return walk; however, there is one direct bus daily from Okama to Yamagata Station at 1pm (¥2050; 1½ hours), running weekends and holidays from 27 April to 31 July, and daily from 1 August to 27 October.

Starting Point

When you exit Jizō Sanchō cable car station, there is a large signboard with the mountain's walking routes mapped (in English) and an even larger stone effigy of Jizō, a Bodhisattva associated with the underworld. Zaō-san is an active volcano: along the trail, signs designate evacuation routes. While an eruption is unlikely, do heed any warnings.

Zaō Onsen

Zaō Onsen (蔵王温泉) is an onsen village halfway up Zaō-san at 880m. The waters here are extremely acidic, with a pH of around 1.5, and high in sulphur, which turns them milky-blue. **Zaō Onsen Dai-rotemburo** (jupeer-zao.com/roten) is a huge, open-air pool above the village. Facilities are scant: strip down in the changing room, ladle some water over yourself and ease in. Bring your own towel. There are also public bathhouses, free foot baths and inns that open their baths to visitors during the day. The tourist information centre can provide information.

SHAWN.CCF/SHUTTERSTOCK ©

01 Take the stone-paved trail, on the right, to **Jizō-san** (地蔵山; 1736m). The parallel trail, on boardwalks, rejoins this one, but misses the peak. This part of the walk is pretty in the conventional sense, with wildflowers in summer.

02 The two paths converge (and split again) at the **9th Station** (1705m). There is an unusual statue here of a *yamanba*, a mountain hag from folklore. Again take the trail on the right.

03 It's a scramble up lava rocks to **Kumano-dake**, (熊野岳; 1841m), the tallest of Zaō-san's peaks. If visibility is low, follow the rocks marked with white paint; tall wooden posts mark the trail in other sections. There's a small shrine, **Kumano-jinja** (熊野神社), on top.

04 From the peak, head down to the magnificent crater lake **Okama** (御釜), its precipitous sides streaked with layers of different-coloured ash deposits. This beautiful crater is known as Okama because of its resemblance to a traditional cooking pot. (Here the trail intersects with the toll road.)

05 Beyond the crater a short trail leads up to **Katta-dake** (刈田岳; 1758m), which also has a small shrine, **Zaō Katta-mine-jinja Oku-no-miya** (蔵王刈田嶺神社奥宮). It honours Zaō Gongen, the principal deity of the esoteric religion historically practised on Zaō-san. Return to the cable car station via the same route, or take the alternative paths.

Take a Break

The main road through Zaō Onsen has restaurants and cafes, though they're not all reliably open once the snow has melted away. (Zaō Onsen is a lively ski town, but quieter in the green season.) **Oto-chaya** (音茶屋; 935-24 Zaō Onsen) serves classic cafe dishes like curry-rice and is a good bet.

33

Dewa Sanzan

Best for

OFF THE BEATEN PATH

DURATION	DIFFICULTY	DISTANCE	START/END
8-9hrs (2 days)	Moderate-hard	12.5km	Zuishin-mon

TERRAIN	Varied, with steps and small boulders

Dewa Sanzan (出羽三山) means 'three mountains of Dewa' (Dewa is the old name for Yamagata) and is made up of Haguro-san (羽黒山; 414m), Gas-san (月山; 1984m) and Yudono-san (湯殿山; 1504m). The mountains have deep significance in esoteric religion and to walk all three is a spiritual undertaking; it's Tōhoku's most famous pilgrim trail. The full circuit takes two days, with a night in a hut on Gas-san (and a bus ride). If you only have one day, you can opt for a six-hour round-trip walk up Gas-san from the mountain's 8th station, or walk one to 1½ hours up Haguro-san. The season is July to mid-September (May to October for Haguro-san).

Getting Here

Regular buses depart for Haguro Zuishin-mon (羽黒隋神門) from stop 1 in front of Tsuruoka Station; four daily continue to Gas-san Hachigōme (the 8th station). Check bus schedules and pick up English maps and brochures at the **tourist information centre** (tsuruokacity.com) across the bus rotary from the train station. Note that return buses from Yudono-san only run on weekends (and weekdays during O-Bon week, 13 to 15 August), so you'll have to set out at those times if you want to complete the circuit.

Starting Point

The red temple-style gate **Zuishin-mon** (隋神門) stands at the foot of Haguro-san and marks the start of the climb. The bus stops right in front. There are some cafes here, and also vending machines.

Three Sacred Mountains

In the Shugendō religion of Dewa Sanzan, a blend of Shintō, esoteric Buddhism and nature worship, the three mountains represent the present (Haguro-san), the past (Gas-san) and the future (Yudono-san), and by completing the circuit worshippers undergo a symbolic cycle of death and rebirth. The steep descent to Yudono-san is the hardest part and few (besides pilgrims) walk this section of the trail, which can become treacherous or impassable during or following heavy rain; check conditions at the Tsuruoka tourist information centre or Midagahara Sanrōjo (p124) before heading out (and carry a bear bell).

01 Pass through the gate, following the path past small shrines, a waterfall, a 1000-year-old cedar tree and **Gojū-no-tō** (五重塔), a five-storey pagoda. First built in the 10th century (and rebuilt in the 14th), the 29m-tall wooden pagoda is the oldest of its kind in Tōhoku.

02 Past the pagoda is Haguro-san's iconic **Ishi-dan** (石段). This **staircase up the mountain** – 2446 stone steps totalling 1.7km – was built in the 17th century (and took 13 years to complete). It's split into three sections: between the first and second is a flat stretch through towering cedars, between 300 and 500 years old.

03 At the top of the second (and steepest!) section is the teahouse, **Ni-no-saka-chaya** (二の坂茶屋). The speciality here is *mochi* (pounded rice cakes) made fresh daily by hand using only local ingredients (hauled up the mountain). Get a set with two and a bowl of *matcha* (powdered green tea) and enjoy the view over the Shōnai plain from the terrace. You can also buy bottled water and other cold drinks here.

04 It takes about an hour to reach the summit, where there is a shrine, **Sanjin Gōsaiden** (三神合祭殿), which honours the deities of the three mountains. It's unknown when a shrine first appeared here, but the current building, painted red with a dense (2.1m-thick) thatched roof, was constructed in 1818.

05 Most of the old 20km pilgrim trail along the ridgeline to Gas-san became overgrown after a road was built in the 1960s, though some parts are still used in ascetic training. Walkers heading on to Gas-san need to take the bus to **Gas-san Hachigōme** (月山八合目; Gas-san 8th station; 55 minutes), which departs from the car park beyond the shrine at 7.05am, 8.05am, 11.50am and 2.05pm (daily July to August; weekends in September); return buses to Tsuruoka Station also depart from here. There are food stalls and a toilet around the car park.

06 From Gas-san 8th station (1390m), it's a five-minute walk up to **Midagahara Sanrōjo** (御田ヶ原参篭所), the pilgrim lodging attached to the Shintō shrine, **Gas-san Naka-no-miya** (月山中の宮). Though accommodation here is exceedingly humble (futons in communal rooms; running water but no showers), it's still the best place to stay on Gas-san. Dinner is a hearty version of *shōjin ryōri* (Buddhist vegetarian cuisine). Reservations are required. The hut is located in the beautiful **Mida-ga-hara** (弥陀ヶ原; pictured), a marshland with numerous small ponds and grasses spotted with over a hundred kinds of alpine wildflowers, including sunny yellow dwarf water lilies. The flowers peak between mid-July and mid-August and this is when Gas-san gets the most visitors. A 2.2km-long, flat boardwalk makes a loop around the area, which is worth doing in addition to the main walk.

REBECCA MILNER/LONELY PLANET ©

07 Most hikers are up for sunrise. Ask the night before to have your breakfast served as a *bentō* (boxed meal), if you plan to head out before 6am. A stone *torii* (shrine gate) marks the entrance to the 5.3km trail up to the summit, which takes around three hours. The path is alternately steep, with some knee-high boulders to climb up, and gentle. Halfway up, at the 9th station (1743m), is the mountain hut **Busshō-ike-goya** (佛生池小屋), fronted by a pond (Busshō-ike). It's known for its coffee made with Gas-san spring water. Bottled water is also available, and food, such as *sansai udon* (wheat noodles with mountain vegetables).

08 The last part of the ascent is through the grassy **Ōmine** (大峰) ridgeline, from where the summit is in sight.

09 At the top is the Shintō shrine, **Gas-san-jinja** (月山神社), which honours Tsukuyomi-no-Mikoto, the moon god. Entrance requires undergoing a brief purification ritual: bow to receive the priest's benediction, then brush yourself head to toe with the slip of paper, placing it afterwards in the fountain. Beyond the gate, photography is prohibited.

10 The descent to Yudono-san begins easily enough along a snaking ridge, from where there are fantastic views of the surrounding mountains, including Chōkai-san (2236m) to the north. In an hour or so, you'll hit **Ushikubi** (牛首; 1729m), the first of several trail junctions; here and elsewhere, follow the signs to Yudono-san-jinja (湯殿山神社).

11 After the junction, the route becomes steadily steeper. Pick your way down

Yamabushi

Yamabushi are Shugendō mountain priests who have completed ascetic training on Dewa Sanzan (which includes austerities, like fasting, and endurance tests, like meditating under cold waterfalls). They're still visible today – distinct in their chequered robes, white pantaloons and straw sandals, blowing *horigai* (conch shell horns) – leading pilgrims on spiritual treks. To learn more about *yamabushi* and Dewa Sanzan's unique culture, visit the **Ideha Cultural Museum** (いでは文化記念館; 72 Inju-minami, Tōge, Haguro-machi), just up the road from Zuishin-mon. If you're interested in trying some traditional ascetic *yamabushi* training in the Dewa Sanzan mountains, check out Yamabushidō (yamabushido.jp) and weigh up the options from basic to intense.

carefully: it's easy to slip here, especially as the path of smooth rock is often wet from mountain streams. The trickiest part comes two-thirds of the way down, where a particularly steep section requires the use of metal ladders bolted to the mountainside. In total, the 5.6km descent takes around three hours, but you'll drop down to 1050m.

12 The final goal of the pilgrimage is the Shintō shrine, **Yudono-san-jinja** (湯殿山神社). You'll likely see pilgrims here, all dressed in white, as well as tour groups (the shrine is accessible by road). There are strict rules for entering, including no photos. Take your shoes off and approach the priest, who will perform a similar ritual to the one at Gas-san-jinja. The object of veneration at Yudono-san-jinja is a large rock over which onsen water flows, and that's all we can say, as the shrine asks visitors to not speak of what they witness here. From the shrine it's a 30-minute walk along the road to pilgrim lodge **Yudono-san Sanrōjo** (湯殿山参籠所), or take the shuttle bus to Sennin-zawa (仙人沢), which drops you off across the street from the lodge. At 10.30am and 2.10pm buses depart from the back of the car park at Yudono-san Sanrōjo for Zuishin-mon (weekends June to October), from where you can connect to a bus back to Tsuruoka. At 4.50pm there is a direct bus to Tsuruoka Station (weekends June to October).

Take a Break

At the top of Haguro-san, **Saikan** (斎館) is a 17th-century temple turned pilgrim lodge. Guests, who stay in humble Japanese-style rooms, can observe morning religious rituals at San-shin Gōsaiden. Meals are *shōjin ryōri* made with foraged mushrooms and seasonal mountain vegetables. It's a wonderful experience, if you can budget an extra day to stay here. Otherwise, lunch (11am to 2pm) is also an option; make a reservation at least one day in advance.

34

Akita Koma-ga-take

DURATION	DIFFICULTY	DISTANCE	START/END
3hrs	Easy-moderate	6.5km	Akita Koma-ga-take 8th station

TERRAIN	Packed earth and gravel; some steps

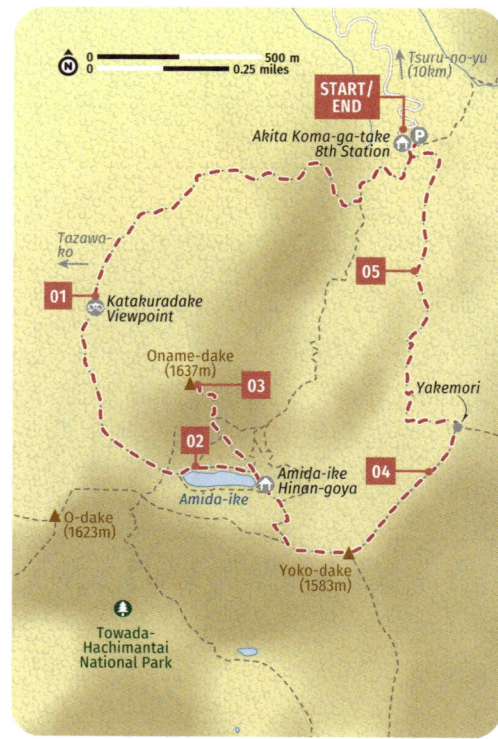

Molar-shaped Akita Koma-ga-take (秋田駒ヶ岳), made up of several peaks, is one of Tōhoku's most popular walking destinations. In mid-summer it puts on what is arguably the region's best display of alpine wildflowers. In late September and early October the mountain's shrubs and grasses turn auburn and gold and pair beautifully with its russet sweeps of volcanic sand. Season: June to October.

Getting Here

Buses run from stop 1 in front of Tazawa-ko Station to Akita Koma-ga-take 8th station (秋田駒ケ岳八合目) on weekends and public holidays between 1 June and 31 October (and daily between 21 June and 19 August). The last bus departs at 1.30pm and the last return bus departs at 5pm (4.25pm in October). The access road is closed to private vehicles on days the buses run. The **tourist information centre** inside Tazawa-ko Station has bus information in English.

Starting Point

A small rest house (hours vary) at the 8th station (1310m) has walking info posted and sells cold drinks and maps. The trail is signposted in Japanese and some English.

01 Take the trail in the direction of Amida-ike (阿弥陀池). After climbing for 30 to 40 minutes, you'll reach the **Katakuradake Viewpoint** (片倉岳展望台; 1456m), from where you can see shocking-blue **Tazawa-ko** (田沢湖), Japan's deepest lake.

Nyūtō Onsen

A morning on Akita Koma-ga-take pairs perfectly with an afternoon visit to **Nyūtō Onsen** (乳頭温泉). There are seven inns here, all of which open their baths during the day to visitors (from around 10am to 3pm; admission around ¥600). Each has different water qualities, from clear to milky-white. Overnight guests can purchase a 'Yumeguri Pass' (¥1800) for access to all of them. Buses run approximately every hour from stop 1 in front of Tazawa-ko Station, or it's a 30-minute drive from Akita Koma-ga-take 8th station. Tazawa-ko's tourist information centre has an excellent map marked with bus stops and walking routes between the inns.

Best for

MOUNTAIN VIEWS

02 Past the viewpoint, the path is gentler as it goes around Oname-dake (男女岳; 1637m) to **Amida-ike**, a shimmering pond sunk in the dip formed by the three major peaks of Akita Koma-ga-take: Oname-dake, O-dake (男岳; 1623m) and Yoko-dake (横岳; 1583m). This is the place to see Akita Koma-ga-take's wildflowers, which include white, five-petalled Aleutian avens and purple Japanese lady bells. There are boardwalks around the lake.

03 A detour up to the top of **Oname-dake** takes about 30 minutes round trip.

As you're smack in the middle of Tōhoku, there are panoramic views over the whole region, including Iwate-san (2038m) to the east.

04 Back at Amida-ike, pick up the path to **Yoko-dake**. At the junction, take the trail heading back to Hachigōme (八合目), which runs along a ridge to **Yakemori** (焼森; 1551m). Here the terrain is finely ground black and red volcanic rock, with patches of shrubs and Siberian dwarf pines. In July look out for the delicate pink *komakusa* (bleeding heart) blossoms.

05 The descending trail passes through thickets of *sasa* (bamboo grass) – it's a good idea to wear trousers and carry a bear bell — and includes some steps. From Yakemori back to the 8th station takes about 45 minutes.

 **Take a Break**

Tsuru-no-yu Onsen (tsurunoyu.com), one of the inns that make up Nyūtō Onsen, has the whole rural ryokan thing nailed: the roof is thatched; meals are served around an *irori* (hearth); and the main bath is a rocky outdoor pool. There are *konyoku* (all-gender bathing) and gender-segregated bathing areas and a soba restaurant open for lunch.

35

Hakkōda-san

DURATION	DIFFICULTY	DISTANCE	START/END
5hrs	Moderate	9.5km	Sukayu Onsen

TERRAIN	Packed earth and gravel; some steps

Hakkōda-san (八甲田山) means 'many peaks and marshlands'; it's the northernmost part of Tōhoku's Oū mountains. This loop is one of the region's classic hikes, passing through strata of beech forest, volcanic rock, alpine marsh and scruffy pines – all quintessential northern landscapes – to Hakkōda-san's highest peak, Ōdake (大岳; 1585m). Season: June to late October.

Getting Here

The trailhead is at Sukayu Onsen (酸ヶ湯温泉). Six JR Mizuumi buses run daily (20 April to 10 November) from the east exit (stop 11) at Aomori Station, via Shin-Aomori Station (only four daily), stopping in the car park of Sukayu Onsen Ryokan.

Starting Point

The ryokan has a shop (7am to 8pm) that sells packaged snacks, like local *nambu sembei* (wheat crackers, often with peanuts or sesame seeds), and a detailed map (¥200, in Japanese). To reach the trail, go out to the road and turn left; the entrance will be on your left shortly, marked by a wooden *torii*. Signs are in English.

01 The walk begins at 900m with a gentle climb through beech forest. After 30 minutes, the grade increases and the vegetation fades as you enter **Jigoku Yunosawa** (地獄湯の沢), a **volcanic landscape** where sulphur springs stain the rocks highlighter-yellow.

02 In another hour, the trail flattens out to cross grassy **Sennin-tai** (仙人岱) on boardwalks. On your right, you'll see a path leading off to Sennin-tai Hutte (仙人岱ヒュッテ). Just be-

Sukayu Onsen

Tōhoku is famous for its onsen and **Sukayu Onsen** (酸ヶ湯温泉) might be the most famous of all. The milky-white water is extraordinarily acidic and rich in sulphur. The beautiful Aomori cypress-wood *sennin-buro* (1000-person bath) here is part of **Sukayu Onsen Ryokan** (sukayu.jp). Admission is free for staying guests; the baths are open to visitors (admission ¥1000) between 7am and 5.30pm. The *sennin-buro* is *konyoku* (all-gender bathing), though there is a screened-off area for women (and the whole bath is women only 8am to 9am and 8pm to 9pm). There are also smaller, gender-segregated baths.

PHUONG D. NGUYEN/SHUTTERSTOCK ©

Best for

ONSEN

yond this point, there's a natural spring where you can fill your water bottle. Shortly after the spring, the trail forks; take the path to Ōdake (大岳).

03 Climbing again, you'll pass through a grove of bushy Aomori *todomatsu* (Maries' fir). It's another hour up a sandy path, which steepens past a small pond, to the summit.

04 At the peak there is a dollhouse-sized shrine and a terrific 360-degree view over the neighbouring mountains. On a clear day, you can see Hachimantai, Iwate-san, Iwaki-san and Tsugaru Bay.

05 Follow the zig-zagging path down for 15 minutes to the hut, **Ōdake Hinan-goya** (大岳非難小屋). At the junction, take the trail towards **Kenashi-tai** (毛無岱), a marshy highland, spotted with wildflowers in June and July (and golden grasses in September and October). It's flat but tiered, with a long wooden staircase connecting the upper level to the lower.

06 After descending for about 90 minutes, there is one last junction; continue straight to Sukayu Onsen. In another half-hour you will emerge from the woods behind the ryokan.

 Take a Break

A stay at **Sukayu Onsen Ryokan** is highly recommended. Rooms in the sprawling old-fashioned inn are simple but comfortable, with shared facilities. Updated, more expensive rooms (from ¥15,000 per person) have en suite toilets. Meals are more filling than fancy, but include lots of local specialities, like *naratake* (honey mushrooms) and *hoya* (sea pineapple). There is also a noodle restaurant open during the day (10.30am to 4.30pm); try the *sansai soba* (buckwheat noodles with mountain vegetables).

36

Tsuta-numa

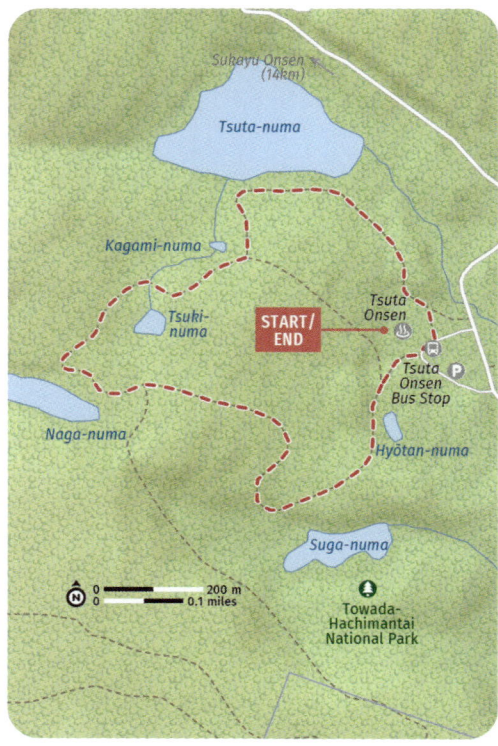

DURATION	DIFFICULTY	DISTANCE	START/END
1-1½hrs	Easy	2.8km	Tsuta Onsen

TERRAIN	Packed earth; some steps

Tsuta-numa (蔦沼; Vine Pond) is the largest of six ponds on this mostly flat circuit through beech forest. The pools were formed by long ago eruptions of nearby Akakura-dake. They're remarkably clear, and make photogenic reflecting pools for the woods surrounding them (especially in late October, when the autumn foliage peaks).

The other ponds are evocatively (and aptly) named Kagami-numa (鏡沼; Mirror Pond), Tsuki-numa (月沼; Moon Pond), Naga-numa (長沼; Long Pond), Suga-numa (菅沼; Sedge Pond) and Hyōtan-numa (瓢箪沼; Gourd Pond). The area is a habitat for many species of birds, including sunset-coloured **ruddy kingfishers** and yellow-bellied **narcissus flycatchers**; it's also home to **green tree frogs**.

This is a great trail for little ones, well defined and even, with boardwalks flanking some of the ponds (look down for **kokanee salmon** and **char**). English signs have information about the local ecosystem.

The trail is behind **Tsuta Onsen** (tsutaonsen.com/en), a handsome, early-20th-century inn built of local beech and horse chestnut wood. The baths (admission ¥800), with clear, sodium carbonate waters, are open to visitors 7am to 9am and 10am to 4pm. However, there are two good reasons to stay the night: in July you can head out in the evening to see the **fireflies** and, in late autumn, the beeches are most photogenic at dawn (when the light turns the normally golden leaves a fiery red).

Tsuta Onsen is a 25-minute drive from Sukayu Onsen, served by the same bus from Aomori Station, via Shin-Aomori Station. Season: late April to November.

Best for

KIDS

37

Oirase Keiryū

DURATION	DIFFICULTY	DISTANCE	START/END
4hrs	Moderate	14km	Yakeyama/Nenokuchi

TERRAIN	Packed earth; some steps

Oirase Keiryū (奥入瀬渓流) is a picture-perfect mountain stream tumbling down waterfalls and over moss-covered boulders. This mostly flat walk follows the river's meandering path through a forest of native broadleaf trees, including *buna* (beech), *keyaki* (zelkova) and *tochinoki* (horse chestnut) trees.

The route unfolds as a series of vistas: **waterfalls** rushing down rock terraces, pebbly beaches, swirling eddies, tiny islands with sprigs of green and frothy rapids – all of this framed by overhanging boughs. Oirase Keiryū is most popular in October, when the leaves change colour, but is also beautiful in May and June, when the *yama-tsuji* (mountain azalea) and *ezo-ajisai* (Ezo hydrangea) bloom, and after the summer rains, when the moss and ferns are thick and lush.

The path is well marked and easy to follow; however, it does run parallel to a road, and in some places it's necessary to walk on the road or cross it (the river mostly masks the sound of traffic). At the midway point, **Ishikedo Rest House** (8.30am-5pm Apr-Nov, closed Wed) sells coffee, local beer and juice. The trail ends in Nenokuchi (子ノ口), which is on the shore of **Towada-ko** (十和田湖), Japan's largest crater lake.

Several JR Mizuumi buses run daily (20 April to 10 November) to Yakeyama (焼山) from Aomori Station, Shin-Aomori Station and Sukayu Onsen. At Nenokuchi, the same bus returns to Aomori, via Yakeyama; it also stops at several points where the trail intersects the road, if you want to cut the walk short. It's best to get an early start, to beat the tour groups. Season: April to November.

38

Tanesashi Kaigan

DURATION	DIFFICULTY	DISTANCE	START/END
3hrs	Easy-moderate	9km	Kabushim/ Tanesashi Kaigan Information Center

TERRAIN	Packed earth; some steps

Tanesashi Kaigan (種差海岸) is a stretch of northern Pacific coast admired for its varied scenery, which includes rocky cliffs, sandy beaches and pine groves. The path that runs along it is the first leg of the 700km-long Michinoku Coastal Trail. It's open year-round, but best walked between April and mid-November.

Getting Here

JR Hachinohe line trains depart hourly for Same (鮫; pronounced 'sahmé') from Hachinohe Station, where the shinkansen stops, via Hon-Hachinohe Station, in town. From Same Station, it's a 15-minute walk to Kabushima (蕪島); turn left out of the station, go left over the tracks and then right along the coastal road. (Fair warning: same is grim and industrial.) If you're driving, there is a public car park across the street from **Kabushima Rest House** (56-2 Same, Same-machi).

Starting Point

Kabushima Rest House has maps in English and displays on *umineko*, the black-tailed gulls that nest here in spring. Below the entrance to the hilltop shrine, Kabushima-jinja, there is a small swimming beach and a sign marking the start of the Michinoku Coastal Trail. Parts of the trail are not clearly defined, marked with short, easy-to-miss wooden posts. Be careful at high tide and retreat to the road (which runs parallel to the route) if necessary.

01 Follow the road for 15 minutes to the end of the fishing port to pick up the path, which crosses pebbly coves where harvested kelp is laid out to dry (careful not to tread on it!).

Michinoku Coastal Trail

The **Michinoku Coastal Trail** (みちのく潮風トレイル; tohoku.env.go.jp/mct/english) runs along Tōhoku's Pacific coast from Tanesashi Kaigan in Aomori Prefecture to Sōma in Fukushima Prefecture. Michinoku means 'end of the road' and is an old name for historically remote Tōhoku. The route, which passes through Sanriku Reconstruction National Park, was initiated in 2013 as part of the region's post-tsunami recovery and was completed in 2019. (It's not all dedicated trail: some sections are on road.) The website has maps and descriptions of the different sections, broken into one- and two-day walks. More information can be found at Tanesashi Kaigan Information Center.

CHENG FENG CHIANG/GETTY IMAGES ©

02 Continue up the rocky sea's edge to **Ashigezaki Lookout Point** (葦手崎展望台), which stands on a craggy point overlooking the very blue Pacific. (A short section of the route is on the road.)

03 Several kinds of **wild lilies** bloom in summer along the stretch down to **Ōsuka Kaigan** (大須賀海岸), a sweeping 2.3km-long beach. Walk along the golden sand or on the (still sandy) path through the grass. At the southern end is a sheltered area, **Shirahama** (白浜), that is generally safe for swimming in summer (the rest of the beach has a dangerous current).

04 Past the beach the trail passes through a **grove of black pines** to a glorious **natural lawn** on a cliff above the sea. Across the road is the **Tanesashi Kaigan Information Center** (14-167 Tanakubo, Same-machi), from where seven daily (four in winter) buses return to Same Station, via Kabushima Kaihin-kōen (for Kabushima Rest House). Infrequent JR Hachinohe line trains depart from Tanesashi Kaigan Station for Hon-Hachinohe and Hachinohe.

Take a Break

Miroku Yokochō (みろく横丁; 36yokocho.com) is Hachinohe's signature nightlife strip, an alley lined with tiny bars and outside seating. While it can seem intimidating, tourists are truly welcome – so long as you're game to drink and banter. Prices are reasonable: from ¥500 for a drink and from ¥700 for food dishes. As Hachinohe is a port city, many restaurants serve locally caught seafood. Miroku Yokochō is a 10-minute walk south of Hon-Hachinohe Station, marked by red paper lanterns.

39

Tōno

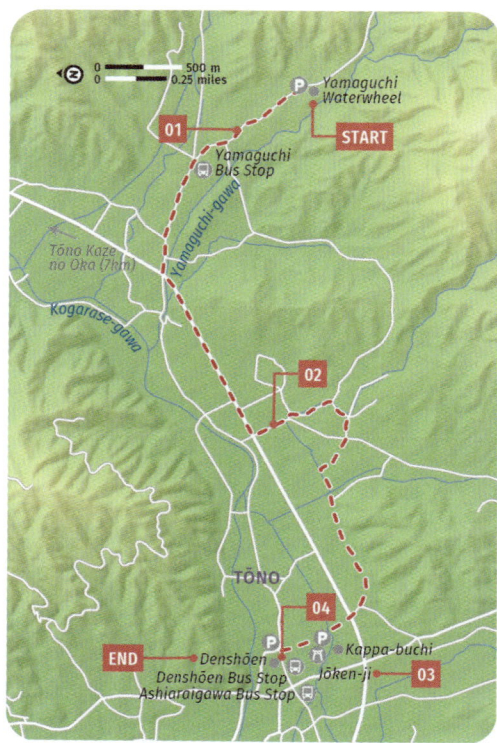

DURATION	DIFFICULTY	DISTANCE	START/END
2hrs	Easy	6km	Yamaguchi Waterwheel/ Denshōen

TERRAIN	Paved road and gravel; mostly flat

Tōno (遠野) is a small town in Iwate Prefecture's mountainous interior. It's famous for looking exactly like what rural Tōhoku should look like, with rice paddies and (some) thatched-roof farmhouses, and also for its colourful folklore, immortalised in the classic work *The Legends of Tōno*.

Getting Here
JR Kamaishi line trains connect Shin-Hanamaki shinkansen station and Tōno. Ontoku- and Nishinai-bound buses, departing at 8.01am, 12.26pm and 3.06pm from in front of Tōno Station, stop at Yamaguchi. From the bus stop, go right at the fork and walk 1km. A taxi from Tōno Station to Yamaguchi Waterwheel costs around ¥3000. The **tourist information centre** (tonojikan.jp) across from the train station has bus schedules and a map in English. Winters in Tōno are cold and snowy; it's best not to visit then.

Starting Point
Yamaguchi Waterwheel (山口の水車), an old-fashioned thatched-roof mill, is one of Tōno's landmarks. It's down a short path across the street from a small car park.

01 From the waterwheel, walk back down the lane (towards the bus stop) through the **Yamaguchi settlement**. This is one of the prettiest parts of Tōno, its farmhouses fronted with colourful flower gardens and rice straw laid out to dry. On the right, a wooden *torii* rises from the fields.

02 When you reach the main road, turn left and follow the road for 15 minutes

Water Sprites

Kappa (カッパ) are impish amphibious sprites who inhabit rivers and ponds. They have webbed feet, pointed beaks, turtle-like shells and an appetite for mischief. Their dish-shaped heads hold a pool of water, which is their essential life force. To outwit a *kappa*, bow in greeting: it will return the bow, spilling the water from its head. To refill a *kappa*'s dish is to earn its gratitude and a future boon. *Kappa* also have a weakness for cucumbers (you may remember that cucumber rolls are called *kappa-maki*). *The Legends of Tōno (Tōno Monogatari)* has more on *kappa* and other mythical creatures that appear in local legends.

until you see a sign pointing to Takamuro Suikō-en (たかむろ水光園); turn left here. After 600m, look for a small wooden sign indicating the route to Kappa-buchi (カッパ淵). A series of these signs will lead you on a wandering path through another **settlement**.

03 Cross the main road and go straight until you see the temple, **Jōken-ji** (常堅寺), on the left. Follow the path with the wooden shrine gates behind the temple to the pool, **Kappa-buchi**, home to Tōno's famous water sprites. It is said that if pregnant women worship at the shrine on the water's edge, they'll produce plenty of milk.

04 Back on the path, keep going until you reach another road; cross it to reach the cultural centre **Denshōen** (densyoen.jp), which has a restored mid-18th-century *magari-ya*, a regional style of farmhouse notable for its attached stable (rare in Japan). Buses return to Tōno Station from Denshōen at 9.21am, 1.37pm and 4.26pm, and also from Ashiaraigawa, a two-minute walk from Denshōen, at 9.40am, 11.25am, 2.25pm and 4.48pm.

 **Take a Break**

Tōno is farm country. Roadside market **Tōno Kaze no Oka** (遠野風の丘; 8-2-1 Nisseto, Ayaori) sells produce from area farmers and also homemade goods like *ganzuki* (steamed cake made with brown sugar). The soft-serve ice cream, made with milk from a local dairy, is especially good. There's also a cafeteria (open 11am to 5pm) that serves *hittsumi* (ひっつみ), a regional hot pot dish with dumplings. It's 3km west of Tōno Station.

Also Try...

Chōkai-san

DURATION	DIFFICULTY	DISTANCE
9hrs	Moderate-hard	11km

With its sloping sides and often snow-capped cone, Chōkai-san (鳥海山; 2236m; pictured) has been nicknamed 'Dewa Fuji'.

The Kisakata Trail (on the Akita as opposed to the Yamagata side of the mountain) is the most popular route. It departs from the visitor centre at Hokodate (鉾立; 1150m), at the mountain's 5th station, and passes the crater lake, Chōkai-ko. There are plants that can only be seen around here, such as Chōkai *azami* (a purple thistle). Just after the 7th station there is a fork, with most climbers opting to go left, and a complete loop at the summit, which will bring you back to this point. It's a mostly steady climb up, with ladders in some places. Public transport is limited to a reservation-only shuttle bus from the nearest train station, Kisakata; a car is recommended. Season: July through mid-October; check weather at chokaizan.com.

Hachimantai Nature Trail

DURATION	DIFFICULTY	DISTANCE
1½hrs	Easy	5km

Hachimantai (八幡平; 1613m) is a vast, jagged plateau that spans the border of Akita and Iwate Prefectures.

The whole, highly volcanic terrain is veined with trails; this mostly flat loop runs around alpine ponds. It's especially popular in late September and early October, when the autumn foliage peaks; wildflowers bloom in summer. In spring, there is still snow on the trail; rubber boots and snow shoes are available to rent at the Hachimantai Park Service Center. There is one bus daily from Morioka Station to Hachimantai Chōjō (八幡平頂上; mid-May to mid-October), where the trailhead is located, and two buses on weekends (from late April to mid-October, when the Aspite Line access road is open) from stop 2 at Tazawa-ko Station; otherwise, you need a car (parking is ¥500).

NIPHAT ROYLAPCHAROENPORN/SHUTTERSTOCK ©

Iwaki-san

DURATION	DIFF.	DISTANCE
6hrs	Moderate	11km

Iwaki-san (岩木山; 1625m) is a dormant volcano rising over the Tsugaru plain.

From the trailhead at Iwaki-jinja, it's a four-hour ascent – with a final climb over boulders – to the summit, which has views over the Sea of Japan and Hakkōda-san. Rather than backtrack, descend (two hours) to Dake-onsen. Both Iwaki-jinja and Dake-onsen are accessible by one of five daily buses (more on weekends) from the nearest city, Hirosaki. With a car, you can do an abbreviated walk (one-hour round trip) from the mountain's 8th Station. Season: July to October.

Goshogake Nature Trail

DURATION	DIFF.	DISTANCE
40mins	Easy	2km

A short circuit with impressive volcanic activity.

English signs explain the natural phenomena, which include bubbling mud pits and an ice-blue pool of near-boiling water. The mostly flat, roped-off trail is behind Goshogake Onsen (後生掛温泉); the bathhouse at the ryokan is open to visitors 9am to 4pm (admission ¥600). On weekends from mid-April to mid-October (and weekdays during Golden Week and O-Bon and from mid-September) buses run here from stop 2 at Tazawa-ko Station.

Nyūtō-san

DURATION	DIFF.	DISTANCE
4hrs	Moderate	9km

Akita's Nyūtō-san (乳頭山; 1478m) has beech forests, alpine meadows and high moors.

There are three trails up Nyūtō-san from Nyūtō Onsen (p127), each named for the hot spring from which it originates. The most popular route starts at Kuro-yu Onsen (黒湯温泉; pictured) and returns to Magoroku Onsen (孫六温泉). A ridge trail connects the summit of Akita Koma-ga-dake (p126) to Nyūtō-san, and it's possible to do an ambitious hike that combines both. Get bus schedules from the tourist information centre (p126) at Tazawa-ko Station. Season: June to October.

Sōunkyō Onsen (p152)

Hokkaidō

40 Shin Sen Numa & Chisenupuri
Lovely boardwalk, swamp, lake and mountain peak with views. **p144**

41 Asahi-dake
Challenging volcanic ascent with alpine meadows and a hot spring. **p148**

42 Kuro-dake
Easy walk with beautiful valley views. **p152**

43 Tokachi-dake
A medium-difficulty walk with a volcanic 'hell' and alpine vistas. **p154**

44 Meakan-dake
Walk up to the lip of an active volcano and peer into the maw. **p156**

45 Mashū-dake
Climb the peak above Japan's clearest and most sacred lake. **p158**

46 Rausu-dake
The wildest of all Hokkaidō's walks and the highest peak in the Shiretoko Peninsula. **p160**

47 Rishiri-zan
Hokkaidō's northernmost 'Fuji' is an ever-steeper cinder cone with a shrine at the top. **p162**

48 Momoiwa Observatory Course
Cross southern Rebun among fields of wildflowers and rocky cliffs. **p164**

Explore

Hokkaidō

One of the wildest and most romanticised regions in Japan, Hokkaidō has day walks (or much longer options) that rival anything one would find in America, Australia or Europe. There's wildlife galore, such as brown bears, foxes and deer, but smaller critters too: flying squirrels, pikas and weasels. With its four distinct seasons, the region always has something new and spectacular to see.

Sapporo

The major hub city of Sapporo (札幌) will likely be where you fly in and depart from. It's got anything you could need, from camping supply stores to great hotels and restaurants should you need to freshen up before or after heading out on your walking adventure. Shin Chitose Airport is about 40 minutes from the centre by train. Nightlife here rivals that of Tokyo, but you may want to get a good sleep if you're planning on walking the next day, as most trails require an early start.

Utoro

A small town bordering the Shiretoko Peninsula, Utoro (ウトロ) is a good spot to base yourself for a Rausu-dake walk (p160), but there are other reasons to come here as well. Depending on the time of year, ice-watching is popular, and you can take sightseeing cruises along the coastline. Seafood is fresh and tasty, especially (in season) *uni* (sea urchin). Don't expect a lot in the way of nightlife, unless you mean nocturnal life: bears, deer, foxes and other critters are easily seen. There is train service to Shari, an hour away, but bus or taxi is the only option after that.

Akanko Onsen

Akanko Onsen (阿寒湖温泉), a delightful, quiet village on the shores of Akan-ko, has the largest Ainu *kotan* (village) in all of Japan. You can see interesting dance and fire performances, eat Ainu traditional food and purchase any kind of Ainu woodcarving – from tiny earrings to giant totem-pole-sized bears – in the many stores that line the streets. The town is not named 'onsen' for nothing: the baths here are wonderfully relaxing, especially after a long day on the trail.

Wakkanai

It's hard to get more remote than Wakkanai (稚内), but if you're going to the islands of Rebun (p164) or Rishiri (p162), you will do. The ferries leave from here, and mainland Japan's most northerly point is about 40 minutes drive to the east – Cape Sōya. Due to its proximity to Russia (you can see the Sakhalin Islands on a clear day) there's Cyrillic as well as English on many of the street signs. At least one camping outfitter is in the shopping arcade, and there are general stores and supermarkets if you need to stock up on supplies. You won't find much selection, though, compared to doing your camping shopping in Sapporo. Train is the easiest way to reach this place.

Niseko

Hokkaidō's closest thing to a mega-resort, the four peaks of Niseko (ニセコ) draw skiers

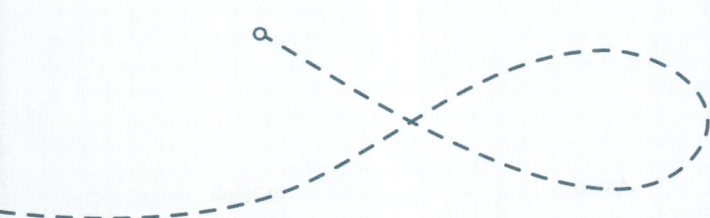

from around the world, who flood in as soon as the slopes are open. For the rest of the year the place remains pretty quiet, with many of the shops completely closed. The walking is fantastic, and there are a number of good onsen to bathe in after you come off the trail. Get there by bus or train from Sapporo.

 ## When to Go

Hokkaidō gets cold, Siberian cold, so winter is not ideal and many roads and trails close from mid-October to May. The ideal times are late spring, summer and early autumn (which can be as early as September). For alpine flower-viewing you'll want July or August; for hills alive with autumn foliage, September.

Most of the walks listed here are doable with public transport, assuming you're willing to get a taxi if needed to/from the trailhead. Japan's network of trains and buses is often poorly timed for walkers, so you'll need to check carefully beforehand. But it's not hard to get to the towns by bus or train. Having a JR Pass may make sense if you'll be doing a fair bit of moving around.

Keep in mind that if you rent a car, usually you'll be required to return it to the same location. Because of this, many visitors find that renting from a location in or near Shin Chitose Airport makes sense, as that's likely to be the location you fly from.

 ## Where to Stay

Hokkaidō has the full range of sleeping options, from cheap business hotels (often located next to train stations) all the way up to fancy luxury ryokan (traditional Japanese inns). The best options may be what's most convenient to your chosen trailhead, as many of these walks are best tackled early in the morning so as to not get stranded in bear territory after dark.

Furano Heso (Belly Button Festival; hesomatsuri.com) This July festival has got to be the area's most unique celebration, where peoples' torsos are painted in elaborate mask designs before a large parade.

Sapporo summer festival For about a month in July/August, much of Ōdori-koen in Sapporo becomes a summer festival, with

Resources

hikesinjapan.yamakei-online.com
A comprehensive walking site with maps and information about all things Japan-hike.

center.shiretoko.or.jp
The Shiretoko Nature Center's website, where you can get info about the area and have questions answered.

nisekotourism.com
The helpful Niseko Tourism website, with contact information and a wide list of resources.

en.kushiro-lakeakan.com
English-language info for the Akan area, including activities and bus access.

games, events and (of course!) lots of Sapporo beer. In fact, a part of the street is a dedicated beer garden, with many domestic and international brewers.

Shiretoko Fantasia An appropriately fantastical simulation of an *aurora borealis* event that was seen in 1958. Though the lights and colours are human-made, the festival gives a sense of what this might have been like. It's on every evening from early February to late March for about 30 minutes in the town of Utoro.

Ainu dance performances All year, once or even several times a day, you can catch traditional dance at the Ikor Theatre in Akanko Onsen's Ainu Kotan. The 2020 award-winning movie *Ainu Mosir* was filmed around Akanko Onsen using mainly local actors, some of whom you'll likely see on stage.

40

Shin Sen Numa & Chisenupuri

DURATION	DIFFICULTY	DISTANCE	START/END
3-4hrs	Easy-moderate	6km	Shin Sen Numa Rest House

TERRAIN	Forest trail, boardwalk, rocks, mud

The best thing about this walk is that it offers a real range of scenery and ecosystems in a tight little package: even with a good break for lunch, it's only three to four hours. You'll start on a boardwalk, which, despite some loose boards and some that are missing, is doable even for those in wheelchairs or using canes and walkers. From there you'll head through forest to a sub-alpine lake and then to a peak which, though small, offers a grand vista of the entire Niseko area.

Getting Here
From Niseko you'll need to plan about 40 minutes by car to reach the trailhead at Shin Sen Numa Rest House or take the hour-long, infrequent and summer-only bus from JR Niseko Station. Since the end of the walk is at a different location you can also leave your vehicle at the endpoint, but either way, you'll need to walk, thumb a ride or take a taxi. The easiest thing is to drive, then call for a taxi when you're at the summit of Mt Chisenupuri, so that it will get there by the time you've descended. Bus users will need to high-tail it back to Shin Sen Numa by 4.05pm.

Starting Point
This route starts at the Shin Sen Numa Rest House (神仙沼レストハウス) car park.

01 Start at the **Shin Sen Numa Rest House**, where you have the luxury of using the toilet (there aren't any on the trail) and grabbing something to eat, if needed. Then head across the street to the boardwalk, where you'll have the option of several different paths. The boardwalk currently could use

Skiing

Walking and onsen-soaking aren't the only reasons people come to Niseko. It's also one of the top skiing destinations in the world, with four resorts together known as **Niseko United** (niseko.ne.jp; Nov-Apr). As soon as the slopes open, the town floods with Australians, Europeans and Japanese ski bums, bears and bunnies, all looking for that perfect powder and a downhill glide.

a little TLC. It's warped in places and here and there a board is missing or broken. Still, it's sturdy enough. And in fact, you'll see plenty of 70- and 80-somethings out and about on it.

02 The longest route option will take you in a large loop around **Shin Sen Numa** (a swamp). It's lovely at any time of year, with wildflowers and various riparian plants. **Birdlife** is plentiful, so birders will want to bring their binoculars. You can even sometimes spot newts and salamanders (as well as frogs, turtles and the occasional snake) in the shallow water. (The entire lake is only 2m at its deepest.) One of the **unique plants** here is woodland horsetail (*Equisetum sylvaticum*), which grows in abundance but is actually quite rare worldwide and is a plant that has likely remained unchanged since the dinosaurs. Less rare is skunk cabbage, which is given an acclaim here not often shared by Western visitors. A species of trillium can be seen here too, as well as Jack-in-the-pulpit. So many flowers bloom here that there's even a separate *Flower Trail* map you can get that lists a number of them, including beautiful purple gentians, lilies, rhododendrons, azaleas, hostas and more.

03 Leaving the swamp, head into the forest, where you'll follow a short trail to **Lake Naganuma**, a mostly dry lake strewn with large boulders that scream 'picnic', so if you've got one, eat it now looking out over the lake. A pump house sits on the opposite side from where the path enters. Despite what one might think, the pump house is not particularly attractive and does not add to the scenic beauty. A bit of a shame.

04 There are two options for getting to the path again: one is to retrace your steps into the forest. Alternatively, if you fancy a walk along the lake first, follow the shoreline all the way to the end. The trail is only a few metres into the forest from the southernmost edge, and can also be found in several other places along the shoreline if you bushwhack just a bit through the bamboo.

05 Those wanting a shorter walk could turn around here, but you'll miss out on a great view from the Chisenupuri peak. To reach it, after leaving the lake, you'll go up, up, up a long series of rocky-formed steps, which are often quite muddy. It's easy to slip here, so use care not to twist an ankle.

06 At one point, the trail continued all the way to the ski resort on the southern slopes and to Yukichichibu Onsen. Now that section (despite still showing on maps) has been closed for so long that it's mainly disappeared, filled in with quick-growing bamboo and scrub brush. At the marker, you will want to turn left, heading uphill towards Chisenupuri. It's a well-marked, if steep and occasionally rooty trail, which gets rockier and rockier as you near the summit.

07 The summit of **Chisenupuri** is broad enough to fit several bus groups, though it's likely you'll have the mountain all to yourself. There's a marker, some stands of stunted pines and some large boulders. If you didn't eat at the lake then dig in now, while appreciating the view. Front and centre is the massive cinder cone of Yōtei-zan, the area's 'Fuji', so-called for a reason. If you didn't know you weren't in Shizuoka,

Nikka Whisky

An hour north of Niseko will bring you to **Yoichi**, the home of **Nikka Whisky**, set up by 'the father of Japanese whisky', Masataka Taketsuru, in 1934. Taketsuru studied whisky-making in Scotland, returned to Japan with his Scottish wife and chose Yoichi as the best place in the country to make Scottish-style whisky. Drop in, tour the museum and taste a dram or two.

KRIS GAETHOPS/GETTY IMAGES ©

you might even think you were looking at the real thing. In winter it's snow-capped, looking even more massive than it normally does. Even in late spring it will still have substantial snow, which stays in the ravines long after most of the mountain is snow-free.

08 The descent from Chisenupuri to the road (visible far below, curving in a serpentine fashion around the mountain) is quite steep, quite rocky, and quite dangerous: use extra care here. Some of the rocks are slippery as well, as is the moss that coats nearly everything once you're down into the trees. Shaded nearly all the time and forever moist from rain and winter's cold, this side of the slope can be tricky. It's gorgeous though: giant rocks, overhanging tree branches, the verdant leaves and rustling *sasa* (bamboo).

09 If you timed it right, the taxi will have just pulled into the Chisenupuri car park by the time you make it down. Ten minutes later you'll be back at the car park of the Shin Sen Numa Rest House. Nicely done.

 Take a Break

There are 25 onsen in the Niseko area, so you'd be remiss not to enjoy a good soak here. And what better spot than **Goshiki Onsen** (五色温泉; 10 Niseko, Niseko-chō). Named for its supposed five-coloured water, the onsen has penetratingly hot water that soothes and relaxes. Day use is 9am to 8pm May to November and 10am to 7pm December to April.

41

Asahi-dake

DURATION	DIFFICULTY	DISTANCE	START/END
6-8hrs	Moderate-hard	12km	Asahi-dake ropeway station

TERRAIN	Volcanic gravel, rocky terrain

Asahi-dake (旭岳) is one of Hokkaidō's greatest hits: awe-inspiring views, some really cool geology (live volcanos!), a challenging yet rewarding ascent and some great alpine air. It is best done in summer or early autumn, as the possibility of injury increases exponentially with ice or snow. Though unlikely, there's a small chance you'll encounter *higuma* (Japanese brown bears), so take appropriate caution if you see one. Drop into the impressive Asahidake Visitor Center for a map and up-to-date weather forecasts before heading to the ropeway base station.

Getting Here

If you're staying in Asahikawa, the nearest large city, you'll have a good drive before you reach the ropeway entry. Parking at the ropeway can be limited, so getting here in the early morning is a grand idea even if you don't plan to do the full circuit. Buses do run, but infrequently, from the bus centre near JR Asahikawa Station.

Starting Point

You'll start and finish this walk at the ropeway station. Reaching the trailhead is simply a matter of leaving the ropeway car and following the signs…or the other walkers.

01 Leaving the ropeway, there's really only two choices: go straight, heading up towards Asahi-dake's formidable peak, or go left, which will eventually lead you to the same place. It's probably best to get the worst (ie steepest) stuff over while

To Bell or Not to Bell...

...that is the question. On the one hand, no one ever wants to run into a bear, especially not a Japanese brown bear, as these animals are considered dangerously unafraid of chomping on a walker or two. (Note: this is actually rare.) But Asahi-dake is like many other Hokkaidō walks in that there is a chance you'll see a bear.

There's a lot *less* chance you'll see one on the initial ascent to the summit, surrounded by 300 other walkers. Even less that you'll see one inside the ropeway cable car or inside the gift shop. Do yourself and those around you a favour by disabling your bear bell (or removing it entirely) when you don't need it.

you're still fresh and energetic. You'll pass a gorgeous little **pond**, often mirror-still in the morning, and if you frame it right you can get pics (or selfies) with the summit of Asahi-dake reflected in the water. In winter, this will be a totally different landscape: a frozen, near-Arctic scene with blindingly white snow.

02 You'll ascend the ever-steeper slope of Asahi-dake, with beautiful alpine scenery if you stop for a water break, and the hissing, sulphur-smelling volcanic vents on the left. This area with the vents is called **Jigokudani (Hell Valley)** and it's easy to tell why. Watch your step along this stretch as it's easy to stumble and the rocks are sharp. Some walkers choose to pick up a pair of cotton gardening gloves for a few hundred yen at a convenience store before starting the walk, which help protect your hands from cuts. Be aware that your footsteps or those of other walkers can dislodge rocks, so be wary as you climb. It's slow going; take it step by step.

03 Making it to **Asahi-dake peak** (2290m), pat yourself on the back and marvel at the 360-degree vista of Daisetsuzan National Park. Several of the other peaks listed in this section are connected by trails here – if you're wanting to turn this into a multi-day walk, it's possible. It's usually quite windy here, so pay attention to any wrappers or foil if you're opening a snack. Another option is to call it a day and head back the way you came, as many will do. But the best is yet to come.

04 Scramble (or bum-slide, if need be) down the steep, gravel-covered slippery backside of Asahi-dake and continue walking. This is possibly the most treacherous section, as it's very easy to slip and even in the best spots it's loose rock that feels like you're going downhill on a bed of marbles. Even in summer, sections of snow and ice are still here, so if you're walking in the spring or late autumn you'll likely need to take extra care with your footing. To the degree possible, try to zig and zag to reduce chances of slipping or injuring yourself.

05 After reaching the bottom, the trail flattens out and you'll walk about 2km until you reach a T-junction near **Mamiya-dake**, passing a small pond and a camping area that's used by overnight walkers on the way. In places it seems nearly Martian: just red and brown rocks, some ochre lichens, a vast expanse of sky. At the T you'll then head left (north), ascending but not reaching the summit of Naka-dake. To the right, as you ascend, you'll see a poisonous, non-batheable 'onsen' that should be avoided due to scalding heat and concentrations of toxic gas.

06 The trail continues to Naka-dake, but turn left again and start your return trip, along a stretch of lovely **alpine tundra**. Wildflower enthusiasts will find many rare Hokkaidō flowers here. Though rare, there are pikas (short-eared relatives of the rabbit) that live in this region (a pika is even inscribed in the Asahi-dake summit marker). They give a shrill call when alarmed, and often perch on the tops of rocks to look around.

07 Take a dip (or soak your feet) in **Naka-dake Onsen**, taking care to find a spot that's not scalding. You may have to wait your turn, as the pool is small and there may be a number of people who want to soak. When you've rested enough, continue onward downhill. The

Going the Distance

Daisetsuzan National Park is a walker's dream, with numerous trails criss-crossing spectacular scenery and numerous entry and exit points. If doing this as part of a longer, multi-day experience seems like your cup of (green) tea, then go for it. All three of the Daisetsu NP walks listed here can be the start or end, and even this walk can be extended into a 10- to 12-hour loop if you feel like pushing it.

THONGCHAI.S/SHUTTERSTOCK ©

trail is now a mix of wooden footpaths, mud and grasses. Walkways, steps and boards (some rotting) make the trail easy to find. Time it right and you'll see not only the last of the wildflowers, but the burning reds and oranges of autumn leaves.

08 At **Susoaidaira**, you'll again turn left, gradually ascending over the foothills of Asahi-dake, which will be clearly visible on your left. Lots of wooden steps make the walking a bit easier. It's possible to spot a snake or lizard catching the last rays of the afternoon sun.

09 Long before you reach it, you'll see the Asahi-dake ropeway station building. By now it may be afternoon, and you'll have another chance to snap photos of Asahi-dake reflected in the mirror-like surface of aptly named **Kagami-ike** (Mirror Lake, aka Meoto-ike). When you're ready, take the ropeway back down to the parking area. You're done.

Take a Break

Otokoyama (男山酒造り資料館; otokoyama.com/en), one of Japan's oldest and most esteemed breweries, was founded in Hyōgo Prefecture centuries ago, but since 1899 its sake has been made here in Asahikawa – all the better to take advantage of that mountain spring water coming from Daisetsuzan. What better way to celebrate after the walk than with a taste (or a bottle!) of a time-honoured Japanese sake? The brewery-museum is easily accessed from Asahikawa's bus route, about 15 minutes away from Asahikawa JR Station.

42

Kuro-dake

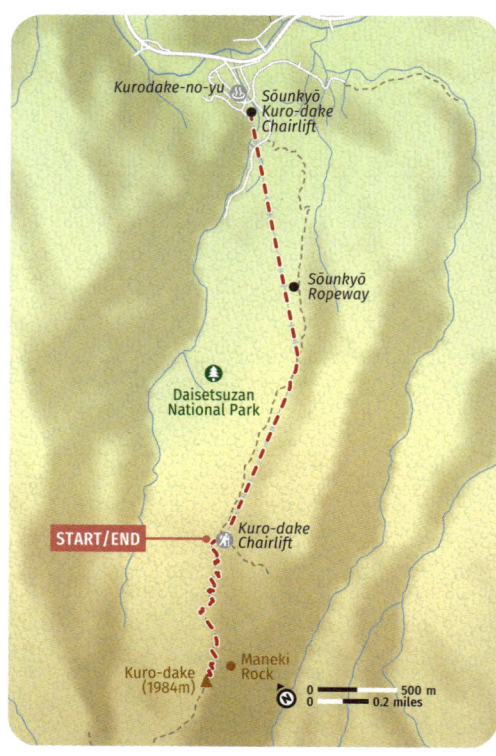

DURATION	DIFFICULTY	DISTANCE	START/END
2-3hrs	Easy-moderate	5km	Kuro-dake chairlift

TERRAIN	Rocky path, gravel, steep inclines

Kuro-dake (黒岳) is a quickie that can be done mostly by ropeway and chairlift, though hardcore hikers may opt to do that part with their feet as well, if they wish to. As described here, it's an easy two- to three-hour walk up a well-travelled path, with the chance to see chipmunks, deer and some lovely scenery along the way. Though steep in most places, it's not usually slippery, so you can make good time if you need to. The chipmunks (do not feed them!) are so used to people that you may need to adjust your step to avoid hitting them.

Take the ropeway and chairlift from the town of Sōunkyō Onsen. From the chairlift, you'll already be near the 7th station waypoint, so you're not far from the peak...and you haven't even started. The walk is simple: just go up the well-trod trail, up and up, with stops for photos and selfies at nearly every point – the views are that gorgeous. **Maneki Rock** is a popular one, in the shape of a *maneki-neko* (beckoning cat). In autumn you'll find the hills ablaze with **stunning panoramas of colour** and surprisingly few walkers. Most opt for the ropeway only, fewer continue on to the chairlift, and still fewer put on their walking boots and go to the summit.

The intrepid can use this walk as an entry for multi-day walking through incredible Daisetsuzan National Park, but for most, it's just a great quick walk that packs a punch: beautiful scenery without much work.

Afterwards, **Kurodake-no-yu** (黒岳の湯; ¥600; ⏰10am-9.30pm) offers handsome hot-spring baths, including a 3rd-floor *rotemburo* (outdoor bath) – it's on Sōunkyō's main pedestrian street.

43

Tokachi-dake

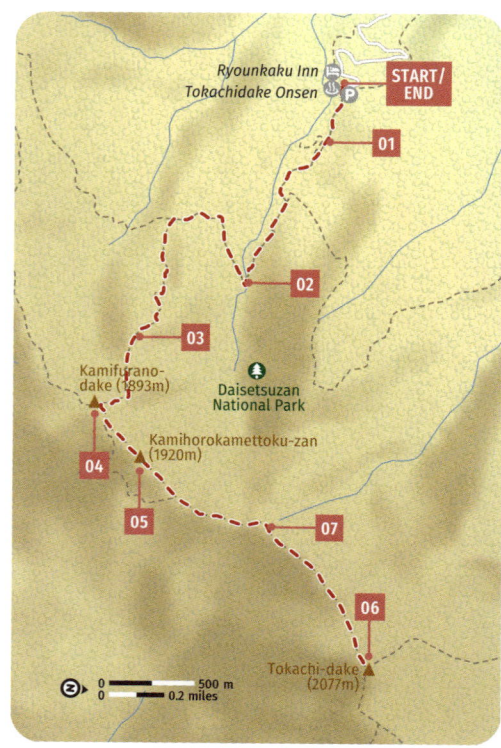

DURATION	DIFFICULTY	DISTANCE	START/END
4hrs	Moderate-hard	12km	Tokachidake Onsen

TERRAIN	Steep inclines, gravel, winds, cliffs

Tokachi-dake (十勝岳) is a challenging walk that's not quite beyond the average walker. It affords great views of multi coloured rock formations, volcanic vents and alpine tundra, as well as lush foliage on either side of the path. Wind can be so fierce here that you may need to abort the mission, and you should pay close attention to weather, as it can change in an instant, going from bright and sunny to overcast in minutes. On the summit of Tokachi-dake you'll be the only – and the most conductive – thing around, so if lightning is in the forecast you'll want to choose a different day to make your ascent.

Getting Here
The town of Tokachidake Onsen in Daisetsuzan NP is the best place to start this walk. You can either stay here overnight or arrive early in your own transportation. Bus service does run, but won't arrive early enough to give you the best departure.

Starting Point
Just beyond the lovely Ryounkaku Inn is a car park and the trailhead.

01 From the car park at Ryounkaku, fill out the trail logbook info and then go uphill, along a two-track road that extends for a kilometre or so before turning into a trail that follows a (usually) dry riverbed.

02 After approximately 1km, the trail leaves the riverbed and heads sharply uphill, crossing over a ridge on its way to the first peak you'll reach, Kamifurano-dake. On the way, a series

Foxes, Foxes, Everywhere

The Japanese red fox is one of the most dapper critters you'll see out and about as you walk or drive to the trailhead. These beautiful animals are highly adaptable, and, unfortunately, this means many of them have adjusted to the many walkers all too happy to offer handouts as they drive by. Yet the saying goes 'A fed fox is a dead fox', and it's all too true – come winter when the tourists dwindle, these animals who depended on handouts either become nuisance animals in yards (and are put down) or they starve. Never offer wild animals food.

RAY BARTLETT/LONELY PLANET ©

of **wooden steps** make the walking a bit easier, though parts of it are quite steep.

03 Before reaching the summit of Kamifurano-dake, you'll pass some incredibly coloured hills above the volcanic 'hell' that formed this side of the mountain: **sulphurous vents**, many of them still gushing steam.

04 Ascending to the summit of **Kamifurano-dake** (pictured; 1893m), you'll be able to see your eventual destination in the distance – if it's clear. High winds here make the walking perilous at times, so be extra careful.

05 You'll cross along a ridge to the next peak, **Kamihorokamettoku-zan**, at 1920m. From here you'll be looking nearly straight down into the volcanic vents. On the other side is stunning alpine tundra.

06 The last stretch, from Kamihorokametto-ku-zan to **Tokachi-dake**, will take nearly two more hours, climbing to 2077m. The views are spectacular, though this entire stretch can be quite dangerous if there are high winds present. Use extreme care.

07 Return the way you came, retracing your steps back to Tokachidake Onsen.

Take a Break

Walkers who chose to spend the night at the **Ryounkaku Inn** will be glad they did: not only do you have perfect proximity to get an early start on the day's walking, but the inn allows previous night's guests to use their *higaeri* (day-use) onsen for free even after checkout, so you can count on having a lovely and refreshing soak after you get down from the climb. The baths here switch genders during the day to allow both sexes to enjoy each bathing area. The *rotemburo* offer sublime views of the mountain you just summited.

44

Meakan-dake

DURATION	DIFFICULTY	DISTANCE	START/END
3-4hrs	Moderate	5.5km	Nonaka Onsen

TERRAIN	Mud, gravel, volcanic scree

Meakan-dake (雌阿寒岳) will bring out the 10-year-old in even the most seasoned climber: you'll reach the top and stare down into a **bubbling volcano** with hissing vents so loud you'll think a jet is flying overhead. It's also got lovely views of the surrounding forest and mountains, a bit of birdlife and (as in many Hokkaidō walks) the chance of bear sightings. Depending on the route you take, you can include a visit to a lake near the trailhead. Either way, you'll start and end at an onsen where you can relax after you come down.

Getting Here
Bus isn't practical, so your best bet is to self-drive or take a taxi out of nearby Akanko Onsen.

Starting Point
There's a car park reserved for walkers just next to Nonaka Onsen; be sure not to park in reserved spaces.

01 From the trailhead, you'll walk uphill through a **dense forest**, with verdant moss on the tree trunks and woodpeckers, nuthatches and other songbirds twittering in the trees. Cross over a gully and then head steeply uphill until you reach the edge of the forest. You will see warning signs that you're within the danger zone should there be an eruption, either of lava or poisonous gas.

02 Ascending in zigs and zags, you'll move parallel to the summit for a while, getting your first glimpses of the vistas once you're above the treeline at around the **4th station**. Depending on where you are, you'll be able to see Lake Onnettō, glimmering in the sunlight far below.

Ainu Culture

Hokkaidō's indigenous culture is little known outside of Japan, but has a rich, interesting tradition that includes highly patterned clothing, wood-carving, a spiritual knowledge that includes animals and plants, dance and cuisine. You can learn about it at Akanko Onsen's **Ainu Kotan** (アイヌコタン), Hokkaidō's largest Ainu village.

Also consider visiting the impressive **Upopoy National Ainu Museum and Park** (ウポポイ; ainu-upopoy.jp) in Shiraoi, opened after the Ainu were legally recognised as an indigenous people of Japan in 2019.

03 The trail continues and by the **6th station** the vegetation changes to primarily wind-stunted pine, with some smaller plants and flowers. The pines offer a nice protective cover from the wind, which could be picking up by now.

04 Between the 7th and 8th stations the pines disappear and you're left walking up a steep, rocky, often treacherous slope that's the final stretch. You'll need to follow the paint-splash markers carefully or risk having to backtrack to reach the safer trail.

05 Nothing prepares you for what it's like to reach the **crater** and look down on the smouldering ochre pool and steaming vents, which roar louder than an aeroplane. In the true sense of the word, it's awesome.

06 The **peak** (1499m) is barren and gravelly, with a few rocks here and there to sit on. Use extreme care when opening food as the wrappers will easily blow away in the strong wind. Hats, too. Two choices for the return: go back the way you came, or head around the crater and down to **Lake Onnettō**, then trek back up along the road to reach your vehicle.

 ## Take a Break

Nonaka Onsen is the unrivalled place to relax here. It's a surprisingly simple onsen, with searingly hot water and a rustic, dark wood *uchiburo* (indoor bath). You'll need to wash off by simply dipping a pan into the *o-yu* (hot water) itself, rather than expecting to soap off. Once you've washed, ease yourself into the milky water and enjoy soaking those tired muscles. Alternatively, head outside to the small *rotemburo*, which has a rocky bottom and a nice view of the trees.

45

Mashū-dake

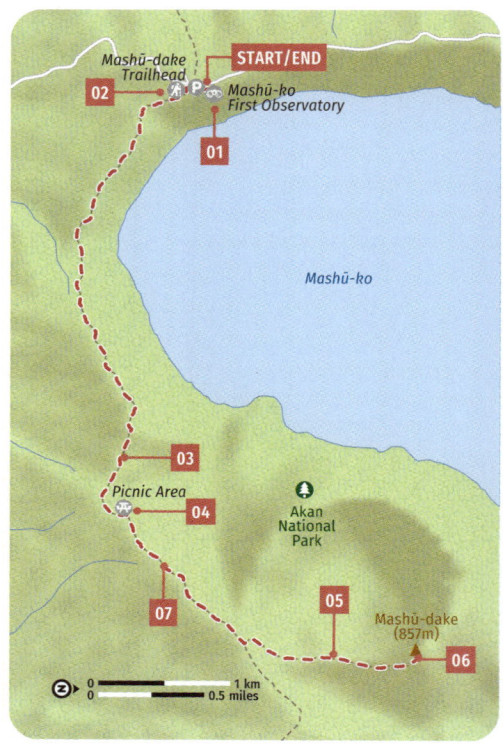

DURATION	DIFFICULTY	DISTANCE	START/END
4-5hrs	Moderate	14km	Mashū-ko First Observatory

TERRAIN	Easy trail, then steep and rocky

Mashū-ko (Lake Mashū) is one of Japan's most sacred spots, so holy that people are not allowed to approach the water's edge. Partly because of this, it's rumoured to have the clearest water in the entire world. The walk is an easy one for most of the way, going through gently rolling hills and copses before finally heading up the steep slopes of Mashū-dake (摩周岳). That last part is quite a haul, but it's worth it when you reach the summit and have an unparalleled view of the lake.

Getting Here

Inconveniently, only two public buses connect the First Observatory and Mashū Station, with the earliest one arriving at 10.55am, and the latest departure at 2.10pm, meaning you will not be able to summit Mashū-dake unless you're Mercury or can do the round trip in under three hours. You'll be best off with a car or taxi hire.

Starting Point

The trailhead begins at the lake's First Observatory, on the southwest shore.

01 Walk up to the **observatory viewing platform** and take a gander at Mashū-ko, one of Japan's most pristine sights. On a clear day the water looks almost electrified.

02 Fill out the trail log and head off around the southern shore. It's mostly light forest for the first kilometre or so, with a few spots where you can see the lake, and lovely hillsides covered with low-growing bamboo.

Wakoto Onsen

Not for everyone, but certainly for those seeking a natural onsen experience, is **Wakoto Onsen** (和琴温泉), a free, mixed-gender, rocky hot spring on the Wakoto Peninsula jutting into nearby Kussharo-ko. What makes it truly special is the perfect sunset view, often reflecting pink or gold in the evening.

There are a number of other free, mixed-gender 'onsen in the wild' scattered around the shores of Kussharo-ko. If they're your thing, drop in to Kotan Onsen Rotemburo in the Ainu *kotan* (village) at the southern end of the lake, Ike-no-yu on its eastern shore, or dig your own onsen in the sand lakeside at Sunayu Onsen.

Best for

OFF THE BEATEN PATH

OSAP/SHUTTERSTOCK ©

03 Further along, you'll find that the forest opens up and is quite sparse, allowing for some excellent **Mashū views**. You'll also notice that the craggy peak in front of you looks larger. You'll be there soon.

04 There's a nice **picnic area** at the midpoint, about 3.5km in, just after the path curves away from the lake. Another 2km and there's a trail heading off to the left, towards the peak that's waiting for you.

05 The hard part begins when you finally reach **Mashū-dake**. This last kilo-metre is *not* easy. The narrow trail has a steep drop-off on one side, and roots and rocks make the footing easy to miss.

06 The reward is a **summit** that almost jumps out on you: turn a final bend and you're there, overlooking a side of the lake you can't even see from the observatory. A bright sunny day will have you exclaiming 'Wow!' out loud.

07 When you're done appreciating the serene beauty of Mashū-ko, retrace your steps and channel your inner mountain goat until you're back on easy street again.

 ## Take a Break

Mashū-ko doesn't have any restaurants, hotels or onsen inns – and that's a good thing. Instead, head to nearby Kawayu Onsen, where you can dine at the friendly **Genpei** (源平; Kawayu Onsen; mains ¥400-1200; ⏰6pm-midnight), an izakaya (pub-eatery) with an English menu and a variety of tasty foods, ranging from ramen to *yakitori* (grilled meat) and fish. There are even a few options for vegetarians as well. On the way, be sure to stop at impressive Iō-zan, an active volcano with sulphur vents you can get disturbingly close to. The same parking ticket can be used here and at Mashū-ko, so hang onto it.

46

Rausu-dake

DURATION	DIFFICULTY	DISTANCE	START/END
8-10hrs	Hard	14km	Iwaobetsu Onsen
TERRAIN		Steep, rocky inclines, alpine trail	

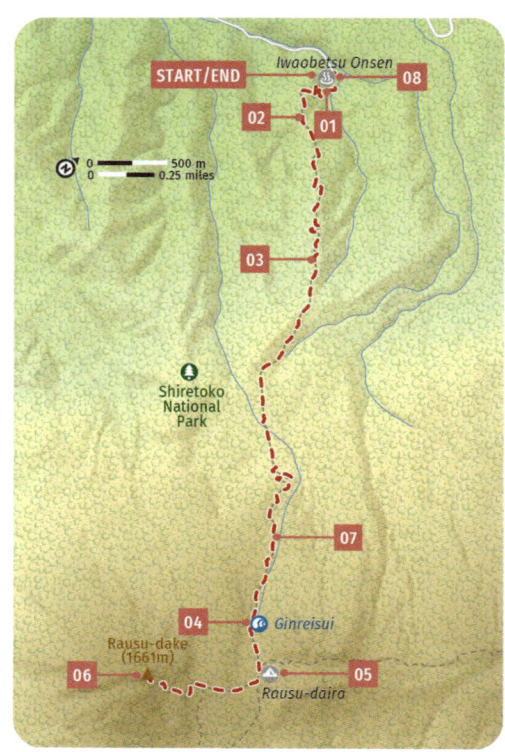

Rausu-dake (羅臼岳) is an austere mammoth that rises above the Shiretoko Peninsula. Climbing it is daunting both because of the altitude rise (about 1500m) and the frequent changes of weather during the day. In fact, the mountain has its own microclimate, making relying on the weather forecast difficult. If you catch it right on a sunny, clear day, it's nothing short of spectacular.

Getting Here

The only way to reach Iwaobetsu Onsen, in Shiretoko National Park, in time for this to be a day walk is by car: either your rental vehicle or a private taxi.

Starting Point

Iwaobetsu Onsen (岩尾別温泉) is the trailhead.

01 Arrive at Iwaobetsu Onsen as early as you can, as this is a day-long, challenging, some might say gruelling, hike. On the winding road to the onsen keep an eye out for *higuma* (Japanese brown bears). They frequent the river once trout and salmon start running in early autumn.

02 Sign yourself into the trail log and turn on your bear bell. Be careful: you may actually need it, as Shiretoko has Japan's highest concentration of brown bears.

03 You'll find that the forest here defies description – in some places it's almost Tolkien-esque, with twisted tree trunks that spider across the ground instead of rising skyward, all stunted by the harsh winters. You'll need to duck in places beneath thigh-thick birches, or step carefully

How to Avoid Bears

Follow local advice to prevent a bear attack. Wear a bear bell when you are in areas that bears frequent; some people opt for a radio turned on instead of the bells. Prior to hiking, chat with rangers about recent bear sightings. Often, they know exactly where you're most likely to encounter one. If you do see a *higuma*, slowly back away and wait for it to leave the area. Be especially careful if you come across a bear cub seemingly on its own, because Mama is unlikely to be too far away and is quite likely to be feeling protective.

Best for

ONSEN

among seedlings that are reaching for the sky.

04 There's a toilet and water at **Ginreisui**. It's pack-out only, so bring ziplock bags for your toilet waste. The trail now heads sharply up a steep ravine on its way to Rausu-daira, passing through a series of rocky crags.

05 At the flat upland area of **Rausu-daira** you're nearly there. Only an hour or two more to go before you're at the summit. Winds can be fierce.

06 Finally, you'll arrive at **Rausu-dake** (1661m) for a stunning panoramic view of Shiretoko in all its glory, with Iō-zan visible to the northwest and Shari-dake off in the distance to the west. On either side you can see the ocean. It's a beautiful place to be.

07 Return by retracing your steps. If you're returning at dusk, there's an increased risk of bear activity so counter this by making sure your bear bell is on…or by singing sea shanties at the top of your lungs.

08 When you're done, you can dip in Iwaobetsu Onsen's day-use bath or (if it's after hours) in the free *rotemburo* to the right of the car park.

Take a Break

You've walked to the top of Rausu and seen Shiretoko from above, so why not take a cruise and see it from the spectacular shoreline? You'll have a chance to see dolphins, whales and other sea life and lots of beautiful, unmarred coastline. **Aurora Cruises** (おーろら; ms-aurora.com/shiretoko/en) has a 3½-hour cruises to the end of the peninsula and back, or 90-minute cruises to Kamuiwakka Falls and back. **Godzilla-Iwa Sightseeing** (ゴジラ岩観光; kamuiwakka.jp/english-booking.php) also offers winter photography cruises among the crift ice.

47

Rishiri-zan

DURATION	DIFFICULTY	DISTANCE	START/END
8hrs	Hard	12km	Hokuroku Campground

TERRAIN	Forest path, rocks, gravel

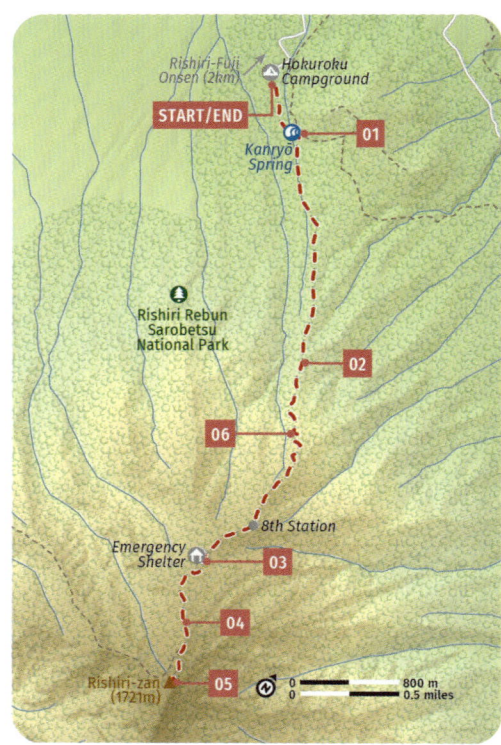

Rishiri-Fuji, as it's known by many, is a near-perfect cinder cone that rises majestically out of the ocean about 40km west of Wakkanai. It's one of the rare spots in Hokkaidō that's bear free, thanks to its isolation, so you can put away your bear bell for this one. It's a long walk that starts out deceptively easy and gets steeper and more challenging as you near the top. The rewards are some lovely changes of scenery, from forest to treeless alpine slopes, some gorgeous eagle-eye views of the island and a cool dormant crater at the top.

Getting Here
To get to Rishiri-tō (Rishiri Island) you'll need to take a ferry from Wakkanai, either direct or via nearby Rebun. From the town centre, it's a five-minute taxi ride to the trailhead. Many hotels offer a shuttle service. And many walkers opt to camp overnight and get an early start the following morning.

Starting Point
The Oshidomari route begins across the street from the Hokuroku Campground bathhouse.

01 After signing the logbook and making sure you have appropriate containers to pack out your waste, you'll walk for only a few minutes before reaching a **spring**.

02 The trail gradually slopes upwards through some lovely forest before coming out at the 5th and 6th stations on a ridge topped with pines made bonsai by the wind. In clear weather you'll have great views back towards town. Higher, you'll reach some official **tenbōdai** (viewpoints) and again want to take out your camera.

Best for

ISLAND ESCAPES

Heartland Ferry

This efficient operation (heartlandferry.jp/english) runs the ferries between the northern city of Wakkanai, Rishiri and Rebun islands. The ferry terminal in Wakkanai has plenty of car parking and is only a short walk from JR Wakkanai station. Ferries depart early to both islands and there are also a number of departures each day that link the two.

03 Just after the 8th station you'll find an emergency shelter, which hopefully you will not need to use. There's also a toilet, which you might very well need to use by this point in the climb. Be sure to pack out all waste, human or otherwise.

04 Between the 8th station and the peak, the going gets tough and the tough keep going: it's slippery, with a gravel trail that easily gives out beneath your feet, and while traction is improved with some steps, some honeycomb-like barriers and ropes, it's still slow and somewhat treacherous.

05 You made it! And wow, what a view! Three hundred and sixty degrees of island vista, with Wakkanai off in the distance to the east and Russia (one of its islands, anyway) to the north. You'll also see nearby Rebun-tō. The winds here are strong and any rubbish left unattended will be blown down the mountainside. Consider having your lunch in a different spot where there's less wind.

06 Return the way you came, heading back down with even more care than you came up, as the chances of slipping seem even greater.

Take a Break

Like so many of Japan's walks, Rishiri-zan has a nice onsen to visit after you're done. It's only a few minutes' drive down the same hill you came up, or about 20 minutes' walk if you're up for a bit more walking. **Rishiri-Fuji Onsen** (利尻富士温泉; ¥500; noon-9pm) has everything you'll need: face and bath towels for rent, several indoor and outdoor baths to soak in and an area for relaxation (complete with coin-operated massage chairs), after you come out. Your hotel may even be able to pick you up here instead of at the trailhead if you tell them your plans.

48

Momoiwa Observatory Course

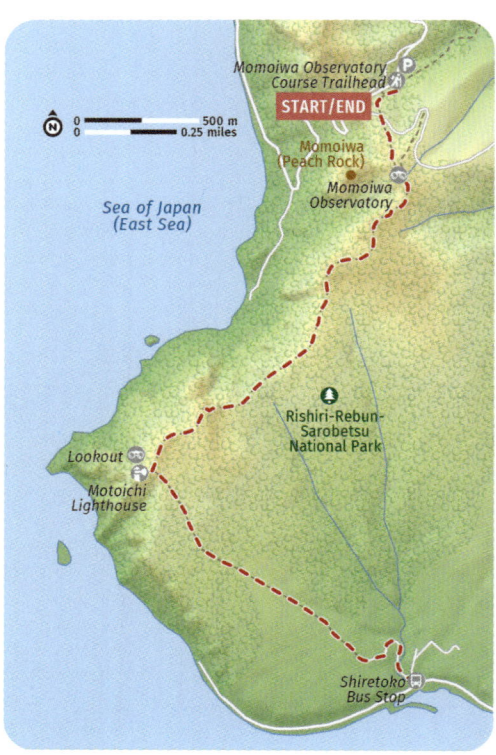

DURATION	DIFFICULTY	DISTANCE	START/END
3hrs	Easy-moderate	2.7km	Momoiwa trailhead/ Shiretoko

TERRAIN	Steps, dirt trail, mild inclines

Rebun-tō (Rebun Island) has an entirely different shape than nearby Rishiri, and much of it is covered with low grasses, giving it a pastoral feel. You almost expect to see sheep grazing among the gentle hills and copses. But look closer and you'll find it's alive with wildflowers, many of them rare or unusual this far north. The easiest and most popular of the island's walks, the Momoiwa (桃岩; Peach Rock) course is well-maintained and offers lovely scenery.

Take a bus from the ferry terminal up to the small car park at the **Momoiwa Observatory Course** (桃岩展望台コース) trailhead. The trail leads up a fairly steep hill, with some rocks and steps and various things to trip over. At the right time of year, you'll already be **flooded with wildflowers** – yellow, purple and white asters, some sunflowers, even cosmos.

Just a quick 20 minutes away is the goal: the **lookout over Momoiwa**, a dome-shaped rock with a small nipple-like protrusion at the top (*momo* can mean breast as well as peach). Far below you can see a car park and info board near the area's only youth hostel. Continue, meandering through green fields with purple and white flowers overlooking cliffs that end in chilly turquoise waves. Most of the time you'll walk along a ridge, with the rolling pasture on your left and the ocean on your right. Breezes can be strong, so bring a hat or scarf if you feel the cold. Finish by coming downhill into the small village of Shiretoko, where you can get the bus back into town.

Best for

ISLAND ESCAPES

Also Try...

FAER OUT/SHUTTERSTOCK ©

Rebun Traverse

DURATION	DIFFICULTY	DISTANCE
8hrs	Moderate-hard	16km

Rebun-tō's heartier walkers will want to try the all-day Rebun Traverse (礼文8時間コース; pictured), which starts on the northern tip of the island at Cape Sukoton and finishes near the middle in Motochi.

It shares much of the same scenery as the Momoiwa Observatory Course (p164), but with a trek through some thicker forest, and several sections – which are often closed – that go along the sea coast. Here it can be tricky, as you may need to time your walk appropriately to hit that section at low tide, and depending on weather and other conditions it can be slippery. A fall out here will be disastrous, as there's no mobile phone reception, so you will need to plan carefully and walk with a friend for safety. At the time of research, parts of this route were closed due to trail conditions. There is a tourist info desk with updates on conditions at the ferry terminal.

Shiretoko Traverse

DURATION	DIFFICULTY	DISTANCE
2 days	Hard	26km

Though this would not be for the casual day walker, the Shiretoko Traverse (知床連山縦走) hike (and it is a true hike!) is a fantastic journey through what many consider to be Japan's last, most wild frontier: no roads, no mobile phone service, just you, your pack, the trail and (perhaps) a bear or two.

This is a two-day journey: day one is described in the Rausu-dake section (p160). Instead of returning to Iwaobetsu Onsen by nightfall, you will camp at Rausu-daira or nearby Mitsumine, then head northeast in the morning, following a trail that runs in the direction of the peninsula's tip, eventually summiting Iō-zan before turning northwest towards Kamuiwakka-yu-no-taki. Among the challenges is that of carrying enough drinking water, as there are few spots to fill up on the trail.

Yōtei-zan

DURATION	DIFF.	DISTANCE
10hrs	Hard	14km

Hokkaidō's Fuji, Yōtei-zan (羊蹄山) rises majestically to tower above the surrounding towns near Niseko. It's beautiful, serene and revered as one of Japan's 100 Famous Mountains.

It's a big climb though, fully 1500m of vertical climb, then descent. Be suitably prepared and don't underestimate the physical challenge. Once at the top, the views out to the Pacific Ocean and Sea of Japan are breath-taking, unless of course, you're inside a cloud!

Kōgen-numa Meguri Hike

DURATION	DIFF.	DISTANCE
4hrs	Moderate	6km

The Kōgen-numa Meguri Hike (高原沼めぐりハイク) is a walking course around the Kōgen-numa (small lakes) and your best chance to see a brown bear in the wild.

It's strictly regulated. Walkers must listen to a lecture at the **Brown Bear Information Centre** (ヒグマ情報センター; ⏲7am-4pm late Jun–mid-Oct) and can only head out on the walk between 7am and 1pm. Walkers must be off the track by 3pm. Staff radio in bear whereabouts and keep an eye on both the walkers and the bears.

Shiretoko-Go-Ko Loop

DURATION	DIFF.	DISTANCE
1hr	Easy	3km

If you're not up for a full-day Rausu-dake jaunt (p160) or the longer two-day Shiretoko Traverse, you can still see lakes, forest, marshland and possibly some wildlife, if you're lucky, in Shiretoko National Park.

The Shiretoko-Go-Ko (Shiretoko Five Lakes) Loop (知床五湖ループ; pictured) extends from the visitors centre along an 800m wooden walkway to a viewing spot overlooking the imaginatively named First Lake. Loop through the others and then head back to the visitors centre.

Temple 19 (Tatsue-ji, p173)

Shikoku

49 **88 Sacred Temples Pilgrimage**
Walk in the footsteps of the pilgrims of old and seek what they sought. **p172**

50 **Ishizuchi-san**
Clamber up chains to the highest peak in western Japan. **p176**

51 **Iino-yama**
Chat with locals on this relaxed walk up Kagawa's Fuji lookalike. **p178**

52 **Tsurugi-san**
Ride the chairlift then amble up to Shikoku's second-highest point. **p180**

53 **Kanka-kei**
Explore Shōdo-shima's famed gorge and scenic spots. **p182**

Explore
Shikoku

In Japan's feudal past, the island of Shikoku was divided into four regions – hence the name *shi* (four) and *koku* (region). The provinces of Awa, Tosa, Iyo and Sanuki are now the modern-day prefectures of Tokushima, Kōchi, Ehime and Kagawa. Despite its geographical proximity to the historical centres of power – Osaka and Kyoto – Shikoku has always been considered somewhat remote. It was accessible only by boat until three bridge links to Honshū were built from the 1980s on. The majority of Shikoku is mountainous, and the island offers excellent walking and a wide variety of choices for anyone seeking outdoor pursuits.

Takamatsu

Kagawa Prefecture's buoyant port city of Takamatsu (高松) boasts the small-town-big-city energy of a prefectural capital, regional culinary specialities including Sanuki-udon and the heritage of traditional gems such as Ritsurin-kōen (park). It's urban Japan at its most pleasant and pretension-free with its heart in the colourful entertainment district and arcades of the central city. Takamatsu is a jumping-off point to catch ferries to Shōdo-shima and the art scene on islands of the Inland Sea, and it has good train links to Okayama on Honshū via the Seto-ōhashi (Seto Bridge).

Matsuyama

Shikoku's largest city is handsome and refined, with a hint of mainland hustle. Matsuyama (松山) is famed across Japan for Dōgo Onsen Honkan, a 19th-century public bathhouse built over ancient hot springs. The finest castle on the island towers above the stylish trams criss-crossing the city streets and the harbour glistening in the distance. Ferries head to Hiroshima and Kyūshū, while the Shimanami Kaidō is an island-hopping series of nine bridges leading from Imabari, north of Matsuyama, to Onomichi near Hiroshima.

Tokushima

With the mountain Bizan looming in the southwest and the Shinmachi-gawa cutting a gentle swathe through the middle, bustling Tokushima city (徳島) is its prefecture's pleasant capital. Temple 1 of the 88 Sacred Temples (p172) is nearby, as Tokushima is the closest point to Kōya-san in Wakayama Prefecture, where pilgrims go to ask for Kōbō Daishi's support on their journey before they begin. Tokushima is a modern, regional city with plenty going on, much busier now that the Akashi Kaikyō-ōhashi (Akashi Kaikyō Bridge) connects it with Kōbe and Osaka via Awaji-shima (Awaji Island).

Kōchi

This smart, compact city of 350,000 has a deserved reputation for enjoying a good time. The castle here is largely undamaged and remains a fine example of Japanese architecture. Excellent access to Muroto-misaki, Ashizuri-misaki and the Iya Valley, plus easy day trips to caves, beaches and mountains, make Kōchi (高知) a perfect base for

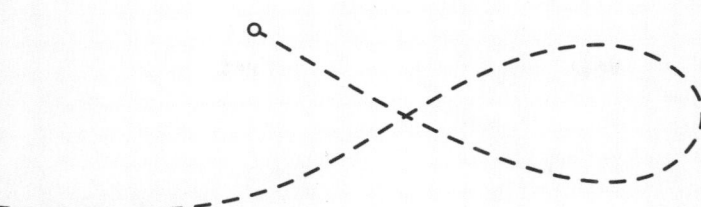

travels around the island. Also claimed by Kōchi is a samurai of great national significance – during the Meiji Restoration, Sakamoto Ryōma was instrumental in bringing down the feudal government.

 ## When to Go

Pilgrims bound for the 88 Temples traditionally set out in April after *taue*, the planting of the rice crops, and undoubtedly spring and autumn are the best times to visit if walking is in your plans. They are pleasant weather-wise and offer cherry blossoms and autumn colours. The high mountains get snow in winter, and midsummer is hot and sticky.

 ## Transport

The big four cities have airports with flights from around Japan, with Takamatsu and Matsuyama airports also receiving international flights.

Three bridge systems link Shikoku with Honshū. The Seto-ōhashi (Seto Bridge) that links Okayama to Sakaide, west of Takamatsu, is the only one of the bridges to carry trains. JR runs regularly from Okayama to Shikoku.

Long-distance buses operate on all three bridge systems to Honshū's major cities.

Ferries connect Shikoku with Honshū, Kyūshū and islands in the Inland Sea.

 ## Where to Stay

Shikoku has been catering to walking pilgrims for 1200 years so there are plenty of places in the full range of accommodation options. The four main cities have lots to offer, but you can also stay in mountain huts and *shukubō* (temple lodgings).

 ## What's On

Awa-odori Matsuri (阿波踊り) Awa-odori in Tokushima is the largest *bon-odori* (folk dance) in Japan, held from 12 to 15 August each year. Each evening men, women and children take to the streets to dance to the samba-like rhythm of the theme song 'Awa Yoshikono', accompanied by the sounds of *shamisen* (three-stringed guitars), *taiko* (drums) and *fue* (flutes). More than a million people turn up every year.

Resources

shikoku-tourism.com
Tourism Shikoku website containing transport maps, info and tips.

visitehimejapan.com
my-kagawa.jp
visitkochijapan.com
discovertokushima.net
Ehime, Kagawa, Kōchi and Tokushima Prefecture websites.

shikokuhenrotrail.com
English-language guide to the 88 Temple Pilgrimage.

Japanese Pilgrimage
Book by Oliver Statler

Yosakoi Matsuri (よさこい祭り) Kōchi's lively Yosakoi Matsuri on 10 and 11 August perfectly complements Tokushima's Awa-odori Matsuri. There's a night-before event on 9 August and a night-after effort on 12 August, but 10 and 11 August are the big days.

Ishizuchi-san Opening Festival In a traditional centre for mountain worship, the first 10 days of July are marked with a 'mountain opening festival' attended by white-dressed pilgrims from all over Japan.

49

88 Sacred Temples Pilgrimage

DURATION	DIFFICULTY	DISTANCE	START/END
40-60 days	Hard	1400km	Temple 1: Ryōzen-ji

TERRAIN	Everything from sealed roads to rough mountain tracks

In the words of the great saint Kōbō Daishi: 'Follow in the footsteps of the men of old and seek what they sought' – ie enlightenment – on this 1200-year-old trek around Shikoku. A two-month pilgrimage is hardly a day walk, however. The full journey is described here, but you can pick and choose sections to suit you. Some options for short walks on the trail are described in the '1 Day on the Pilgrimage' box and in the Uwajima Temples walk and the Unpen-ji to Daikō-ji walk (both p184).

The full 88 Sacred Temples Pilgrimage (四国八十八ケ所) is an arduous task: 1400km circumnavigating the island. But not as hard as it was 1000 years ago when *henro* (pilgrims) virtually disappeared into the unknown.

The first guidebook was published in 1685, and these days everything you need to know is online, but it's still a mighty adventure. No instant gratification here. There are 88 little goals to be achieved. Make that 89. For the pilgrim must return to Temple 1, Ryōzen-ji, to finish the journey. It is vital that the pilgrim completes the circle of Shikoku, for a circle is like the search for enlightenment: never-ending.

Getting Here

To get to Temple 1, Ryōzen-ji (霊山時), take a local train from Tokushima to Bandō. The temple is a 10-minute walk from there.

A Day on the Pilgrimage

The first five temples are within easy walking distance, making it possible to get a taste of the *henro* trail on a day trip from Tokushima. From Temple 1, look for wooden signposts, pointing fingers on stone pillars or small white signs by the roadside marked *henro-michi* (へんろ道 or 遍路道), indicating the way. Don't miss the 500 *rakan* (disciples of Buddha) statues at Temple 5. From Rakan bus stop near Temple 5, catch a bus back to Tokushima Station or take a taxi to Itano Station and train back. Temple 1: Ryōzen-ji (霊山時) – 1.1km – Temple 2: Gokuraku-ji (極楽寺) – 2.4km – Temple 3: Konsen-ji (金泉寺) – 5km – Temple 4: Dainichi-ji (大日寺) – 2km – Temple 5: Jizō-ji (地蔵寺).

Starting Point

Everything you need is available at Temple 1, Ryōzen-ji (pictured), including an English-language guidebook, pilgrim clothes, hat, staff and temple stamp book. Show respect at the Main Hall and Saint's Hall before you start.

01 The prefecture of Tokushima-ken (徳島県) is home to the first 23 of the 88 temples and is known as *Hosshin-no-dōjō*, the 'place to determine to achieve enlightenment'. The first 10 temples are more or less on an east–west line with about 40km between them on the north side of the Yoshino river valley. The route then heads south, crossing the Yoshino-gawa to **Temple 11**, Fujii-dera, before becoming a full-fledged mountain trail, heading up and over to **Temple 12**, Shōzan-ji, which is perched high in the mountains. This track has the reputation of being the steepest and hardest climb on the pilgrimage. The trail then heads east to a cluster of temples in and around Tokushima city. **Temple 19**, Tatsue-ji, to the south of the city, is a barrier temple – only those who are 'pure of intention' can pass. The following two temples are high in the mountains, but then pilgrims head out to the coast and the last temple in Tokushima, **Temple 23**, Yakuō-ji in Hiwasa. This is a *yakuyokedera*, a temple that wards off bad luck in unlucky years. The unluckiest age for men is 42, while for women it is 33. The stairway to Yakuō-ji is split, with 42 steps on the men's side and 33 steps on the women's. Pilgrims approach on the appropriate side and put a coin on each step – on busy days the steps are virtually overflowing with money.

02 The largest of Shikoku's four prefectures, Kōchi-ken (高知県) spans the entire Pacific coastline from east of the cape at Muroto-misaki to west of the cape at Ashizuri-misaki. Historically known as the land of Tosa, the region was always considered wild and remote as it's cut off from the rest of Japan by a barrier of rugged mountains on one side and the Pacific Ocean on the other. Consequently, the Tosa character is thought of as strong, independent and proud. Kōchi-ken is known as *Shūgyō-no-dōjō* (the Place of Practice) and has a notorious reputation as the pilgrim's testing ground. Although the trip through Tosa makes up more than a third of the pilgrimage in walking distance, only 16 of the 88 temples are located in the province. There are 84km between the last temple in Tokushima-ken at Hiwasa and the first temple in Kōchi-ken at Muroto-misaki. Kōchi's first temple, however, marks the spot where Kōbō Daishi achieved enlightenment and holds huge significance to pilgrims. The route then follows a wide arc around Tosa Bay, visits the nine temples in and around Kōchi city, then drops to the end of Shikoku's second great cape, Ashizuri-misaki. The distance from **Temple 37** (Iwamoto-ji) in Kubokawa to **Temple 38** (Kongōfuku-ji) at Ashizuri-misaki is 87km, the longest distance between temples on the pilgrimage. Ashizuri-misaki is known for ascetic training, for believers setting out by boat looking for the Pure Land of the South, and for its suicides. There are few places this remote in all Japan, and *henro* tend to breathe a sigh of relief after moving on to Ehime-ken.

AMEHIME/SHUTTERSTOCK ©

03 Occupying the northwestern region of Shikoku, Ehime-ken (愛媛県) is known as *Bodai-no-dōjō* (the Place of Attainment of Wisdom), and has the largest number (26) of pilgrimage temples. As with Tosa, the southern part of the prefecture was always considered to be wild and remote. Uwajima is known for its bullfighting and the notorious Taga-jinja sex shrine and museum. The temples are few and far between in this isolated part of the island. The trail turns into Shikoku's deep mountains. **Temple 45**, Iwaya-ji, which hangs high on a cliffside above the valley floor, oozes sacredness, but by this stage, pilgrims are looking forward to arriving in Shikoku's largest city, Matsuyama, as they know that the hardest part of the pilgrimage is over. Eight temples are clustered around the island's most cosmopolitan city, plus there is the opportunity to soak away aches and pains in legendary Dōgo Onsen, not far from Ishite-ji, **Temple 51**. There are a further six temples in and around Imabari, where the Shimanami-kaidō bridge system now links Shikoku to Honshū. After a long, testing climb on a mountain track to **Temple 60**, Yokomine-ji, the trail turns east for another climb to **Temple 66**, Unpenji, the highest of the temples at 900m.

04 Formerly known as Sanuki, Kagawa-ken (香川県) is the smallest of Shikoku's four regions, and the smallest of Japan's 47

prefectures. It's known as *Nehan-no-dōjō*, 'the Place of Completion', as it has the last 22 of the 88 temples. The region's hospitable weather and welcoming people have always been of great comfort to *henro*. Each little prize of 'one more temple' comes rapidly. At Kannonji there are even two of the 88 temples in adjoining compounds. Zentsu-ji, **Temple 75**, is significant as the boyhood home of Kōbō Daishi and is so large that most of the other temples could fit in its car park. The trail then heads further east to Takamatsu, the prefectural capital. Yashima-ji, **Temple 84**, to the east of the city, sits atop a 280m mountain that was once the site of a battle between the Heike (Taira) and Genji (Minamoto) clans in the Gempei wars, immortalised in the book *Heike Monogatari* (The Tale of the Heike). You can see the Pond of Blood in which the victorious warriors cleaned their swords. Ōkubo-ji, **Temple 88**, is back in the mountains in the south of the prefecture. It's worth a visit even if you aren't doing the pilgrimage. The walls of the Main Hall are hung with crutches, braces and plaster casts – testament to the faith of pilgrims for more than 1000 years. Holding pride of place is a stone pillar on which is written: 'The place of fulfilment of the vow'. Remember that the journey is not complete when you get to Temple 88 though – there is still a 40km journey back to Temple 1 in Tokushima to complete the circle.

Kōbō Daishi

Pilgrims have been walking clockwise around Shikoku for some 1200 years, following in the footsteps of the great Budchist saint Kōbō Daishi (774–835 CE), who achieved enlightenment on the journey. Shikoku-born Kōbō Daishi founded the Shingon sect of Buddhism in 807 and his body is enshrined at the great Kōya-san temple complex in Wakayama-ken on Honshū (p90). Shingon, commonly referred to as Esoteric Buddhism, is the only major Buddhist sect that believes that enlightenment can be achieved in this lifetime. Pilgrims traditionally start and end their journey at Kōya-san – asking for Kōbō Daishi's support on their upcoming journey and thanking him for that support on their return. You never walk alone – Kōbō Daishi is always at your side.

 Take a Break

Visiting walkers are nothing new here. Pilgrims have been walking around the island for 1200 years, so there are plenty of places providing the essentials – somewhere to sleep, eat and bathe. It's not too hard to find a place to stay each night, be it in a *shukubō* (temple lodging), at a *minshuku* (Japanese guesthouse), ryokan, hotel or, if you're on a tight budget, on a park or temple bench. Kōbō Daishi himself is said to have once slept under a bridge – and to this day, pilgrims never tap their staff on a bridge in case they wake him up.

50

Ishizuchi-san

DURATION	DIFFICULTY	DISTANCE	START/END
5-7hrs	Moderate	7km	Ishizuchi Ropeway

TERRAIN	Rough, rocky track, steepish sections

At 1982m, Ishizuchi-san (石鎚山) is known as 'the roof of Shikoku' and is the highest peak in western Japan. With its name meaning 'stone hammer mountain', Ishizuchi has long been a centre for mountain worship, attracting pilgrims and climbers alike. It can be summited relatively easily thanks to an aerial ropeway that whisks climbers from 455m up to 1300m.

Getting Here
Come using your own wheels or by Setouchi Bus from JR Iyo-Saijō Station to the Ishizuchi Ropeway's Shimo-dani lower station.

Starting Point
Take the ropeway (ishizuchi.com; return adult/child ¥2200/1100; every 20 minutes) up to Sanchō-jōju upper station.

01 From the top of the ropeway at 1300m, follow the signs to Jōju (成就) for around 20 minutes to reach the shrine **Ishizuchi-jinja Jōju-sha** (石鎚神社成就社). After an initial descent, head uphill through the forest to reach Zenja-ga-mori (前社森), from where a zig-zagging slope continues up to Yoakashi-tōge (夜明かし峠) pass at 1652m. Shortly you'll encounter your first of three sets of chains, Ichi-no-kusari (一の鎖), at 33m in length. This is an opportunity for walkers to test their mettle! Don't feel you have to haul yourself up the chains, though, as there's a bypassing track. Carry on to **Ni-no-kusari-goya** (二の鎖小屋), a small hut, where the track from Tsuchi-goya comes in from the left.

02 This is where the real challenge begins. Although there's a path all the way to the

Opening Day at Ishizuchi-san

The biggest annual event on Ishizuchi-san is **Ōyama-biraki Matsuri** (Mountain Opening Festival), which takes place from 1 to 10 July. During this period up to 150,000 pilgrims and Shugendō practitioners gather from across Japan to climb to the summit. They come, dressed in white, to worship Ishizuchi Ōkami, the god of Ishizuchi-san, who stands for kindness, wisdom and courage. From a distance the mass of humanity on the trail resembles a great white stripe stretching for the 3.6km from Jōju-sha to the summit! Most participants ride the ropeway, but in centuries past, they climbed the whole way. Note: women are not allowed to climb Ishizuchi-san on 1 July.

top, the most popular way to make the final ascent is up the *kusari* (heavy chains; pictured) draped down the rock faces. Clambering up these chains is the approved pilgrimage method – and great fun! You may have shinnied up the first set earlier on, but the second set is twice as long at 65m, as is the third at 68m. Avoid the chains in inclement weather and take the track, which has been tamed by the installation of ugly steel steps almost to the top. When you reach the first peak, **Misen** (弥山; 1974m), you'll find **Ishi-zuchi Jinja** (石鎚神社) and **Ishizuchi-jinja Chōjō-sansō** (石鎚神社頂上山荘), a popular mountain hut. The ascent from the ropeway will have taken three to 3½ hours.

03 There's one final test. **Tengu-dake** (天狗岳; 1982m), the highest point, is reached by carefully climbing along a sharp ridge with a big drop-off to the left. On a good day it's clearly visible and will take 10 minutes, but would be best avoided in bad weather. On a clear day there are incredible views and you'll understand why Ishizuchi-san is called 'the roof of Shikoku'.

04 When you're ready, head down on the track using the steel staircases to descend back below the chains. From Ni-no-kusari-goya, follow the track back down the way you came up to the top of the ropeway. The descent from the peak should take around 2½ to three hours.

 Take a Break

Perched at the peak, **Ishizuchi-san Summit Hut** (Ishizuchi-san Chōjō-sansō; 石鎚山 頂上山荘) is open from the start of May to the start of November. You can eat here, just buy snacks and drinks or stay the night as the hut sleeps 50. There's nothing luxurious, just hot meals, bedding on a tatami mat in a warm shared room, and a solid roof and walls. A real Japanese mountain experience!

51

Iino-yama

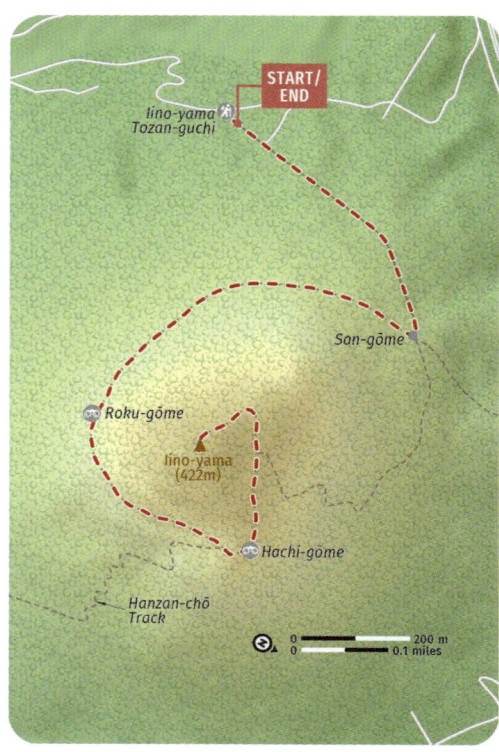

DURATION	DIFFICULTY	DISTANCE	START/END
2-3hrs	Easy-Moderate	4.5km	Iino-yama Tozan-guchi

TERRAIN	Rocky mountain track, not too steep

Known to locals as Sanuki-Fuji because of its similar shape to Fuji-san, Iino-yama (飯野山) offers panoramic views out over Japan's smallest prefecture, despite being only 422m in height. Somewhat surprisingly, considering its shape, Iino-yama is not a volcano. This is a popular walk with both locals and visitors with easy access and a variety of paths. Three different routes head up to the peak from three different sides, and you'll likely meet locals getting their daily exercise and nattering with buddies on your way to the top.

Iino-yama Tozan-guchi (飯野山登山口), with parking and toilets, is at the southwest of the mountain and can be reached by bus from JR Marugame Station (丸亀駅). Head up the stone steps. The trail initially turns to the west, climbs steadily, and at **San-gōme** (三合目; third staging point) runs into the Sakaide Track coming up from the northern side of the mountain. This is the third staging point of 10, number 10 being at the peak.

Turn right at San-gōme and the track will curl around towards the east of the mountain, continuing to climb, passing **Roku-gōme** (sixth staging point), from where there are **great views south** of the central mountains, and running into the Hanzan-chō Track coming up from the east. There are **spectacular views north** out to the Inland Sea and Seto-ōhashi at **Hachi-gōme** (eighth staging point). When you get to the peak at 422m, you'll have completed a 360-degree curling climb around Iino-yama, enjoying views out in all directions. There's a small **temple** up the top, but no views. Head back down the way you came up when you're ready.

Best for
KIDS

52

Tsurugi-san

DURATION	DIFFICULTY	DISTANCE	START/END
3-4hrs	Easy-Moderate	4km	Mi-no-koshi

TERRAIN	Rough, rocky mountain track

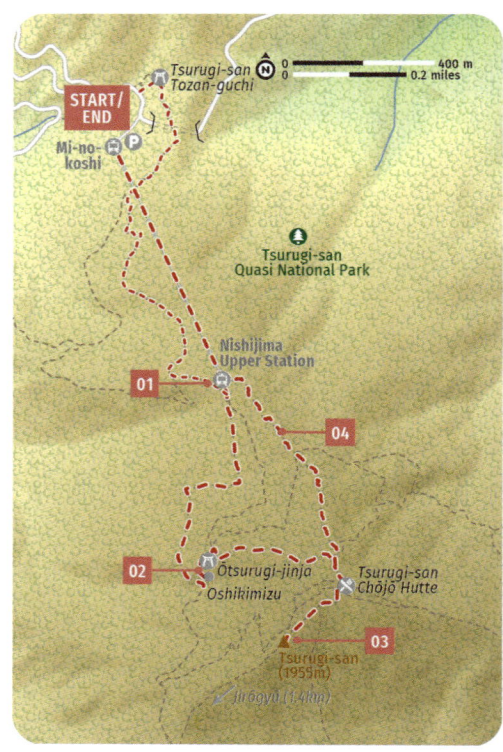

At 1955m, Tsurugi-san (剣山) is the second-highest mountain on Shikoku and easy to climb thanks to a chairlift. The gently rounded summit is known as Heike-no-baba; it is said to have served as the 12th-century training field for military horses of local Heike warriors. When the Heike clan succumbed to the rival Genji at the Battle of Dan-noura in 1185, legend tells us they buried their emperor's sword at the peak of Tsurugi-san; hence the mountain's nickname of Kenzan (Sword Peak).

Getting Here

This is one where you're going to want your own wheels. Tsurugi-san is at the head of the Iya Valley, so if you've been exploring Iya, carry on up Rte 439 to Mi-no-koshi. Alternatively, drive south on Rte 438 from the Yoshino Valley to the north.

Starting Point

There's plenty of free parking at Mi-no-koshi at 1420m. The single-seater chairlift up to Nishijima station at 1750m (return ticket adult/child ¥1900/900; turugirift.com), taking 15 minutes, is at the far end of the car park.

01 If you opt to walk rather than take the chairlift up to **Nishijima station**, it will take 45 minutes to an hour extra. The trailhead at Mi-no-koshi is at the big *torii* (shrine gate) at the entrance of the village. It is marked Tsurugi-san Tozan-guchi (剣山登山口). Head straight up the concrete steps to the top and turn right in front of the shrine. You'll pass under the chairlift in a small tunnel after about 10 minutes, then wind your way up the forest path to the top of the chairlift at Nishijima (西島).

Vine Bridges & Scarecrows

Tsurugi-san sits at the head of one of Japan's infamous 'hidden regions', the Iya Valley. Head down Rte 439 from Mi-no-koshi to **Oku Iya Ni-jū Kazura-bashi** (奥祖谷二重かずら橋), two secluded wisteria vine bridges hanging side by side, glorious remnants of a remote and timeless Japan. They were originally constructed by bandits who took refuge in the valley gorges. Downriver is **Nagoro** (名頃), known as Scarecrow Village. Those 'people' waiting at the bus stop, gossiping on a porch, and toiling in the fields are scarecrow-type dolls made by lonely residents as a way of memorialising former members of their dwindling population.

Best for

OFF THE BEATEN PATH

02 From here, take the right of the three tracks, ignoring the *torii* over the middle one. Follow the signage to **Oshikimizu** (御神水), the 'Spring of God', rated one of Japan's 'top 100 water sources', and dip into the refreshing, delicious spring water. After the spring, climb to the small shrine, **Ōtsurugi-jinja** (大剣神社), set among some intriguing rock formations, before heading up to the summit. From the Nishijima, this will have taken about 45 minutes to an hour.

03 At the top of the track, pass between the weathered buildings to come out on the rounded peak of **Tsurugi-san** (剣山). The highest point at 1955m is a couple of hundred metres away and from there, enjoy the views in all directions. On a clear day, you can see as far as the Chūgoku range on Honshū and if you feel like some more walking before you descend, take the trail down from the summit to the southwest to the clearly visible summit of Jirōgyū (次郎笈) at 1930m. It will take two hours to go to Jirōgyū and back.

04 For the descent back to Mi-no-koshi, go back between the buildings, start on the track you came in on, then stay right and head down the ridge to the Nishijima chairlift station. From there, either take the lift or the signposted track down to Mi-no-koshi.

Take a Break

Tsurugi-san Chōjō Hutte (剣山頂上ヒュッテ; tsurugisan-hutte.com; late Apr-early Nov), just below the peak, is the place to take a break for a meal such as curried rice, udon or soba noodles or drinks. It's simple, as you'd expect at a remote mountain hut, but the food tastes great at 1950m. Staying overnight here is a superb experience; book ahead online in English. Rooms are simple and there's even a bath.

53

Kanka-kei

DURATION	DIFFICULTY	DISTANCE	START/END
3-4hrs	Moderate	8km	Sanchō ropeway station

TERRAIN	Mountain track, unpaved road and concrete pavement

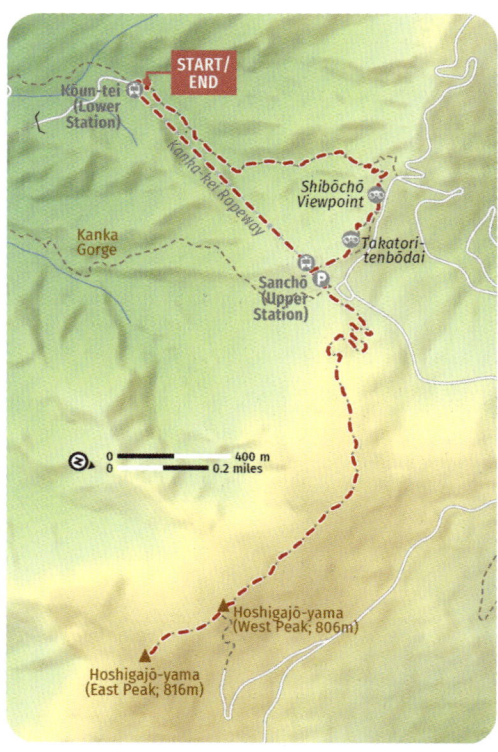

On the Inland Sea island of Shōdo-shima, officially part of Shikoku's Kagawa Prefecture, Kanka-kei (寒霞渓) is known as one of Japan's three most beautiful gorges and for its magnificent autumn colours. An aerial ropeway carries visitors up from Kōun-tei lower station at 295m to Sanchō station at 612m, from where walkers can climb Hoshigajō-yama (816m), the island's highest peak, then descend on the Omote 12 Scenic Places walking trail back to the lower ropeway station.

From the **Kōun-tei lower station** (紅雲亭), where there's a bus stop and parking, ride the **Kanka-kei Ropeway** (kankakei.co.jp; one-way adult/child ¥980/490) up to the **Sanchō upper station**. Views out over the Inland Sea are superb. Make the most of the day by walking one hour to Shōdo-shima's highest peak of **Hoshigajō-yama** (星ヶ城山), away to the east. Follow signage for a steady climb to first reach the mountain's **West Peak** (星ヶ城西峰; 806m), then the high point at **East Peak** (星ヶ城東峰; 816m). After admiring the views, follow your tracks back to the ropeway's upper station.

The **Omote 12 Scenic Places walking trail** (表12景) initially heads west from the ropeway station. It should take an hour or more to descend back to Kōun-tei lower ropeway station. The first section features **Takatori-tenbōdai** (鷹取展望台), a viewpoint at a spot where it is said that early emperors of Japan used to practise falconry. After **Shibōchō viewpoint** (四望頂), the track descends into the gorge and dense forest with cobbled concrete paving. The 12 scenic spots are at impressive rocks and views of rock formations. It's a fun and interesting descent back to where you started.

Best for

ISLAND ESCAPES

Also Try...

CRAIG MCLACHLAN/LONELY PLANET ©

Uwajima Temples

DURATION	DIFFICULTY	DISTANCE
2-3hrs	Easy	5km

For a taste of the 88 Temple Pilgrimage in southern Ehime-ken, try this mini-circuit that starts at Uwajima.

This walk between Temple 42, Butsumoku-ji (佛木寺), and Temple 41, Ryūkō-ji (龍光寺), covers about 5km. Take a bus from Uwajima Station direct to Temple 42, Butsumoku-ji. After admiring the thatched bell-house and the statues of the *shichi-fukujin*, the seven gods of good fortune, follow the clearly marked *henro* trail back through picturesque farming villages and rice paddies to Temple 41, Ryūkō-ji. Here, a steep stone staircase leads up to a pleasant temple and shrine overlooking the fields. The temple is said to have been founded by Kōbō Daishi in 807 CE and dedicated to rice growing. From outside Ryūkō-ji there are signs to Muden Station (務田駅), a 15-minute walk away. From here, you can catch a train or bus back to Uwajima.

Unpen-ji to Daikō-ji

DURATION	DIFFICULTY	DISTANCE
2-3hrs	Moderate	9.5km

Many modern *henro* ride the aerial ropeway (雲辺寺ロープウェイ; shikoku-cable.co.jp) up from Kanonji to Temple 66, Unpen-ji (雲辺寺).

Unpen-ji, the highest of the 88 Temples at 900m, means 'Temple of the Surrounding Clouds', but on a clear day, views out over the Kagawa plains are phenomenal. There are 500 marvellous *rakan* (disciples of Buddha; pictured) statues here. It is said that everyone has a lookalike among the 500. See if you can find yours before following the *henro* trail down out of the mountains to the north. You've got 4.5km of walking track, some of it steepish, to drop out of the mountains, followed by 5km of flattish rural roads to get to Daikō-ji, Temple 67. The large camphor tree here is said to have been planted by Kōbō Daishi.

MITUMAL/GETTY IMAGES ©

Omogo-kei

DURATION	DIFF.	DISTANCE
2-3hrs	Easy	9km

The gorges at Omogo-kei (面河渓) are famous for their autumn colours, cliffs, waterfalls and bizarre rock formations.

There is a popular walking route along the banks of the Omogo-gawa (pictured), taking about two hours round trip. It will be much more enjoyable if you've got your own wheels, although there is a bus service. There's also a strenuous five-hour route from Omogo-kei to the summit of Ishizuchi-san. The route climbs from 700m at Omogo-kei to the south of the mountain, to 1525m at Omogo-yama (面河山), and up to 1982m at Ishizuchi-san's peak.

Kuishi-yama

DURATION	DIFF.	DISTANCE
3-4hrs	Easy-moderate	5km

In the mountains north of Kōchi city, climbing Kuishi-yama (工石山) is a relatively easy jaunt, good for families and popular with school groups.

There are a couple of tracks both starting at Kōchi City Kuishi-yama Seishonen-no-ie (高知市工石山青少年の家) on Rte 16, about 30km north of Kōchi city. You'll need your own wheels to get here. Signage is only in Japanese, but the trails are easy to follow and there are all sorts of interesting trees, birds and rock formations as you climb to great views from the peak at 1177m.

Miune-san

DURATION	DIFF.	DISTANCE
2 or 3 days	Moderate-hard	17km

Climb Tsurugi-san (1955m) and walk along the mountaintops to Miune-san (三嶺山; 1894m), before dropping into the Iya Valley on a multi-day walk.

After summiting Tsurugi-san (see p180), follow the ridge southwest to climb Jirōgyū (1929m) before continuing west to Miune-san. You can either descend to Iyashi-no-onsen-kyo to make a two-day walk, or continue along the tops to Tengutsuka (1812m) and descend north to Kubo from there as a three-day walk. There are unstaffed mountain huts to stay at along the way. Get the map and prepare well.

Kirishima mountains (p198)

Kyūshū

54 Hiko-san
Sacred walk once used by *yamabushi* (mountain monks) for training. **p190**

55 Yufu-dake
Beautiful views from this twin-peaked climb. **p192**

56 Kujū-san
The island's highest peak, often known as the 'Ceiling of Kyūshū'. **p194**

57 Aso-san
Hike within the massive caldera of one of Japan's most active volcanoes. **p196**

58 Karakuni-dake
A quick zip to the top of the Takachiho mountain range. **p198**

59 Kaimon-dake
Kyūshū's 'Fuji' and southernmost peak. **p200**

60 Miyanoura-dake
The tallest mountain in all of Kyūshū is on a remote island famous for giant trees. **p202**

Explore
Kyūshū

Kyūshū is often overlooked by tourists, which is a shame, for it holds some of the country's most spectacular walks and usually has far fewer crowds than many of the other walks this book offers. Bear-free, the island's trails are not jingling and jangling like department-store Santas doing Christmas collections. The food is fantastic, the people warm and friendly, and it's a region well worth devoting walking time to.

Fukuoka

Kyūshū's largest city, Fukuoka (福岡) is big enough to have it all without being a vast metropolis like Osaka or Tokyo. It has a great food scene (ramen is huge here!), plenty of business hotels (often convenient to the train stations) and free public wi-fi in many parts of the city. Purchase equipment and supplies here, as they may not be available once you get to other parts of the island.

Kagoshima

The southernmost city in the region, Kagoshima (鹿児島) is connected to Fukuoka by shinkansen (bullet train). The airport is inconveniently located about 40 minutes by car from the city, closer to the town of Kirishima. But it's linked with Kagoshima city by buses and a highway. There's no train station at the airport, but a train runs nearby in Aira town. A camping supply store is located near the city's central park.

Yufu

Yufuin, once its own town, is now a district within the larger city of Yufu (由布). Regardless of the name, it's a small spa town that's known for its hot springs, which draw hundreds, even thousands, of people per day. As such, you'll find walking streets and plenty of souvenir stands, but it's not a great spot for stocking up on hiking supplies. It's hard to find much to do in the evening – by 8pm nearly everything has closed. By 10pm it's a ghost town. If you prefer nightlife, you'll be better off in nearby Beppu, a hot-springs town about 40 minutes away, with big supermarkets, camping supply stores and things to do after darkness falls.

Yakushima

You'll likely arrive in Yakushima (屋久島) by ferry or by plane. Either way, you'll be well advised to rent a car, as the island is not well set up for walking and to do Miyanoura-dake (p202) in a day requires getting up well before the buses are running. When running, with few exceptions, the buses only travel around the circumference of the island, and they do not go the entire way. No service (other than by car) can circumnavigate the entire island. You'll want to do your major camping purchases in Kagoshima city, as here there are no camping chains.

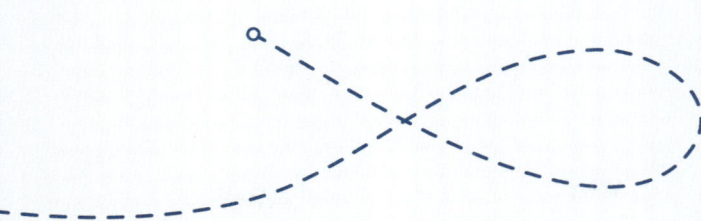

Resources

visit-kyushu.com/en
An English site with a variety of outdoor activities in Kyūshū.

kagoshima-yokanavi.jp/en
Kagoshima's tourist website, with lots of useful information and contacts.

gofukuoka.jp
Fukuoka city's official website for visitors.

yakushimatourism.com
Info on World Heritage–listed Yakushima.

kumamoto.guide/en
Guide to Kumamoto city and central parts of Kyūshū.

When to Go

Kyūshū is warmer than other parts of Japan and thus has a longer walking season, with little snow even in the coldest months. However, summers can be a beastly combination of heat, humidity and sun, so the ideal walking windows are spring and autumn. Autumn has the potential for typhoons, but the changing leaves are spectacular, making it a great time to come.

Where to Stay

This really depends on which walks you plan to do, but if you're heading to Kaimon-dake (p200), you'll want to stay in nearby Ibusuki town, which is famous for its unique *sunaburo* (sand bath) experience: you don a cotton robe and walk down to the beach, where a shallow, body-sized trench has been dug for you in volcanically heated sand. Lie down and let them shovel hot sand over you, where you'll sweat and steam for 10 minutes.

Transport

The island's major cities and towns are well connected by trains, planes and buses, but getting to trailheads is another story. If your budget allows, rent a car to give you the best flexibility and independence. In Yakushima you may find that a rental is far less expensive than taking taxis to and from the trailheads, as buses do not get near the trails in most cases, and if they do, it's not until long after daybreak.

What's On

Kagoshima Spring Matsuri Held in late April, this is a fill-the-streets with singing and dancing kind of affair, with people dressed in traditional garb and lots of participation. Come join in the fun.

Contest Sometimes just getting things off your chest – loudly – is therapeutic. In mid-October in Yufu, 100 people are drawn by lottery from the participants to shout out whatever they want to say. There's also a barbecue.

Full Moon Festival Nagasaki's streets are filled with lanterns, there are moon cakes aplenty, and celebration heightens as the September moon becomes full. Held yearly in the island's largest Chinatown, it's a cross-cultural event that draws thousands.

Aso Fire Festival This month-long festival in March celebrates the end of winter and upcoming growing season. On the second Saturday, Dai-himoji-yaki sees the lighting of a giant fire character (火) on the slopes of Ōjō-dake.

54

Hiko-san

DURATION	DIFFICULTY	DISTANCE	START/END
4hrs	Moderate	4km	Hiko-san Slope Car upper terminal

TERRAIN	Rocky, steep steps

Hiko-san (英彦山) is a beaut: a steep, rewarding walk that *yamabushi* (mountain monks) used for training. Expect your thighs to hurt after this one. The trail is mostly in thick forest, going from the upper terminal of the Hiko-san Slope Car (a funicular vehicle), past several shrines, to a deserted shrine at the summit. Coming down there are several options, but the 'moderate' rating above switches to 'hard' if you opt for the longer, far less frequented 'Devil Cypress' route.

Getting Here
Train service runs from Fukuoka to a Hiko-san station, from where you can take a bus to the Slope Car. Be very cautious about timing your return to meet the infrequent buses or you'll end up stuck.

Starting Point
Get off the bus or park at the Slope Car terminal and ride it to the top, where the trail begins. The Slope Car runs every 20 minutes, the first one heading up at 8.40am, the last one descending at 5.10pm. The cost is one-way/return ¥350/700.

01 You'll come out of the Slope Car next to the **Hiko-san Jingu** shrine complex.

02 From the shrine, head through the giant circle and follow the stairs: the trail only goes up, and for a good while it will be mainly **steps**, most of them stone that's been worn and rounded by millions of feet over the centuries.

03 Along the way, signs (some in English) describe the local history, much of it centred on the shrine and the monks who lived here. There are some **picnic tables** along the way

Kyūshū's Mountain Monks

The *yamabushi*, Buddhist monks who live and train in the mountains, have used Hiko-san for centuries. Only a few *yamabushi* routes in Kyūshū exist. These are noted for their difficulty, as the trail-hardened monks would challenge themselves and walk the routes daily the way joggers might go for a morning run. They also developed skills such as using wild edible and medicinal plants and martial arts. Formed as early as the 8th century, by the 13th century these groups exerted significant power and monks were found in high-ranking positions in the courts and offices.

Best for

KIDS

as well, making it easy to rest if you need a break.

04 This walk is never high enough to be alpine or to break entirely free of the treeline, but nearing the top you'll have some **stunning views** of the valley below, and many tall, old-growth trees poke out of the canopy.

05 After the beautiful shrine at the start, the **summit** (1199m) is almost disappointing: a seemingly abandoned building that's boarded up with a sign (in Japanese) that cautions you to watch for falling shingles. Yet you are allowed to open the shutters and even go inside (be sure to take off your shoes). It's a bit eerie, but where else in Japan will you have a shrine all to yourself?

06 Though staff at the Slope Car may tell you that going down via the 'Nature Trail' is nearly the same as returning the way you came, be aware: it's *not*. The Nature Trail (though beautiful, with the incredible Devil's Cypress) is very infrequently walked, and the trail gets extremely rough, requiring chains, cables and care to descend safely.

07 If you come down the way you came up, it's a quick downhill breeze to get back to the shrine and Slope Car terminal. Enjoy the shrine if you haven't already, and then head back to your car.

 Take a Break

Not far from the Slope Car's bottom station, **Cafe Cairn** (カフェ けるん) is an excellent spot for a break after coming down off the mountain. Relax with sandwiches, cake, ice cream or coffee, outside if it's warm or inside near the toasty fire if it's cold.

55

Yufu-dake

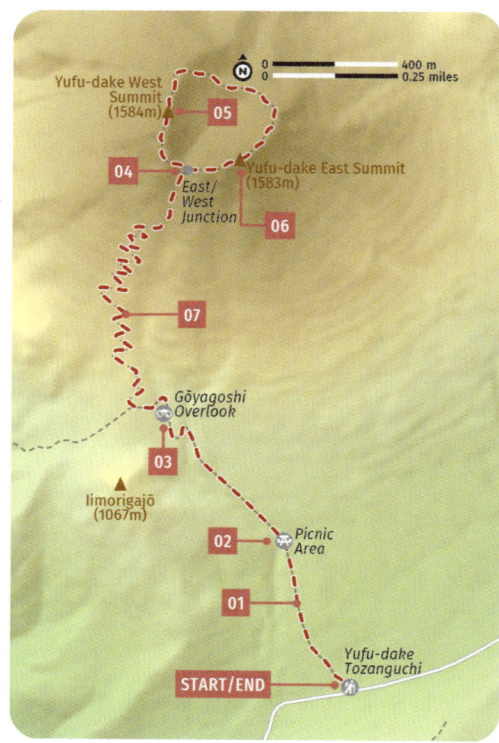

DURATION	DIFFICULTY	DISTANCE	START/END
4hrs	Moderate	6.5km	Yufu-dake Tozanguchi bus stop

TERRAIN	Dirt of rocky trail

Twin-peaked Yufu-dake (由布岳) is easily doable in a morning or afternoon and affords a great view of the surrounding Yufu valley. You'll pass a number of interesting terrains, from grassland at the start to thick forest (keep an eye out for deer, which frequent the areas near the trail), to *sasa* (low-growing bamboo) and scrub and eventually rocky mountaintop. It's short enough that it's a good option for families with kiddos, too, who may scamper like mountain goats up the trail.

Getting Here
Coming by bus from Yufuin is doable, though Yufuin-bound buses pass by the trailhead as well. The earliest buses arrive around 7am, and they depart as late as 5pm in the afternoon.

Starting Point
You'll begin and end this walk at the Yufu-dake Tozanguchi bus stop, where you'll find a decent-sized car park, restrooms and information. The trail starts across the street.

01 One of the prettiest parts of this walk is the first and final 20 minutes: you'll go gradually up a large field, as verdant green as pasture gets.

02 At the end of the field there's a small **picnic area**. On a good clear day you'll catch glimpses of nearby Iimorigajō (飯盛ヶ城), a near-perfect, if small, cinder cone.

Yufu's Shouting Contest

Say you've got something on your mind that you think the world needs to hear. Loudly. What better place to make it known than at the Yufuin Shouting Contest? It's been held annually in mid-October for more than 40 years. It's arguably Japan's most unusual festival. You don't need to have that much to say, but say it loudly enough and you may just win. Even if you don't, you can enjoy the barbecue and mix and mingle with other attendees. About 600 to 800 people attend each year, and from them, 100 are chosen by lottery to say what they have to say. Loudly.

03 At the forest you'll want to head left, going up through dense, moss-coated conifers (mainly Japanese cypress) and eventually reaching the **Gōyagoshi** (合野越) overlook, with lovely Iimorigajō now below you.

04 You'll zig and zag, and eventually you'll come to the Y intersection where you can go east (東) or west (西). Most choose west, as that's the highest peak. There's a steep scramble required on either (going west there's even a chain), but you're almost there.

05 After another 20 to 30 minutes of careful scrambling over rocky terrain, you'll reach the **west summit** (1583m). It's a beautiful spot, large enough to sit down and have a picnic. In season, the azaleas, bursting in bloom, will light up the entire mountain in giant splashes of pink.

06 The intrepid will continue around the lip of the crater, passing the **east summit** (1584m) before returning to the Y intersection. Pick your way carefully, as it's narrow and rocky, and it's easy to tumble.

07 Returning to the Y, you'll retrace your steps down the mountain to the car park.

 Take a Break

If you're looking for an onsen to soak in that's truly a unique, Japan-only experience, you'll want to head to **Shitan-yu** (下ん湯; ☏0977-84-3111; ¥200; ⏱10am-9pm). It's over 200 years old. Most notably, it's mixed-gender bathing (混浴) in simple pools of wondrously hot water. (The modest may want to opt for nearby **Nurukawa Onsen** (ぬるかわ温泉; hpdsp.jp/nurukawa), where there are rinsing areas and separated genders.)

56

Kujū-san

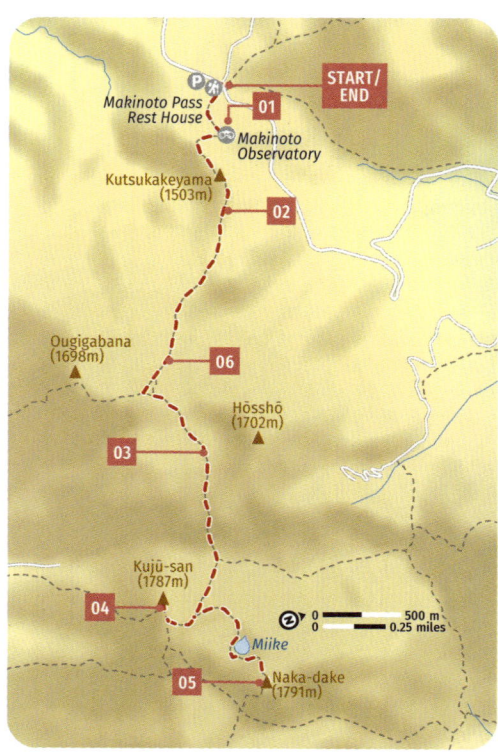

DURATION	DIFFICULTY	DISTANCE	START/END
4–5hrs	Moderate	9km	Makinoto Pass Rest House

TERRAIN	Dirt trail, rocky slopes, wooden steps

Known as the 'Ceiling of Kyūshū', the Kujū (九重) mountain range is the island's highest, not counting Miyanoura-dake, on Yakushima, thus technically not part of *this* island. It's a range of spectacular peaks and really begs to be walked with overnights rather than as a day trip. But the five-hour round trip from Makinoto Pass will delight, offering you some lovely looks at peaceful, rural Ōita and Kumamoto. (The range lies between the two prefectures.) It's often snow-covered from late autumn to spring.

Getting Here
A bus runs several times daily by this part of the Yamanami Hwy.

Starting Point
Start at Makinoto Pass Rest House (牧ノ戸峠レストハウス), where there's a toilet and plenty of parking.

01 The trail and logbook are to the left of the car park. It is paved initially and heads gradually up, leading (after 15 minutes) to the nice **Makinoto Observatory**, where even non-walkers can enjoy a bird's-eye view.

02 When you're done watching the horizon, head back up the trail. Less than an hour into the walk it's easy to see why they call this the 'Ceiling of Kyūshū': the sky stretches wide and azure above you, and the **rolling hills** fade into a blur of green. It's so pastoral you might almost be in England. For parts of the walk the trail can be quite difficult to find in fog or mist, and walkers routinely get lost. Use care and consider turning back if the visibility is poor.

Kujū in Kanji

You'll notice if you read kanji that there are several different ways to refer to what, in English, is written as Kujū. Homonyms, the words for the range and the peak differ, so you'll see it written as 久住山 (the latter character, 'san', means peak) when discussing the actual mountain. To add to the problem, there was a Kujū town (now renamed Taketa, as even locals were getting confused) located nearby and also spelled differently. When in doubt, you can always use the hiragana to be safe: くじゅう.

03 At the **wide meadow**, you are nearing the most popular peak, Kujū-san (久住山). Though slightly less high than its sister Naka-dake (中岳), to the east, Kujū-san is more frequently summited, as the highest peak requires an extra hour.

04 Summit **Kujū-san** (1787m) and then come back down, turning right on the trail towards Naka-dake. By now you may be getting whiffs of sulphur gas. At times this can be so strong that walkers are advised to wait for the wind to change. Before walking talk to park staff about current conditions.

05 **Naka-dake!** 1791m. The tallest spot in all of Kyūshū island. There's not a lot of room here, though, so chances are you'll descend soon after you take that selfie, but if visibility allows, get a shot of little Miike pond cupped among the azaleas before you go down.

06 Retrace your steps, taking care to not get lost, as some trails will take you across entirely different sections of the park rather than back to the Makinoto Pass car park.

Take a Break

With all that sulphur there's got to be an onsen around here somewhere, right? There is. And it's a good one. The pretty hot-spring town of **Kurokawa Onsen**, tucked in a valley at the bottom of the Kujū range, consistently ranks as one of Japan's top spots to bathe, and despite its popularity and the crowds it's retained a lot of the charm of a quaint onsen village. A popular activity is an *onsen meguri* (onsen tour) with a discounted pass that allows access to three day-use baths among the town's 24 ryokan.

57

Aso-san

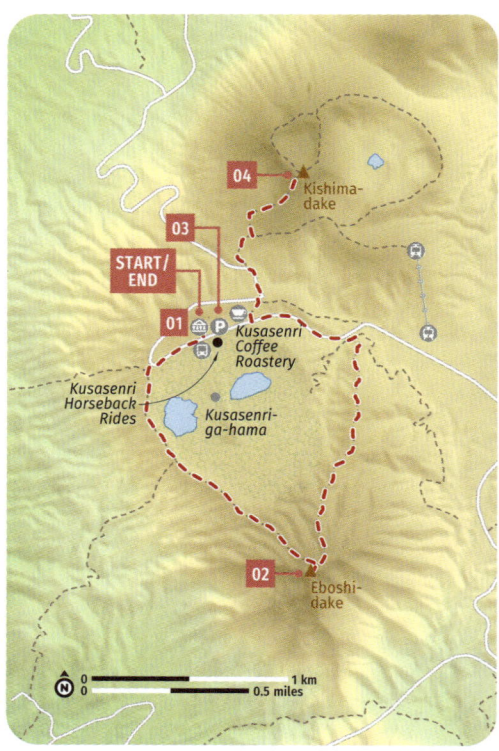

DURATION	DIFFICULTY	DISTANCE	START/END
3hrs return	Easy-moderate	6km	Aso Volcano Museum

TERRAIN	Variety of trail: stepped, paved, unpaved

Spectacular Aso-san (阿蘇山) is one of the world's largest calderas, with a circumference of 120km. The caldera was formed by four huge volcanic eruptions between 300,000 and 90,000 years ago, and the present-day Five Peaks of Aso (Aso Go-gaku) were formed by later minor eruptions. While Naka-dake is the most spectacular of the five, with seven craters, it's an active volcano and often off limits to visitors. The route we describe here climbs two more of the famous five peaks, Eboshi-dake and Kishima-dake.

Getting Here

Aso is best reached by rental car, but can be accessed by bus from JR Aso Station on the northern side.

Starting Point

Start at the Aso Volcano Museum bus stop, where you'll find a huge car park, the museum, shops, a cafe and a restaurant.

01 From in front of the **Aso Volcano Museum** (阿蘇火山博物館; 1135m), look almost directly south across the Kusasenri-ga-hama grasslands to Eboshi-dake, your first target peak for the day. Cross the main road and turn right (west) for 300m to the first corner, where you'll pick up the trail along the western side of the grasslands, which feature two large freshwater ponds and a variety of flowers and insects.

02 The easy-to-follow trail climbs gradually above the southern end of the grasslands, with wooden steps in places, up to the peak of **Eboshi-dake** (烏帽子岳; 1337m; pictured). If it's

Eruptions & Earthquakes

Aso-san is very active, with the most recent eruptions in 2016 and 2021. Check online (aso-volcano.jp/eng) for the latest conditions as to whether it's possible to visit Naka-dake, which is sometimes closed due to poisonous volcanic gases, bad weather or the risk of volcanic activity. Those with respiratory problems should refrain from approaching the crater altogether.

Mt Aso is in Kumamoto Prefecture, barely 40km east of Kumamoto city. In April 2016, a series of earthquakes, including a 7.0-magnitude main shock, killed 273 people and caused major damage to the city and surrounding region; in October, Naka-dake erupted for the first time in 36 years, volcanic smoke rising from the crater up to 11km into the sky.

spring, you're likely to see purple azaleas blooming along the way. The peak reveals excellent views back to the north of Kusasenri-ga-hama, the Aso Volcano Museum car park, and Kishima-dake (your second target peak for the day). Often-smoking Naka-dake is out to the east and if the wind is blowing from that direction, you may be engulfed with aromas from the active volcano.

03 Follow the descending trail down to the eastern side of the grasslands, which will eventually bring you back to the eastern (opposite) end of the large car park from where you started. Take a break with an ice cream or a coffee here. The relatively easy loop track you've completed should have taken around two hours.

04 If you're keen for more, it's a 60- to 90-minute return walk up **Kishima-dake** (杵島岳; 1326m), another of the Five Peaks of Aso and the peak you viewed from atop Eboshi-dake. The well-marked, paved trail heads out the eastern end of the car park, near where you arrived back from the first part of the walk. Allow 40 minutes to climb the paved, then stepped trail to the peak. You'll get opposite views from the first part of this hike, looking south across the Kusasenri-ga-hama grasslands to Eboshi-dake.

Take a Break

There's a lot going on at the start/end point of this hike. The fascinating **Aso Volcano Museum** (entry ¥1100) is also home to a visitors centre, a good cafe and some shops. For excellent coffee, at the far end of the large car park you'll find the **Kusasenri Coffee Roastery**, and in between are a couple of restaurant options. Across the road on the grassy plain is **Aso Kusasenri Horseback Rides**.

58

Karakuni-dake

DURATION	DIFFICULTY	DISTANCE	START/END
3hrs	Easy-Moderate	3km	Ebino Visitors Centre car park

TERRAIN	Rock and gravel trail, steep in places

The Kirishima mountain range spans the border between Kagoshima and Miyazaki Prefectures, a dramatic landscape of craters, forests, ponds and rocky crags. Takachiho is the iconic mountain visible for kilometres in all directions, but Karakuni-dake (韓国岳) is the area's highest peak.

The path starts out from the visitors centre at the **Ebino-kōgen Eco Museum Centre** (えびのエコミュージアムセンター; ebino-ecomuseum.go.jp; 9am-5pm) and enters a wooded forest, quickly going uphill. It's muddy in places, with lots of protruding roots and branches, and ropes border the trail on either side, preventing you from detouring into the forest (or getting lost).

By the **3rd station** you're back on the official trail, which is a well-trodden rocky path the rest of the way. There's low forest here that soon gives way to a wind-stunted scrub, much of it a species of azalea called **Miyama Kirishima**, unique to this region, that explodes in pink blooms each spring and is famous throughout Japan. Enjoy the lovely **views of Ebino-kōgen and Kirishima-Kinkō-wan National Park**. After the 6th station you'll be at the crater edge – pay close attention to the guard signs, and do not get too close. It's a sheer drop.

At the summit, pick your way carefully over the rocks to the marker. You're at 1700m, with an **eagle-eye view** in all directions. Far off in the distance you can see Sakurajima, perhaps with a cinder cloud rising above it. On a clear day, the perfectly circular caldera lake of Ōnami-ike is visible to the southwest. In winter, the daring will be rewarded with fantastical ice and snow 'sculptures' in the bushes and trees.

Best for

MOUNTAIN VIEWS

59

Kaimon-dake

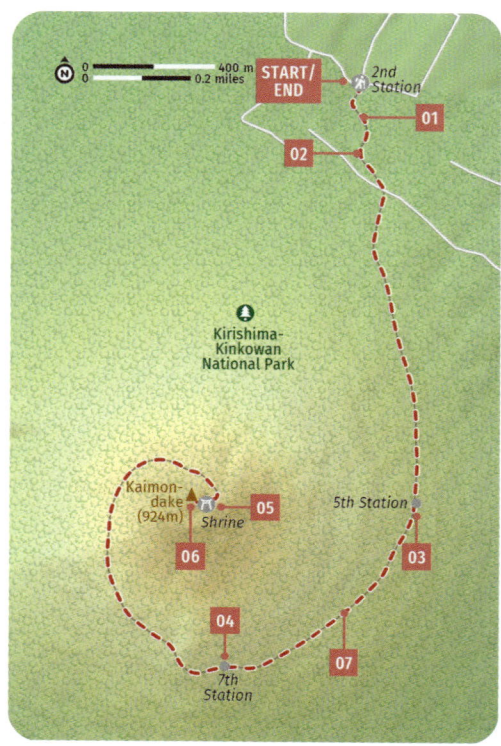

DURATION	DIFFICULTY	DISTANCE	START/END
4-5hrs	Moderate	7km	2nd station

TERRAIN	Gravel, rock, roots

Picture-perfect cinder cone Kaimon-dake (開聞岳) isn't super tall (just 924m), but it rises up like a Mt Fuji from the southernmost tip of the Satsuma Peninsula – indeed, this lovely mountain is known as the region's Fuji. It is a stellar climb, winding around the peak in a clockwise fashion all the way to the top, and passing lush green forest, small grottoes and cliffs along the way. Reaching the top gives you a spectacular view of the mouth of Kagoshima Bay, with the town of Ibusuki (famous for its sand baths) below.

Getting Here
Buses run to and from Ibusuki with enough time for the four to five hours needed to walk. The earliest departs around 8.10am and there's a return bus at 4.46pm. Trains on the JR Ibusuki Makurazaki line stop at JR Kaimon station at the foot of the mountain.

Starting Point
The best starting point is the 2nd station marker, which is up a paved road from the bus station.

01 The trail from the 2nd station follows a gully for 15 minutes before turning and going through a lovely forest – unfortunately, a forest that is often used for logging.

02 There's an almost prehistoric vibe here, with **giant ferns**, **moss-covered tree trunks** and **twisted roots** conspiring to make you feel like you've stepped back in time. Keep going; there are some sections with steps now, and you'll go even deeper into a forest unlike any you've yet seen.

Isshie the Ikeda Lake Monster

Move over Nessie, now there's something...leaner? Smaller? Cuter? Whatever. Isshie, the lake monster of Ikeda-ko, is likely a figment of someone in the tourism industry's fine imagination. Be that as it may, plenty of people come to take selfies with a remarkably Nessie-like cement creature that adorns the car park next to this impressive lake. Monster or no, the lake deserves a callout both for its size (the largest in Kyūshū) and for the size of its eels: up to 2m in length and as thick as a man's thigh.

Best for

OFF THE BEATEN PATH

03 By the **5th station**, you'll see the very southernmost tip of the Satsuma Peninsula, and beyond it, the water of Kagoshima Bay. If there's not haze, you'll even see the Ōsumi Peninsula and Cape Sata, the southernmost point in mainland Japan.

04 At the **7th station**, the forest is thinning a bit and the trail is quite rocky, with several sections requiring ladders and ropes or chains. The panorama now includes views of far-off Yakushima, Tanegashima and a number of smaller, lesser-known islands. Rescue Point 3, should there be an emergency, is also nearby.

05 As you near the top you'll come to a small **shrine**, an atmospheric *torii* (pictured) and small Jizō (guardian) statue. You're almost there.

06 The **summit** has the requisite marker post, but also a map carved in granite, showing the two peninsulas of Kagoshima and its islands. Due east you can see Ikeda-ko (Ikeda Lake), known for its giant eels and its own version of the Loch Ness monster.

07 Return to the 2nd station the same way you came, watching your step carefully.

 **Take a Break**

Ibusuki, where you'll likely spend the night (if you don't make this a day trip from Kagoshima city), is famous as a holiday spot, mainly for its unique kind of onsen: sand. Instead of dipping in hot water, you'll strip, don a rental cotton *yukata* (robe), and walk down to a bathhouse, where a row of shallow grave-like holes await. Bake there as long as you like and then, lightheaded and oh-so-nicely warm, stumble back to the bathhouse, where you can rinse off the sand and soak in water if you so desire before donning your clothes.

60

Miyanoura-dake

Best for

ISLAND ESCAPES

DURATION	DIFFICULTY	DISTANCE	START/END
10-12hrs	Hard	16km	Yodogawa trailhead

TERRAIN	Steep trail, rocks, gravel

There's no question that this is a bit more trail than most folks will want to call a 'walk', but Miyanoura-dake (宮之浦岳) is unquestionably one of Kyūshū's must-do hikes (let's call it that) and one of the most rewarding. It's on the island of Yakushima, a destination in itself (Japan's first UNESCO World Heritage Site), with fantastical giant cypress trees – unique to the island – and a host of animal sub-species that includes deer and monkeys. This is a long hard, hike from 1365m at the Yodogawa trailhead up to 1936m at the peak – and back. While that's only 570m of vertical gain, there's quite a bit of up and down over the one-way 8km distance.

Getting Here

Fly or take a ferry to Miyanoura Port, where you'll need to arrange for transportation to the trailhead. Most hikers either rent a vehicle or take a taxi to the Yodogawa trailhead.

Starting Point

There are several routes. This walk uses the Yodogawa trailhead (淀川登山口), which is located a long drive up a windy narrow road. Watch for monkeys, which frequent the roadside and are distractingly cute. Do not feed them (or any wildlife).

01 If you're driving, arrive early for a parking spot, as it often fills up as early as six in the morning. Signage here is mostly in Japanese but there's a map with English that explains how the region has a variety of different ecosystems, including the southernmost alpine marsh in Japan. Sign the guest log and start up the trail.

Ancient Cypress Trees

The island of Yakushima is famous for its giant *sugi* trees. Often mistranslated as 'cedars', the *Cryptomeria japonica* is a unique variety of cypress known for its long lifespan, but the tree known as Jōmon Sugi puts them all to shame. It is believed to be as old as 7200 years, and is named for the hunter-gatherer period in Japan's history in which it may have been a seedling.

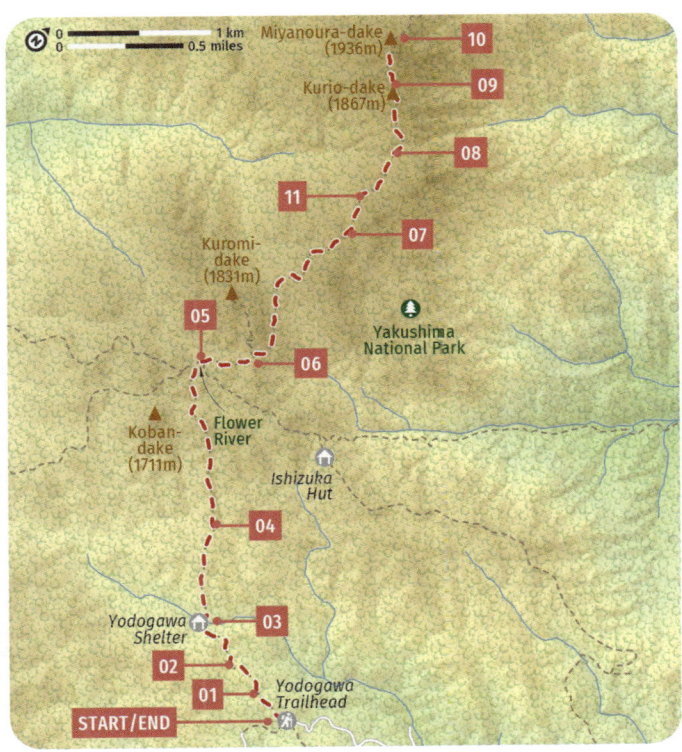

02 The trail is immediately a treat, with tall, moss-covered **cypresses**, a lovely fresh scent in the air and quiet stillness – thanks to the lack of bears, few walkers bring a bear bell (and those who do... shouldn't!). You will likely be walking part of this in the dark, which is contemplative and calming – it's just you, the forest and the other walkers. Depending on your luck, you may be sharing it with dozens or you may have the trail all to yourself.

03 After about 45 minutes you'll reach the **Yodogawa shelter**, a rest area and emergency hut. Some people opt to begin their walk the night before and camp here overnight, giving them an early start the following morning. Still others will walk up much of a day from the island's shore, camp here, and reach the summit on day two. There's a toilet – a real one (how luxurious!). But after this you'll need to pack out any waste, human or otherwise.

04 Day breaks, giving you your first **full vistas of the cypress forests** that were the reason this island was given UNESCO World Heritage status. It almost seems like a forest sprite will pop out from behind a rock and surprise you, as it might in a Ghibli cartoon. Already you'll feel you've gone up, ascending on steps and boarded walkways much of the way. You'll get **lovely views** of some of the smaller peaks as you go. Many are capped with wind- and rain-smoothed boulders, ringed with old-growth forest and a few protruding dead trees.

05 After about two hours of ascent you'll come to a section of alpine marsh known as the **Flower River** (花之江河), a lovely spot to stop for a snack. In season, this will be covered with a variety of wildflowers, but even in early spring or late autumn it's a beautiful place, with the water trickling around little copses and through the peat bogs. Keep an eye out for **deer**, which often come to the water's edge to drink.

06 Another 30 minutes will bring you to the turn-off for **Kuromi-dake** (黒味岳; 1831m), where you can detour, summit, call it a day and return. Alternatively, superhikers will want to check this peak out before continuing on to the real deal. You needn't feel bad if you opt for Kuromi-dake only, as it's only 100m less high than Miyanoura-dake. You'll also have some stretches that are steep, requiring you to use the anchored ropes and chains.

07 Continuing onward, you'll notice now that the trees get shorter and shorter, until they're so stunted they're hardly worth calling trees. Long gone are the famous giant cypresses; now you're looking at brush pines and other evergreen shrubs, if you're still seeing any trees at all. A type of mountain laurel blooms in great abundance here in the spring and early summer. Some walkers find it hard to follow the trail, so take care not to get lost.

08 At this point you'll want to be paying close attention to the weather. Yakushima is the rainiest part of Japan, so there's a good chance it will be wet. If it's raining, or looks like it, determine if there's a risk of lightning. Do not walk exposed during a lightning storm. Instead, seek shelter away from tall trees that themselves have a risk of being struck. Three to four hours in, you'll be able to spot Miyanoura-dake in the distance as you cross the **higher passes**.

JAPAN IMAGE/SHUTTERSTOCK ©

When It Rains It Pours

There's a good chance you'll be experiencing some 'weather' during your Miyanoura-dake walk, and if so, don't worry that you're just unlucky. In fact, the joke among locals is that it rains 35 days a month here. True or not, Yakushima experiences more rain per year than any other part of Japan, nearly 800mm per month in the peak rainy season. It's caused by warm ocean currents adding moisture to the air, which then gets trapped by the island's numerous high peaks. Nearby Tanegashima, a flat island, gets only half the rain of Yakushima. Some of this rain comes in the form of severe thunderstorms, so walkers be wary and be prepared to get wet and take shelter if you need it.

09 As you near the peak, you'll find that the vegetation is almost entirely a low-growing rush, a relative of bamboo. Its yellow and green leaves are very beautiful, and if the wind is strong you'll see it rippling along the hills in waves. **Large boulders**, dropped here by the volcano's eruption, look almost lunar.

10 The **summit** (1936m): if the weather is clear you'll see the entire island stretching out below you, water surrounding it on all sides. This is the Yakushima walker equivalent of winning the lottery, so don't be disappointed if you don't get a spectacular view: more than likely, it'll be cloudy or even raining as you reach the top.

11 Retrace your steps to return to the Yodogawa trailhead. Most walkers find it takes nearly as long to descend as to climb, about 10 or 11 hours in total.

Take a Break

You won't be able to get here without transport, but a dip at **Hirauchi Kaichū Onsen** (平内海中温泉; Hirauchi, Kumage) will be as memorable as the walk. A naturally heated pool right on the ocean's edge, this mixed-gender spot is not for the bashful. Several pools, ranging from tepid to decently warm, are only usable at certain times of day, depending on the tide. As the waves roll in you can let the chilly ocean water hit your face and shoulders even as the rest of you is bathwater warm. Keep an eye out for mudskippers, amphibious fish that 'walk' around on the rocks with modified fins.

Also Try...

KS BIOGEO/ISTOCK/GETTY IMAGES ©

Sobo-san

DURATION	DIFFICULTY	DISTANCE
6hrs	Moderate-hard	8km

One of the *Hyakumeizan*, Japan's 100 Famous Mountains, Sobo-san (pictured) is in the middle of Kyūshū, 20km almost directly east of the Aso caldera. The characters for Sobo-san (祖母山) mean 'grandmother mountain' and the peak is said to be named for Toyotama-hime, the grandmother of the first emperor of Japan, Jimmu.

Best walked as a loop track from the Kitadani trailhead, the ascent of Sobo-san involves a 650-vertical-metre climb to the 1756m summit via Fuketsu, then a relatively easy return via Sengen-daira. The climb from Fuketsu to the peak involves some steep rocky sections and the occasional ladder; families might find it easier to do a return hike via Sengen-daira. Along the way you'll get great views of the Kyūshū mountains, including Yufu-dake, the Kujū mountain range and the Five Peaks of Aso (Aso Go-gaku).

Kuro-dake

DURATION	DIFFICULTY	DISTANCE
6hrs	Moderate-hard	9km

Kuro-dake (黒岳) is to the northeast of Kujū-san. Its highest peaks are Takatsuka-san (高塚山; 1587m) and Tengu-iwa (天狗岩; 1550m). Because the volcanoes in the area have been dormant for a long time, there are large tracts of virgin beech forest, plus azaleas and rhododendrons. Accordingly, the area has been listed as one of Japan's 100 Famous Nature Spots.

The most popular route starts at and returns to Otoko-ike (男池) – a famous freshwater spring – directly north of Kuro-dake. Access is difficult without your own transport or a willingness to use your thumb. This also, of course, means fewer people go there, a bonus if you are after your own space.

BEEBOYS/SHUTTERSTOCK ©

Unzen

DURATION	DIFF.	DISTANCE
3hrs	Easy-moderate	3km

At the top of the Shimabara Peninsula, in Nagasaki Prefecture, lies Unzen (雲仙; pictured), one of Japan's first national parks and famous for its onsen baths, its beauty and its volcanic activity.

A loop walk, part of which can be done by ropeway, takes you around the beautiful peaks, quite close to where the mountain erupted in 1991, killing dozens of people, including several volcanologists.

Takachiho-dake

DURATION	DIFF.	DISTANCE
3-4hrs	Moderate	5.5km

Takachiho-dake (高千穂岳) is not the Kirishima region's highest peak, but it is the most iconic – a massive, unbroken molar visible in all directions that presides over the Ebino-kōgen (えびの高原), a highland plateau shared by Kagoshima and Miyazaki Prefectures.

At the summit a sword marks the fabled spot where the ancestors of Japan's emperor stepped down from the sky.

Raizan

DURATION	DIFF.	DISTANCE
3hrs	Moderate	6km

Not far from Fukuoka, Raizan (雷山) is an excellent afternoon walk that's got lovely bamboo groves, rivers, waterfalls and incredible moss, and which ascends dramatically to a rock-topped peak.

If you're lucky you'll see a variety of wildlife, such as deer, *tanuki* (raccoon dogs), land crabs or even *mamushi* (vipers). The hardy will continue on to Ibarayama (井原山), a nearby and slightly higher peak.

TOOLKIT

The chapters in this section cover the most important topics you'll need to know about in Japan. They're full of nuts-and-bolts information and valuable insights to help you understand and navigate Japan and get the most out of your trip.

Arriving
p210

Getting Around
p211

Accommodation
p212

Hiking
p213

Health & Safe Travel
p214

Responsible Travel
p215

Nuts & Bolts
p216

Subashiri Trail (p44)
DOWRAIK/SHUTTERSTOCK ©

# Arriving

Virtually all international visitors arrive in Japan by air, most flying into Tokyo's Haneda or Narita airports, or into Osaka's Kansai International Airport (KIX). A number of other cities also receive international flights. All airports have efficient ways to get into their respective cities, usually by train or bus.

Travelling with Hiking Gear

Everything you could possibly need for any of the hikes in this book is available in Japan. If you're on the bigger side, especially when it comes to shoe size, consider taking your own hiking shoes. Outdoor-goods stores are everywhere in Japan and there are lots of high-quality local brands and makers. You may even consider buying hiking gear in Japan and taking it home as a souvenir of your visit. Walking poles are popular, and if rain is forecasted, you may be surprised that many Japanese take an umbrella when they go hiking.

Baggage-forwarding services (called *takkyūbin*) are popular, and many domestic tourists use them to send bags to where they're going or back home when they're done. This system is very useful for international visitors too, though in most cases, your bags won't get to where you send them until the following day.

	Narita Airport	Haneda Airport	Kansai Airport
TRAIN	60 mins ¥3000	30 mins ¥670	45 mins ¥3000
BUS	80 mins ¥3000	40 mins ¥1000	60 mins ¥1600
TAXI	60 mins ¥30,000	30 mins ¥5000	50 mins ¥15,000

IMMIGRATION
Entering and exiting Japan is usually hassle-free. Temporary visitor visas, normally for 90 days, are given on arrival for many nationalities. Foreigners are photographed and fingerprinted on arrival.

WI-FI & SIM CARDS
Free wi-fi is usually available at airports, train stations, accommodation and at hotspots across Japan. Alternatively, pick up a SIM card or a pocket wi-fi device on arrival at all major airports.

CASH OR CARD?
Most places will accept international credit cards such as Visa or Mastercard; there has been an increase in mobile payment options like Apple Pay. If you're heading to remote areas, take some cash.

TOURIST INFORMATION
All airports, major train stations, big cities and many smaller towns will have a tourist information office, most with an English-speaker on hand, plus free wi-fi. Staff tend to be extremely helpful.

Getting Around

Japan is renowned worldwide for its remarkably efficient transport network, from bullet trains to buses and ferries. If it's on the map, you'll be able to get there.

TRAVEL COSTS

Car rental
From ¥7000/day

Petrol
Approx ¥175/litre

Tokyo–Kamikōchi bus
from ¥8200

Tokyo–Hokkaidō flight
from ¥10,000

Air
With a number of budget airlines, such as Peach, Jetstar, Skymark and AIRDO, it's often faster and cheaper to fly than to take a train, especially if travelling from Tokyo or Osaka to places like Hokkaidō, Shikoku or Kyūshū.

Train
Japan's rail network is legendary for its efficiency; shinkansen (bullet trains) run on major routes, while regular trains fan out through the countryside. Japan Rail (JR) passes are available for seven, 14 or 21 days, plus regional passes are available.

Bus
Long-distance and overnight buses are a cheap option. Bus is often a good way to get from train stations to trailheads and back; popular hikes will usually have a bus option. Overnight buses run from Tokyo and Osaka to various North Alps hikes.

Rental Vehicle
It's much easier to drive around Japan these days, thanks to multi-language car navigation systems. Driving is the best way to get to trailheads in remote areas such as in Hokkaidō; trailheads usually have a parking area nearby. Japanese drivers are courteous.

LIKE CLOCKWORK!

Japan's transport network is incredibly efficient, be that in cities, regional areas or even at remote mountain trailheads. Bus and train drivers will depart dead on time if they can, so make sure you are where you need to be to meet schedules. The wildcard, however, is the weather. The typhoon season from June to October coincides perfectly with the season for high mountain hiking; if a typhoon is in the forecast, most Japanese will cancel their hiking plans.

DRIVING INFO

Drive on the left.

60
Speed limit is 60km/h on ordinary roads.

.03
Blood alcohol limit is .03%.

LEFT: SAKARIN SAWASDINAKA/SHUTTERSTOCK ©,
RIGHT: RBAGUSDIANI/SHUTTERSTOCK ©

Accommodation

HOW MUCH FOR A...

Regional business hotel room ¥8000

Stay at a *shukubō* ¥12,000/person

Tent site in Kamikōchi ¥1300/person

Camping

On a budget and keen to mix with locals? Camping is a great option, especially in the July to September 'camping season' when many mountain, coastal and hiking areas have open campgrounds. There are campgrounds along renowned multiday hikes, but you'll have a lot of gear to carry. Kamikōchi (p54) in the North Alps is a particularly good spot.

Ryokan

These Japanese inns are the kind of place you imagined yourself staying at before making the trip to Japan. You'll be sleeping on a futon mattress on tatami matting, with Japanese-style meals. Ryokan range from gorgeous and pricey *onsen ryokan* in resort towns, serving *kaiseki* (traditional haute cuisine) meals, to small, simple, relatively inexpensive places not serving meals.

Minshuku

Simpler than ryokan, *minshuku* are smaller family-run places, though you'll still be sleeping on a futon on tatami, usually with shared toilet and bathroom facilities. With a pre-booking, *minshuku* usually provide dinner and breakfast – or stay *sudomari* (room only). Often found in country areas, they may be introduced by the local tourist office; you're unlikely to find them on search engines.

Shukubō

Lodgings at Buddhist temples were historically on offer to pilgrims and official visitors, but these days, many temples are happy to accept casual travellers. While there's a wide variety of *shukubō*, most provide two meals of *shōjin-ryōri* (Buddhist vegetarian cuisine), a futon, plus the opportunity to attend evening and morning prayer sessions. Kōya-san (p90) is a great place to stay at a *shukubō*.

BUSINESS HOTELS

Originally built to house businessmen staying away from home, business hotels are economical and functional, with beds in compact rooms with private bathrooms. There are huge chains that have hotels all over Japan, usually near train stations, major road intersections or expressway on/off ramps. Most have parking, serve breakfast and some have onsen as their point of difference.

MOUNTAIN HUTS

In for a real Japanese mountain experience? Overnight at a *yamagoya* with locals, many of whom will be planning to summit the nearest peak for sunrise. Most huts offer dinner, bed and breakfast for around ¥10,000 to ¥12,000. You'll be in a shared room with futon supplied. Meals will be simple, both served early (think 6pm and 5am). The hut may feel like a packed sardine can during busy holiday periods. If you're lucky, there may even be a bath or onsen. Try Mikuri-ga-ike Onsen at Tateyama (p51) or Tsurugi-san Chōjō Hutte (p181).

Hiking

Hiking in Japan

Throughout history, the mountains were considered the realms of the gods, ascetics, mystics and hermits – no place for the common person trying to eke out a living and survive, such as farmers or fishers. It took an Englishman, Walter Weston, to spark interest in alpinism and the mountains as places of recreation in the late 1800s. New magazines and books were soon published, creating a flow of information out to the public on hiking in Japan. Post-WWII, the government promoted outdoor activities and with increasing private car ownership, the mountains became more accessible for camping and walking. In 1964, Kyūya Fukada's book *Hyakumeizan (100 Famous Mountains of Japan)* became widely known; then in the 1980s and '90s, Japan went through an 'outdoor boom', which continues to this day. An ageing population of retirees, with time on their hands, helps account for a land of increasing numbers of outdoor enthusiasts.

Trail Etiquette

As you'd expect, Japanese hikers tend to be courteous and enthusiastic. In general, downhill walkers give way to those heading uphill, there is very little rubbish on the trails, and local hikers almost religiously take responsibility for their own rubbish. An important aspect of Japanese society is not to create hassles for others or make other people worry – if, at a remote trailhead, you are required to post your intentions, such as at Hakusan (p70), make sure you do so; arrive reasonably early at mountain huts if overnighting (by 4pm at the latest), and leave early the next morning. You'll be expected to be gone by 5am at some huts in the Japan Alps!

Yama-to-Keikoku
Yamakei; hikesinjapan.yamakei-online.com
Japan's best-known hikers' resource, with an excellent English website.

Japan Meteorological Agency
jma.go.jp
Info on weather and natural disaster risk reduction.

Mapple Hiking Maps
mapple.co.jp
Produces detailed Yama-to-Kōgen Chizu hiking maps for popular hiking areas around Japan.

Health & Safe Travel

Drinking Water

Tap water is generally safe to drink throughout Japan. Bottled water is available everywhere, in vending machines and convenience stores, but is expensive in places such as remote mountain huts, especially if it has been helicoptered in. Don't drink untreated water in the mountains unless that spot is specifically marked as a *mizu-ba* (水場) on the map – a known source of safe water.

Lightning

Mountain weather is very changeable. One reason that hikers in the high mountains both start and finish their day early in summer is that humidity builds during the day, meaning that thunderstorms and lightning are common in the afternoons. Don't get stuck on a summit or high ridge during a lightning storm and keep away from exposed metal such as walking poles.

IN CASE OF EMERGENCY

Police
110

Ambulance & Fire
119

Disaster Safety Confirmation
171

INSURANCE

Make sure to have some form of travel insurance when visiting Japan. Japanese medical providers will require payment on the spot, with you getting recompensed later by your insurance company. If you are planning on climbing the high peaks or going on extended hikes, consider getting some 'hiking and adventure sports' insurance, such as with Yamakifu (yamakifu.or.jp).

Natural Disasters

Japan is a land of erupting volcanoes, typhoons, earthquakes and tsunami – any of which might mess up your travel and hiking plans. Nobody will forget footage of the tsunami that followed the 9.0-magnitude Great East Japan Earthquake of 2011. When Ontake-san erupted in 2014, 63 hikers perished. If a typhoon is in the forecast, no one will be out there.

WILDLIFE

Japan is hardly a high-danger region when it comes to wildlife. Bears are out there, though, and many Japanese hikers wear *kuma-yoke* (bear bells) to alert bears to their presence. There are a couple of species of poisonous snakes, and you don't want to be stung by a *suzume-bachi* (murder hornet). There are usually warning signs if they are present.

LEFT: JUBIPULSE34/SHUTTERSTOCK ©,
RIGHT: SUMMIT ART CREATIONS/SHUTTERSTOCK ©

Responsible Travel

Climate Change & Travel

It's impossible to ignore the impact we have when travelling, and the importance of making changes where we can. Lonely Planet urges all travellers to engage with their travel carbon footprint. There are many carbon calculators online that allow travellers to estimate the carbon emissions generated by their journey; try resurgence.org/resources/carbon-calculator.html. Many airlines and booking sites offer travellers the option of offsetting the impact of greenhouse gas emissions by contributing to climate-friendly initiatives around the world. We continue to offset the carbon footprint of all Lonely Planet staff travel, while recognising this is a mitigation more than a solution.

Japan National Tourism Organisation
japan.travel
Planning info, including sustainable travel.

Government of Japan
japan.go.jp
Everything about Japan, including sustainability topics.

Kamikatsu
why-kamikatsu.jp/en
Zero-waste town.

SUPPORT LOCAL
Japan is known for its unique culture, arts and crafts, and different parts of Japan have their own versions. Show your support by shopping, eating and drinking local to make the most of your visit.

RESPECT THE CULTURE
Study up on dos and don'ts before going to Japan. Take off your shoes when appropriate, queue in neat lines, speak quietly and respectfully, and learn some easy phrases in Japanese.

REDUCE WASTAGE
Japan goes through an incredible number of *waribashi* (disposable chopsticks), plastic bottles and plastic shopping bags. Carry around reusable chopsticks, have your own refillable water bottle and use your own bag when shopping.

Nuts & Bolts

GOOD TO KNOW

Time Zone
GMT/UTC + nine hours

Country Code
81

Population
125 million

CURRENCY: YEN ¥ (PRONOUNCED 'EN')

Best Ways to Pay

Credit cards are accepted almost everywhere, but if you're going out on remote mountain hikes, make sure to have cash with you. Some mountain huts will require cash for an overnight stay. Be prepared: get cash from an ATM before you leave the last sizeable town. Credit cards are accepted almost everywhere, but if you're going out on remote mountain hikes, make sure to have cash with you. Some mountain huts will require cash for an overnight stay. Be prepared: get cash from an ATM before you leave the last sizeable town.

ELECTRICITY 100V TOKYO & THE EAST 50HZ, OSAKA & THE WEST 60HZ

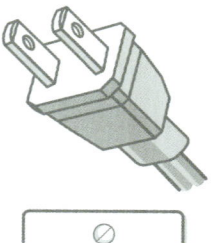

Handing Over Cash

Most hotels, restaurants, shops and even taxis will provide a small tray for you to put money on, instead of giving it directly to the cashier. Some places will require you to put cash directly into a money-handling machine rather than to a person.

Tipping Etiquette

Tipping is not a part of Japanese culture and you may cause confusion if you try to tip.

Smoking

Smoking in restaurants, hotels and offices is prohibited. Smoking on the streets and in public places, except in designated areas, is also banned.

Weights & Measures

Japan uses the metric system. Speed limits are in kilometres per hour; if you're used to miles per hour, work things out before hitting the road in your rental car.

Toilets

Increasingly, toilets are sit-down style with fancy features. In remote areas, such as on hikes, expect squat toilets; the correct position is facing the hood.

HOW MUCH FOR A...

Rice ball (onigiri)
¥180

Coffee
¥450

Draught beer
¥600

Bowl of ramen
¥1000

By Difficulty

EASY

Akiyoshidai 115
Akiyoshidō 112
Bijodaira 73
Goshogake Nature Trail 139
Fushimi Inari 78
Hachimantai Nature Trail 138
Kamikōchi 54
Minō Falls 97
Ōdai-ga-hara 97
Omogo-kei 185
Shiretoko-Go-Ko Loop 167
Tōno 136
Tsugaike Nature Park 73
Tsuta-numa 130
Uwajima Temples 184
Yama-no-be-no-michi 88
Yoshino-yama 96

EASY–MODERATE

Akita Koma-ga-take 126
Aso-san 196
Hakuba Happō-ike 52
Iino-yama 178
Karakuni-dake 198
Kasuga-yama 86
Kogorōyama Loop 115
Kōya-san 90
Kuishi-yama 185
Kumano Kodō 92
Kurama to Kibune 82
Kuro-dake 152
Miyajima 108
Momoiwa
Observatory Course 164
Nakasendō 66
Oku-Nikkō Marsh 36

Old Hakone Hwy 42
Panorama-dai 34
Sandan-kyō 106
Shin Sen Numa
& Chisenupuri 144
Takao-san 24
Tanesashi Kaigan 134
Tsurugi-san 180
Unzen 207

MODERATE

Atago-san 96
Daimonji-yama 80
Hakkōda-san 128
Hibayama 115
Hiko-san 190
Ishizuchi-san 176
Iwaki-san 139
Kaimon-dake 200
Kanka-kei 182
Kiso-koma-ga-take 64
Kōgen-numa Meguri Hike 167
Kōyō-dai 45
Kujū-san 194
Mashū-dake 158
Maya-san 97
Meakan-dake 156
Mitsu-tōge-yama 32
Norikura-dake 60
Nyūtō-san 139
Oirase Keiryū 132
Oku-Takao 45
Ontake-san 62
Ōtake-san 26
Oze National Park 38
Raizan 207
Rokku Gaaden 84
Sanbe-san 110

Takachiho-dake 207
Tateyama 50
Unpen-ji to Daikō-ji 184
Yufu-dake 192
Zaō-san 120

MODERATE–HARD

Asahi-dake 148
Daisen 102
Dewa Sanzan 122
Chōkai-san 138
Kuro-dake 206
Miune-san 185
Nantai-san 44
Nishiho-Doppyō 58
Rebun Traverse 166
Sobo-san 206
Shibutsu-san 45
Tokachi-dake 154

HARD

88 Sacred
Temples Pilgrimage 172
Hakusan 70
Hyōnosen 114
Jōnen-dake 73
Mitoku-san 114
Miyanoura-dake 202
Mt Fuji Subashiri Trail 44
Mt Fuji Yoshida Trail 28
Myōkō-san 72
Rausu-dake 160
Rishiri-zan 162
Senjō-ga-take 68
Shiretoko Traverse 166
Yatsu-ga-take 73
Yōtei-zan 167

Index

88 Sacred Temples Pilgrimage 172-5, **173**

A

accommodation 14, 212
  business hotels 212
  Chōzō-goya 41
  Fujisan Hotel 31
  Hakusan Murodō 71
  Kamikōchi Imperial Hotel 57
  Komadori Sansō 27
  Midagahara Sanrōjo 124
  minshuku 212
  mountain huts 212
  Onsen-goya 40
  onsen ryokan 59, 129
  ryokan 212
  Ryounkaku Inn 155
  Sandan-kyō Hotel 107
  shukubō 91, 212
  Sukayu Onsen Ryokan 129
  Tsuru-no-yu Onsen 127
  Yarimikan 59
activities 14-15
Ainu culture 142, 143, 157
Ainu Mosir 143
air travel 210
Akanko Onsen 142
Akita Koma-ga-take 126-7, **126**
Akiyoshidai 115
Akiyoshidō 112, **112**

Trails 000
Map Pages 000

animals, *see* bears, birds, deer, foxes, snakes
Aomori 118
Asahi-dake 148-51, **149**
Aso Volcano Museum 196, 197
Aso-san 196-7, **196**
Atago-san 96
autumn leaves 130, 152

B

bathrooms 216
bears 149, 161
beer 25, 143, 151
Bijodaira 73
birds 37, 73, 130, 145
books 17
Buddhism 76, 91, 93, 104-5, 175, 191
Buddhist temples, *see* temples & shrines
bus travel 211
business hotels 212

C

cable cars & ropeways
  Hakuba 52
  Kanka-kei Ropeway 182
  Komagatake Ropeway 64
  Mitake Tozan 26
  Miyajima 109
  Ontake Ropeway 62
  Shin-Hotaka Ropeway 58
  Sōunkyō Onsen Ropeway 152
  Zaō Ropeway 120
Cafe Cairn 191

camping 212
car travel 211
cash 210, 216
caves 112
Central Honshū, *see* Japan Alps & Central Honshū
cherry blossoms 14
  Shikoku 171
  Yoshino-yama 96
children, travel with 73, 84-5, 130, 178, 190-1, 192-3
Chōkai-san 138
city breaks 6
climate 14-15, *see also individual regions*
climate change 215
clothing 16
costs 211, 212, 216
credit cards 210, 216
currency 216
cypress trees 202-3

D

Daibutsu 87
Daimonji-yama 80-1, **80**
Daisen 102-5, **103**
Daisetsuzan National Park 149, 150, 152, 154
dangers 214
deer 87, 108-9, 204
Dewa Sanzan 122-5, **123**
drinking venues, *see* food & drink
drinks, *see* beer, whisky
driving 211

E

earthquakes 197, 214
Eboshi-dake 196
electricity 216
emergency numbers 216
environment 214
events, *see* festivals & events

F

family travel 73, 84-5, 130, 178, 190-1, 192-3
festivals & events 15, *see also individual locations*
films 16
flora 145
food & drink
   Amazake-chaya 43
   Baccano 109
   Bakery & Table 43
   Beer Mount 25
   Bononsha 91
   Café 2612 65
   Café わわ 89
   Cafe Cairn 191
   Cafe Shibutsu 39
   Chōzō-goya Baiten 41
   Genpei 159
   Gyōshintei 37
   Hatomachi-tōge Rest House 38
   Ishikedo Rest House 132
   Ishizuchi-san Summit Hut 177
   Miroku Yokochō 135
   Mizuya-chaya 87
   Momiji-ya 27
   Ni-no-saka-chaya 123
   Nishi-Hotaka-guchi station 58
   Nishimura-tei 79
   Ōdaira-sansō 69
   Oto-chaya 121
   Otokoyama 151
   Saikan 125
   Sanbe Burger 111
   Seasons 40
   Sukumo 43
   Tenka-chaya 33
   Tokusawa-en 57
   Tōno Kaze no Oka 137
   Tsurugi-san Chōjō Hutte 181
foxes 79, 155
Fuji Five Lakes 22, 23, 32, 34, 45
Fukuoka 188
Fushimi Inari 78-9, **78**

G

galleries, *see* museums & galleries
gear rental 213
gorges
   Kanka-kei 182
   Ōdai-ga-hara 97
   Omogo-kei 185
   Sandan-kyō 106-7
Goshogake Nature Trail 139

H

Hachimantai Nature Trail 138
Hachinohe 118
Hakkōda-san 128-9, **128**
Hakone 22
Hakuba Happō-ike 52-3, **52**
Hakusan 70-1, **70**
Hatajuku 43
health 214
Hibayama 115
highlights 6-13
Hiko-san 190-1, **190**
Hiroshima 100
Hiroshima & Western Honshū 99-115
   accommodation 101
   climate 101-2
   festivals & events 101
   resources 101
   transport 101
   travel seasons 101-2
history of hiking 213
Hokkaidō 141-67
   accommodation 143
   climate 143
   festivals & events 143
   resources 143
   transport 143
   travel seasons 143
Honshū, *see* Japan Alps & Central Honshū, Hiroshima & Western Honshū
Hyakumeizan 10, 206, 213
Hyōnosen 114

I

Ibusuki 200-1
Iino-yama 178, **178**
Ikeda-ko 201
immigration 210
insurance 214
internet access 210
internet resources, *see* resources
Ishizuchi-san 176-7, **176**
islands 13
   Hokkaidō 141-67
   Honshū 47-73, 99-115
   Kyūshū 187-207
   Miyajima 108-9
   Miyanoura-dake 202
   Rebun-tō 164, 166
   Rishiri-tō 162-3
   Shikoku 169-85
   Shōdo-shima 182
   Yakushima 202-5
Iwaki-san 139

J

Japan Alps & Central Honshū 47-73
   accommodation 49
   climate 48-9
   festivals & events 49
   resources 49
   transport 49
   travel seasons 48-9
Japanese language 17
Jōnen-dake 73

K

Kagoshima 188
Kaimon-dake 200-1, **200**
Kamikōchi 54-7, **55**
Kanka-kei 182, **182**
Kansai 75-97
  accommodation 77
  climate 77
  festivals & events 77
  resources 77
  transport 77
  travel seasons 77
Karakuni-dake 198, **198**
Kasuga-yama 86-7, **86**
Kawaguchi-ko 22
Kibune 82
Kishima-dake 197
Kiso-koma-ga-take 64-5, **64**
Kōbe 76
Kōbō Daishi 90, 175
Kōchi 170-1
kofun 89
Kōgen-numa Meguri Hike 167
Kogorōyama Loop 115
Kōya-san 90-1, **90**
Kōyō-dai 45
Kuishi-yama 185
Kujū-san 194-5, **194**
Kumano Kodō 92-5, **93**
Kurama to Kibune 82, **82**
Kuro-dake (Hokkaidō) 152, **152**
Kuro-dake (Kyūshū) 206
Kyoto 76
Kyūshū 187-207
  accommodation 189
  climate 189
  festivals & events 189
  resources 189
  transport 189
  travel seasons 189

Trails 000
Map Pages 000

L

lakes
  Amida-ike 127
  Fuji Five Lakes 22, 23, 32, 34, 45
  Happō-ike 52-3
  Kagami-ike 151
  Lake Naganuma 145
  Lake Onnettō 157
  Mashū-ko 158
  Okama 121
  Shiretoko-Go-Ko 167
  Shōji-ko 34
  Towada-ko 132
  Tsuta-numa 130
  Ukinunoike 110
  Yu-no-ko 37
language 17

M

Magome-juku 66
maps 213
marshes & wetlands
  Dake-sawa-shitsugen 56
  Kenashi-tai 129
  Mida-ga-hara 124
  Nushiri 40
  Oku-Nikkō Marsh 36-7, **36**
  Oze-ga-hara 39
  Senjō-ga-hara 37
  Shin Sen Numa 144-7
  Tsugaike Nature Park 73
Mashū-dake 158-9, **158**
Matsumoto 48
Matsuyama 170
Maya-san 97
Meakan-dake 156-7, **156**
measures 216
Michinoku Coastal Trail 135
Minō Falls 97
minshuku 212
Misasa Onsen 100
Mitake-san 26
Mitoku-san 114

Mitsu-tōge-yama 32-3, **32**
Miune-san 185
Miyajima 108, **108**
Miyama Kirishima 198
Miyanoura-dake 202-5, **203**
Mizunomi-ōji 93
money 210, 216
Momoiwa Observatory Course 164, **164**
mountain huts 212
mountain views 10
mountains
  Akita Koma-ga-take 126-7
  Atago-san 96
  Chōkai-san 138
  Daimonji-yama 80-1
  Daisen 102-5
  Hakusan 70-1
  Hibayama 115
  Hiko-san 190-1
  Hyōnosen 114
  Iino-yama 178
  Ishizuchi-san 176-7
  Kaiun-san 33
  Kasuga-yama 86-7
  Kiso-koma-ga-take 64-5
  Kuishi-yama 185
  Kujū-san 194-5
  Kuro-dake 152
  Maya-san 97
  Mitoku-san 114
  Mitsu-tōge-yama 32-3
  Miune-san 185
  Miyanoura-dake 202-5
  Mt Aso 197
  Mt Fuji 28-31, 44
  Myōkō-san 72
  Nabewari-yama 27
  Nantai-san 44
  Nishiho-Doppyō 58-9
  Nyūtō-san 139
  Oku-hotaka-dake 55
  Ontake-san 62-3
  Ōtake-san 26-7

Raizan 207
Rausu-dake 160-1
Rishiri-zan 162-3
Sanbe-san 110-11
Senjō-ga-take 68-9
Shibutsu-san 39, 45
Takachiho-dake 207
Takao-san 24-5
Tateyama 50-1
Tsurugi-san 180-1
Yatsu-ga-take 72
Yoshino-yama 96
Yōtei-zan 167
Yufu-dake 192-3
Zaō-san 120-1
Mt Fuji 28-31, 44, *see also* Tokyo, Mt Fuji & Around
Mt Fuji Subashiri Trail 44
Mt Fuji Yoshida Trail 28-31, **29**
museums & galleries
   Daisen Museum of Nature and History 105
   Ebino-kōgen Eco Museum Centre 198
   Ideha Cultural Museum 125
   Sanbe Azukihara Buried Forest Museum 111
   Takao 599 Museum 24
music 17
Myōkō-san 72

N

Nagoro 181
Nakasendō 66, **66**
Nantai-san 44
Nara 76
national parks 9
   Daisen-Oki 102-5
   Daisetsuzan 149, 150, 152, 154
   Nikkō 22, 44
   Oze 38-41, 45
   Shiretoko 160, 167
   Unzen 207
   Yoshino-Kumano 97

natural disasters 214
Nikka Whisky 146
Nikkō 22, 44
Niseko 142
Niseko United 145
Nishiho-Doppyō 58-9, **58**
Norikura-dake 60, **60**
Nyūtō-san 139

O

Ōdai-ga-hara 97
off-the-beaten-path walks 9
Oirase Keiryū 132, **132**
Oku-Nikkō Marsh 36-7, **36**
Oku-Takao 45
Omogo-kei 185
Old Hakone Hwy 42-3, **42**
onsen 12
   Akanko Onsen 142
   Gokuraku-yu 25
   Goshiki Onsen 147
   Happō-no-yu 53
   Hirauchi Kaichū Onsen 205
   Ibusuki 201
   Kawa-yu Onsen 95
   Kurodake-no-yu 152
   Kurokawa Onsen 195
   Mikuri-ga-ike Onsen 51
   Mimizuku-no-yu 53
   Misasa Onsen 100, 101
   Nabedaira-kōgen 58
   Naka-dake Onsen 150
   Nonaka Onsen 157
   Nurukawa Onsen 193
   Nyūtō Onsen 127
   Rishiri-Fuji Onsen 163
   Ryounkaku Inn 155
   Sandan-kyō Hotel 107
   Sato-no-yu 53
   Sennin-buro 95
   Shitan-yu 193
   Sukayu Onsen 129
   Tenzan Tōji-kyō 43
   Tsubame Onsen 72

   Tsuru-no-yu Onsen 127
   Tsuta Onsen 130
   Wakoto Onsen 159
   Yarimikan 59
   Yumoto Onsen 37
   Zaō Onsen Dai-rotemburo 121
onsen ryokan 59, 129
Ontake-kyō 63
Ontake-san 62-3, **62**
Osaka 76
Ōtake-san 26-7, **26**
Oze National Park 38-41, **39**

P

Panorama-dai 34, **34**
Philosopher's Path 80-1
pilgrimage routes
   88 Sacred Temples Pilgrimage 172-5
   Dewa Sanzan 122-5
   Kōya-san 90-1
   Kumano Kodō 92-5
   Hakusan 70-1
   Ishizuchi-san 176-7
planning 6-17
   highlights 6-13
   packing 16
   transport 211
   weather 14-15
podcasts 17
population 216

R

Raizan 207
Rausu-dake 160-1, **160**
Rebun Traverse 166
religion 63, 71, 93, 123
resources 213, 215
   Hiroshima and Western Honshū 101
   Hokkaidō 143
   Japan Alps & Central Honshū 49
   Kansai 77
   Kyūshū 189
   Shikoku 171

resources continued
  Tokyo, Mt Fuji & Around
  Tōhoku 119
responsible travel 215
Rishiri-zan 162-3, **162**
Rokku Gaaden 84-5, **84**
ropeways, see cable cars & ropeways
ryokan 212, see also onsen ryokan

S

safe travel 214
salamanders 107
Sanbe-san 110-11, **110**
Sandan-kyō 106-7, **106**
Sapporo 142
Scarecrow Village 181
seasons 14-15
Sendai 118
Senjō-ga-take 68-9, **68**
Shibutsu-san 45
Shikoku 169-85
  accommodation 171
  climate 171
  festivals & events 171
  resources 171
  transport 171
  travel seasons 171
Shin Sen Numa & Chisenupuri 144-7, **145**
Shintōism 93
Shirakaba-daira Station 59
Shiretoko Traverse 166
Shiretoko-Go-Ko 167
Shirouma-dake 53
Shōji-ko 34
shrines, see temples & shrines
shukubō 91, 212
SIM cards 210
skiing 52, 72, 145
smoking 216

Trails 000
Map Pages 000

snakes 214
Sobo-san 206
South Alps 68-9

T

Takachiho-dake 207
Takamatsu 170
Takao-san 24-5, **24**
Takayama 48
Tanesashi Kaigan 134-5, **134**
Tateyama 50-1, **50**
Tateyama-Kurobe Alpine Route 50-1
temples & shrines
  Daisen-ji 105
  Daishō-in 109
  Fushimi Inari 78-9
  Fushiogami-ōji 94
  Gas-san Naka-no-miya 124
  Gas-san-jinja 124
  Gojū-no-tō 123
  Hiko-san Jingu 190
  Hōkura-jinja 85
  Hosshinmon-ōji 93
  Hotaka-jinja 56
  Ishizuchi-jinja Jōju-sha 176
  Isonokami-jingū 88
  Itsukushima-jinja 108
  Jōken-ji 137
  Kasuga Taisha 87
  Kawaguchi Asama-jinja 33
  Kongōbu-ji 91
  Kumano Hongū Taisha 95
  Kusushi-jinja 30
  Mizunomi-ōji 93
  Musashi Mitake-jinja 26
  Nanzen-ji 81
  Nenbutsu-dera 89
  Oku-no-in (Kōya-san) 91
  Oku-no-in (Ōtake-san) 27
  Okunomiya 104
  Onsen-ji 37
  Ōtsurugi-jinja 181
  O-yama 51

Ryōzen-ji 173
Sanbutsu-ji 114
Sanjin Gōsaiden 123
Shirataki-jinja 33
Shirayama Hime-jinja Oku-miya 71
Yakuō-in 24
Yudono-san-jinja 125
Yuki-jinja 82
Zaō Katta-mine-jinja Oku-no-miya 121
Tenri-kyō 88
time 216
tipping 216
Tōhoku 116-39
  accommodation 119
  climate 119
  festivals & events 119
  resources 119
  transport 119
  travel seasons 118-19
toilets 216
Tokachi-dake 154-5, **154**
Tokushima 170
Tokyo, Mt Fuji & Around 21-45
  accommodation 23
  climate 22-3
  festivals & events 23
  resources 23
  transport 23
  travel seasons 22-3
Tōno 136-7, **136**
tourist information 210
trail etiquette 213
train travel 211
travel seasons 14-15, see also individual regions
travel to/from Japan 210
travelling with kids 73, 84-5, 130, 178, 190-1, 192-3
travel within Japan 211
Tsugaike Nature Park 73
Tsumago 66
tsunami 214
Tsurugi-san 180-1, **180**

Tsuruoka 118
Tsuta-numa 130, **130**
typhoons 214

U

Uchiyama-Eikyū-ji 88
Unpen-ji to Daikō-ji 184
Unzen 207
Utoro 142
Uwajima Temples 184

V

vegetarian food 37, 91, 124, 212
views 10
visas 210
volcanoes
  Asahi-dake 148-51
  Aso-san 196-7
  Goshogake Nature Trail 139
  Iwaki-san 139
  Kaimon-dake 200-1
  Karakuni-dake 198
  Kuro-dake 206
  Meakan-dake 156-7
  Norikura-dake 60
  Ontake-san 62-3
  Sanbe-san 110-11
  Tokachi-dake 154-5
  Zaō-san 120-1

W

Wakkanai 142
waterfalls
  Ayashiro-no-taki 27
  Biwa-taki 25
  Deai-taki 107
  Haha-no-shirataki 33
  Kōza-no-taki 84
  Minō Falls 97
  Mitsu-taki 107
  Oirase Keiryū 132
  Ryūzu-no-taki 36
  Sandan-taki 107
  Shimaidaki 106
  Uguisu-no-taki 87
  Yu-daki 37
weather 14-15
websites, *see* resources
weights 216
wetlands, *see* marshes & wetlands
Western Honshū, *see* Hiroshima & Western Honshū
Weston, Walter 56, 57, 213
whisky 146
wi-fi 210
wildflowers
  Asahi-dake 150
  Hakkōda-san 129
  Momoiwa Observatory Course 164

Norikura-dake 60
Ontake-san 62
Oze National Park 38
Tanesashi Kaigan 135
wildlife 103, 107, 130, 145, 155
World Heritage sites
  Kansai 76
  Kasuga-yama Primeval Forest 86-7
  Kii Mountain Range 90, 92, 96
  Miyajima 108
  Yakushima 202-3

Y

Yakushima 188
yamabushi 125, 191
Yamagata 118
yamagoya 212
Yamaguchi 136
Yama-no-be-no-michi 88-9, **88**
Yatsu-ga-take 72
Yonago 100
Yoshino-yama 96
Yōtei-zan 167
Yufu 188
Yufu-dake 192-3, **192**

Z

Zaō-san 120-1, **120**

THE WRITERS

This is the 2nd edition of this guidebook, updated with new material by Craig McLachlan. Writers on previous editions whose work also appears in this book are included below.

Craig McLachlan

Craig has climbed the *Hyakumeizan* (Japan's 100 Famous Mountains), summited all 21 of Japan's 3000m peaks, hiked the 3200km length of the country and walked the 88 Sacred Temples of Shikoku pilgrimage; he's been writing Lonely Planet guidebooks for 25 years. Find Craig on Instagram @yuricraig

Contributing writers

Ray Bartlett, Rebecca Milner

SEND US YOUR FEEDBACK

We love to hear from travellers – your comments keep us on our toes and help make our books better. Our well-travelled team reads every word on what you loved or loathed about this book. Although we cannot reply individually to your submissions, we always guarantee that your feedback goes straight to the appropriate writers, in time for the next edition. Each person who sends us information is thanked in the next edition.

Visit **lonelyplanet.com/contact** to submit your updates and suggestions or to ask for help. Our award-winning website also features inspirational travel stories and news.

Note: We may edit, reproduce and incorporate your comments in Lonely Planet products such as guidebooks, websites and digital products, so let us know if you are happy to have your name acknowledged. For a copy of our privacy policy visit **lonelyplanet.com/legal**.

BEHIND THE SCENES

This book was produced by the following:

Commissioning Editor
Darren O'Connell

Production Editor
Hannah Cartmel

Book Designer
Clara Monitto

Cartographer
Mark Griffiths

Assisting Editors
Anne Mulvaney,
Brana Vladisavljevic

Cover Researcher
Kat Marsh

Thanks to
Imogen Bannister, Charlotte Orr,
Vicky Smith

Product Development
Amy Lynch, Marc Backwell,
Katerina Pavkova, Fergal Condon,
Ania Bartoszek

ACKNOWLEDGMENTS

Cover photograph
Springtime, Toyama;
yoshimi maeda/Shutterstock ©